CN01460422

Beyond the Tigers

BEYOND THE TIGERS

Tracking Rajiv Gandhi's Assassination

Rajeev Sharma

Foreword by

Vijay Karan

Introduction by

T R Ramachandran

Kaveri Books

New Delhi - 110 002

First Published 1998
Edition 2024

ISBN-10: 81-7479-030-6
ISBN-13: 978-81-7479-030-9

Published by
Kaveri Books
4832/24, Ansari Road
New Delhi-110002 (India)
Tel: 011-23288140, 47072321
E-mail : info@kaveribooks.com
kaveribooks@gmail.com
Website: www.kaveribooks.com

Printed at
Chawla Offset Printers, New Delhi - 110 052.

PRINTED IN INDIA

''Dedicated to my father, Dr Rattan Lal Sharma, who is a living embodiment of single-minded devotion to one cause—do something constructive so that the posterity remembers you.''

ACKNOWLEDGEMENTS

I am thankful to :

* My wife, Dr Pratima, whose sustained cooperation over the years, whose proddings, suggestions and encouragement made it possible for me to complete this book ;
* My several sources in different agencies who gave me valuable briefings and material but wish to remain anonymous;
* Mr T R Ramachandran for giving me his utmost cooperation;
* The publishers, Mr Anil Kumar Jain and Mr Rakesh Goel, for toiling along with me in completion of this book and publishing it;
* And Mr Anik Basu, my former colleague in Newstime-Eenadu, who edited this book.

Rajeev Sharma

CONTENTS

PART V ANNEXURES

Foreword

On that fateful night of May 21, 1991, I was at home with my family, doing really nothing. The telephone rang, and we got the terrible news. How could anyone do it, we thought. First Indira Gandhi, now Rajiv - in a country with an over-riding ethos of non-violence. A country that gave to the world Buddha, Mahavira, Ashoka and Gandhi.

I was then the Director of the Central Bureau of Investigation (CBI) and it did not take me long to realise that soon enough, I would be summoned and asked to take over the investigation of the case. Yes sadly, the case, as it had forthwith become for an investigating agency. I called one of my officers and fixed a meeting of the senior CBI officers in my office somewhat early next morning. As I was getting ready on the morning of May 22, Naresh Chandra, the cabinet secretary, called on the RAX.

"You will have to take over the investigation", he said without emotion.

"Yes I know", I said, and explained that I had already called a meeting of my officers to work out the mechanics of the investigation."

"Good," he said, "Come to my office at eleven. I have called the others also. And do come with whatever may be your requirements."

I watched the morning news on TV and raced through the newspapers to see if anyone had been caught, if there had been an instant kind of breakthrough.

There was none, and my heart sank. Of-course, we had been taught in the course of our training that no case is really beyond detection, however heinous, however perfect. If an investigator looked hard, he would find clues in even the most flawless of crimes. But we were also taught that of all the crimes, political assassinations are the hardest to crack. They are planned and executed so meticulously that they are an investigator's biggest challenge. Prime minister Olaf Palme of Sweden was shot dead on a street in Stockholm some years ago and till today, no one knows who did it. Nearer home, President Zia of Pakistan was blown up in his aircraft in 1989 and again till today, no one seems to have a clue about the perpetrators. As the US Ambassador was also in the ill-fated aircraft, the CIA would have surely tried to assist in the solution of the case, but obviously without success.

In the CBI headquarters that morning, the first matter to engage our attention was to set up a Special Investigation Team (SIT) headed by an officer, who I thought, should be at least of the rank of inspector general of police. As the assassination had taken place in Tamil Nadu, the head of the SIT should preferably be Tamil-knowing, I deliberated. During those days, the air was thick and talk that the Tamil Nadu police had become politicised, with one group of officers aligned with Karunanidhi and another with Jayalalitha. I sent for the civil list of IPS officers and we went through names of several Tamil-knowing officers of states other than Tamil nadu. With my mind made up, we started selecting the other members of the team. The Madras office of the CBI was told that it would have to suspend all other activities "until further orders" and concentrate only on the assassination case.

To the cabinet secretary I made two requests: One, that we should be given D R Karthikeyan to head the Special Investigation Team and two, that the chief secretary of Tamil Nadu should be requested to provide us all the infrastructure that we would require. Both the requests were granted. Karthikeyan was then Inspector General of the CRPF in Hyderabad. When I called him, he was somewhat overcome by the awesome responsibility that was being thrust on him. Being a committed kind of person that he is, he readily agreed. I told him to join me in Madras next morning.

Early next morning (it was May 23), I flew to Madras in a special aircraft, accompanied by S K Datta, our additional director and some other officers then working in Delhi but selected to join the Special Investigation Team. About thirty six hours had passed since the assassination and there were still no clues. What would future hold for us, I wondered. Were we also doomed to failure, like so many other top investigating agencies of the world that had drawn a blank in so many other assassination cases? But I was determined and I could see that kind of expression on the faces of all the others with me. Come what may, we had to succeed. The prestige of not just the CBI but of the nation was at stake.

We were also determined to investigate with an open mind. After all, it could be anybody, not just the LTTE, though the LTTE had already emerged as the main suspect in the media. Hadn't the Punjab militants gunned down Indira Gandhi? How could we rule out the Kashimiri militants, or the insurgents of the North-eastern states, or even the Naxalites of Andhra Pradesh or Bihar? Or for that matter, any other foreign hand?

The distance between May 23 and June 12 is a mere twenty days. On May 23, we had taken on a totally blind case. By June 12, we had all but solved it. The journey was not so long but arduous and very stressful. All that we now needed to do was to try and identify and apprehend the remaining accused, collect as much clinching evidence as possible to back our case and tie up all the loose ends. To my mind, our breakthrough came largely on account of the following three factors. The first of-course was the fortuitous discovery of the Hari Babu photographs. To our great dismay, the photographs made their way to the newspapers even before we could take them into our custody. The damage had been done - Sivarasan saw his photograph in the newspapers and started taking elaborate counter-measures to evade arrest, within a few days of the assassination, even before we knew who he was. Had the pictures not leaked, who knows, may be we could have caught him unawares and captured him alive.

Initially, the Hari Babu pictures only constituted a possible lead. Nobody came forward to identify Dhanu or Sivarasan. We speculated that Dhanu could be the unidentified woman whose dismembered body had been recovered from the blast site. We also speculated that she could be the human bomb. But we could not be sure till we had clinching forensic and circumstantial evidence.

On May 30, I flew to Colombo with S K Datta and Karthikeyan, looking for clues, but still not sure that the LTTE had done it or that Sivarasan and Dhanu were LTTE operatives. All the Sri Lankan agencies who could help us opened their doors to us, more than ready to help. But none of the Sri Lankan intelligence or investigative agencies could throw any light on whether the LTTE had actually committed the deed or on the identity of the two persons in the Hari Babu pictures. We were loaded with conjectures and presumptions, but nothing really of tantalising use, except one clue.

We had been five days in Colombo and everyone was getting restive in Delhi. What's new, I was repeatedly asked everyday. Eventually, I was told to return to Delhi and brief the government on the progress of the investigation. On my last day in Colombo, we got the information, provided by a leader of a Tamil outfit other than the LTTE that the man in one of Hari Babu's pictures was one-eyed and that his name was Pakyaraj. It was in fact one of so many leads and conjectures that we did not know what to make of it. Leaving behind Datta and Karthikeyan in Colombo, I flew to Madras late in the evening. The entire SIT was there at the airport to meet me. In no time, we locked ourselves in a room and in a marathon meeting that lasted till the early hours of the next morning, I briefed my officers on everything that we had been able to gather in Colombo and they in turn, apprised me about the progress of their investigation. There was no common ground, except one, and it seemed to scream at us. I was told that the investigation in Madras had shown that the unidentified man of the Hari Babu photographs was a one-eyed LTTE operative called Shivraj Master. Again, one-eyed! Bull's-eye, we thought.

After sleeping for just about half-an-hour at the airport retiring room, I flew to Delhi in the morning. As I reached my home, I was told that the cabinet secretary had been repeatedly calling. I rang him up and he said impatiently, "come at once".

"Can I at least have a bath?" I asked.

He hesitated for a moment and then said, "Okay, but come as soon as you can. The PM is losing his patience."

When I entered the cabinet secretary's room, the home secretary and the chiefs of the Intelligence Bureau and R&AW were already there. I made a somewhat long-winded presentation, articulating various theories and conjectures and finally telling them that our investigation till then seemed to indicate that the LTTE had done it. In substantiation, I said that the crucial man in the Hari Babu pictures had been identified as a one-eyed LTTE operative by two independent sources, one in Colombo and one in Madras. And the clue was far too specific to be ignored, I said. My colleagues of the IB and R&AW shook their heads in disbelief.

"The LTTE track does not seem to be correct" I was cautioned. "So don't get carried away by just one bit of coincidental information."

Of-course the SIT was on the right track. The jigsaw pieces started falling into place in just a few days. By June 12, Nalini, her mother, her brother and her LTTE boyfriend had been arrested. The rest, as the cliche goes, is history.

No one who has seriously studied the case has doubted the SIT investigation. No one has also doubted the LTTE hand. The court has in fact upheld and lauded the SIT investigation. But the question that seems to rankle in the minds of many has been: is that it? Does the conspiracy stop with Prabhakaran and the LTTE or are there others? Several theories abound and Rajeev Sharma's microscopic eye does not miss any of them. He also feels that the wider conspiracy has still not been unravelled.

Soon after the assassination, the Congress party announced that if voted to power, it would set up a commission of enquiry to look into the conspiracy aspect of the assassination. Not long after PV Narasimha Rao took over as prime minister, I briefed him about the SIT investigation at some length. While he did not fail to compliment us for working out the case, he said that the commission of enquiry would have to be set up. I tried my best to reason with him, pointing out the investigation of the conspiracy also was a part of the investigative process and it was anyhow engaging the attention of the investigating team. On the other hand, a commission of enquiry could hardly have the competence to do a professional job. Even in the USA, the Warren Commission had been able to achieve little while probing the John F Kennedy case. There could also be complications and the SIT could be placed in embarrassing situations vis-a-vis the commission. Rao listened carefully. He said he agreed with whatever I had said but was helpless as the party had already made a commitment to the people. As I had warned the prime minister, the Jain commission, that was set up in August 1991, exposed itself thoroughly by the time it was wound up in March 1998. Its entire probe was anything but professional; it could not say anything substantive on the conspiracy; and it eventually turned out to be a national embarrassment.

When Jayalalitha became the chief minister of Tamil Nadu, I decided to call on her. Karthikeyan came with me. A lot of infrastructure of the SIT had been provided by the state government and we were in need of help of the local authorities all the time. She received us at her Poes Garden residence. After I had given her a brief account of our investigation, her first question was "When are you going to arrest Karunanidhi?"

I told her that if any evidence came our way that showed Karunanidhi's involvement, we would not hesitate to arrest him. I told her categorically that we were investigating the case with an entirely open mind and that if she or anybody else had any leads and clues pointing to the involvement of Karunanidhi or the DMK or anybody else in the assassination, they should be shared with us so that we could look into them thoroughly. Jayalalitha said nothing. Nor did we come across any evidence linking Karunanidhi or the DMK with the case.

When we were in Colombo in the first week of June 1991, we were told in whispers by various persons that Premadasa could be behind it. There is a lot of difference between could be and is. I am not trying to say that there was no larger conspiracy. Should any fresh evidence come to the notice of the CBI any time in the future, no one can stop it from reopening the case and filing fresh charge sheets against the persons concerned.

Rajeev Sharma's book brought back so many memories which I would have liked to record but I guess I have to draw the line somewhere. One needs to also exercise discretion as the case is still subjudice. And I would not like to come between the reader and this very readable book. There are areas where one may not agree with Rajeev or his deductions. But to his credit, he has without doubt done a very professional job, not missing out even the smallest of details. I can see that a lot of painstaking research has gone into the work. And yet, the book is racy and gripping and at times highly suspenseful. I have no doubt that it will not only stimulate discussion of this very important case but also contribute to its greater understanding.

In several ways, the book reminds me of a police case diary. So much material has been harnessed and in such painstaking details, that it appears as though the author was the Chief Investigating Officer of the case.

VIJAY KARAN*

---

* *Vijay Karan was the director of CBI at the time of Raiv Gandhi's assassination. He personally supervised the investigation*

PREFACE

"Why this book ?", several people asked me in mid-1996 when I had completed nearly ninety per cent of it.

There are several reasons. Never before had such a prominent world figure been assassinated in so unconventional a manner. Never before had a 'whodunit' of such dimensions stared people in the face when they read their newspapers for weeks after the event. Every day something sensational was being reported about the assassination and the assassins. Many found it difficult to believe that a gang of assasins could so easily infltrate into the country from across the sea and carry out such an audacious killing.

For the first time, not one but two judicial inquiry commissions probed different aspects of the same assassination — one headed by a sitting Supreme Court judge on security lapses and another presided by a retired Chief Justice of Delhi High Court on conspiracy aspects. There were occasions when the SIT investigations and both the inquiry commissions generated news simultaneously. The nation was glued to the Rajiv Gandhi assassination case.

I was baffled by intriguing developments, bizarre theories doing the rounds and the amazingly high degree of sophistication shown by the conspirators. Unconvinced by the SIT version, I started collecting material on Rajiv's assassination. I took pride in the fact that I was among the very few reporters in the country to have covered every single hearing of the Verma commission and the Jain commission. This came in handy. Apart from throwing up valuable information by way of depositions, arguments, affidavits and applications, the two commissions provided brilliant opportunities to get access to usually inaccessible officials and interact with them 'off-the-record'.

By 1995, I had enough material to write several volumes. By middle of 1996, I had completed the book. But it could not be published because of certain legal difficulties. Besides the proceedings of the two commissions, their voluminous reports, and extensive briefings from the right officials in the right places, I also carefully studied the bulky judgment of the trial court in Rajiv assassination case.

Over and above all this, I went through nearly twenty thousand press clippings of newspapers and magazines, Indian and foreign. My sincere endeavour has been to make this book objective, apolitical and illuminating. It is not without purpose that this book is sans exclamation marks.

I have raised some questions which I believe have a direct bearing on the Rajiv Gandhi assassination case. It has not been my intention to castigate any individual or agency. My sole objective has been to raise pertinent questions, many of which people do not even know exist at all.

I don't dispute the involvement of the LTTE in Rajiv's assassination. But what about the forces who helped the Tigers carry out the plot?

The murder of Rajender Jain last year, just a day before he was to make some disclosures before the Jain commission, and the failure of the investigators to track down the murderer, is testimony to the fact that a massive cover-up is still on.

This book pinpoints several areas which have been neglected by the SIT and even the Jain Commission. The arms shipments to LTTE just before and after Rajiv's assassination the dubious role played by the late Sri Lankan president R Premadasa and the Indian angle of the BCCI are some of these areas.

I strongly believe that there is evidence already available with the Central agencies which points to people other than the chargesheeted accused, Beyond the Tigers. To crack the real conspiracy behind Rajiv's assassination and take the already-conducted investigations to their logical conclusion, it is essential that the government orders a fresh police investigation into the case immediately.

If it happens, I will consider my mission accomplished.

RAJEEV SHARMA

July 15, 1998
SG-2, Xavier Apartments, Delhi-110 034

INTRODUCTION

May 21, 1991. Sriperumbudur near Madras (now Chennai). Congress president and former Prime minister Rajiv Gandhi is killed by a human bomb. The nation is dumbstruck that transborder militancy has reared its ugly head in the tranquil south. The gruesome incident brings to the fore the diabolical plans of the Liberation Tigers of Tamil Eelam (LTTE), the dominant militant organisation across the Palk Straits in Sri Lanka, in targeting politicians inimical to its cause. Barely seven years before, on October 31, 1984, Rajiv's mother Indira Gandhi was ruthlessly mowed down by her own bodyguards at her official residence on Safdarjung Road in New Delhi. That was the sacrifice the country's top leadership had to make for ordering "Operation Bluestar" to flush out militants from the Golden Temple in Amritsar.

Chronicling the assassination of leading lights in politics is not everyone's cup of tea. The work involves going through voluminous material available with the investigating agencies, commissions of inquiry, besides interviewing scores of experts and others with single minded fervour and devotion. The endeavour is to unravel something which might have missed the eye of overworked sleuths and lawyers who made lengthy submissions in the trial court. Just about everything, even if remotely connected, with the brutal slaying has to be literally put under a microscope. And the task is anything but easy when an aspiring author has to deal with the labyrinth of files gathering dust in various offices. It is a Herculean effort to get hold of every piece of paper especially when a lot of it is labelled confidential.

Right to information continues to be a subject of intense debate in the golden jubilee year of the country's independence. Ground realities do not match the pious averments of the governments of the day. Even at the best of times and in spite of the freedom of speech and expression enshrined in our Constitution, one could be inexorably caught in nerve wrecking red-tape and babudom which can dampen one's spirits. And extracting vital information from investigating officers probing sensitive matters like the Rajiv Gandhi assassination case can be a mind-boggling exercise.

Let us also not forget the various forces at work which made the task of the Special Investigation Team headed by D R Karthikeyan that much more difficult. The former director of the Central Bureau of Investigation did not swerve or get sidetracked from the highly sensitive job at hand with just about everyone keeping a hawkish eye on the SIT. If Karthikeyan is now receiving bouquets it was well deserved for he knew he was walking on razor's edge. The Congress government with P V Narsimha Rao at the helm of affairs from 1991 to 1996 came under attack from Sonia Gandhi for dragging its feet in completing the investigations. Narasimha Rao tried his best to clear the air in this regard but the stoic lady at 10, Janpath was not pacified as she had reasons to believe that the country's chief executive and the then Congress president was charting his own course. Narasimha Rao's oft repeated statement that the ''law will take its own course'' irritated Sonia loyalists no end. His relationship with Sonia Gandhi was never on an even keel, and it is no secret she was just biding her time to see Narasimha Rao's back.

Then Justice M C Jain, who as the chairperson of the one man-commission vested with the onerous responsibility of probing the conspiratorial aspects of Rajiv Gandhi's assassination, found innumerable impediments in getting down to the brasstacks. First he encountered the problem of getting suitable space for setting up the inquiry commission. Then it was putting together a team and beginning open and in-camera hearings. There were constant face offs between Justice Jain and the government, which the former seeking certain sensitive information from the government to facilitate his probe, and the government stonewalling him on the plea that making these available would have an adverse impact on the country's security environment.

Rarely has a government instituted a commission of inquiry with specific terms of reference but changed them at a later date and expressed resentment at having to part with sensitive information. Subsequently, after a record number of extensions the commission finally submitted an interim report and then a final one to the government, which again whipped up a controversy.

The book on Rajiv Gandhi's assassination by Rajeev Sharma has, therefore, to be viewed in its totality. The dynamics of the changing environment in the Indian subcontinent and South Asia cannot be wished away as this region abounds in pockets of conflict and severe ethnic strife. Transborder terrorism aimed at stoking tension has continued for nearly two decades. The LTTE, as a highly motivated militant outfit in neighbouring Sri Lanka fighting for a separate homeland, has received training from Israel's Mossad and managed to stay afloat against the might of the Indian Peace Keeping Force and in the wake of the offensive launched by Chandrika Kumaratunga's armed forces in the island nation. Rajiv Gandhi's slaying is not the handiwork of some misguided elements in this country. India and Rajiv Gandhi should be blamed for creating Frankenstein monster out of the LTTE by allowing it initially to use India as a staging ground for its activities in Jaffna peninsula, which in the ultimate analysis, boomeranged. The LTTE was banned after Rajiv Gandhi's assassination.

There are some interesting insights in the book about various aspects of the investigation and the theories thrown up initially which had to be revised and changed with startling facts gradually surfacing. "The first breakthrough in the case can also be seen as the first evidence of foreign hand. A few days after the assassination, investigators recovered from the site a 9-volt battery of foreign-make with two switches for setting off the explosion. The investigators used a powerful magnet after the explosion to collect steel pellets strewn all around. It was then that the sleuths realised the assassin wore a vest jacket and waist belt with the explosive charge on the back." I am sure a lot more theories will be floated about Rajiv Gandhi's assassination as time goes by. The LTTE has emerged as an enigmatic set up with supporters across the globe. They use different tactics in pursuit of their objectives.

A case in point is that of John F Kennedy's assassination in the United States; new books, throwing up new angles, keep getting published even though more than two decades have elapsed.

The book is peppered with racy passages connected with the investigations and the foreign hand in the Rajiv Gandhi assassination case. " Rajiv Gandhi's assassination would have been a perfect murder with no clues but for the nine colour photographs taken by freelancer Haribabu who perished with the last shot. The picture showed a section of the public with the two wanted women - Nalini and Subha - seated in the crowd. The camera remained intact. That the camera survived the Claymore effect of the bomb is a miracle. The camera was taken to the police headquarters in Madras where the lab assistant found that it contained a colour film roll. He returned it saying the police did not have the facility to develop colour film rolls. It was then passed on to the state forensic lab in the next compound."

The escape of the One-eyed Jack Sivarasan in a tanker to Bangalore, the modus-operandi of the LTTE in familiarising itself by staging dry runs and befriending local people to avoid arousing suspicion coupled with the meticulous attention given to drawing up the plans to the minutest detail flummoxed some of the most seasoned investigators. "Even as Sivarasan and Subha continued to elude one of the biggest ever dragnets in the crime history of the country for nearly 90 days, the raids by security agencies brought to light the vast and complex network of the LTTE had established in Tamil Nadu. The unearthing of a grenade manufacturing unit in Coimbatore and seizure of sophisticated wireless communication sets in Tiuruchirapalli and a huge cache of explosives in Thanjavur district revealed that the state had become an operational base for the LTTE." The dedication of the Tigers to complete the task assigned and avoid being captured by swallowing a cyanide pill strung around their neck or shooting themselves proved to be a dampener for the investigators who wanted to capture Sivarasan and company alive. That was not to be. "The storming of the house in Konankunte on the outskirts of Bangalore where six militants were holed up including a woman was delayed because a medical team was on its way from Gwalior with the antidote for cyanide poisoning. They wanted to catch Sivarasan and Subha alive. They somehow entertained the idea that the assassins would be oblivious to the high voltage drama that was being enacted all around and wait until the house is stormed."

With public memory being all too short, Rajeev Sharma has tried to put on paper the enormity of the investigations, the hit and trial method adopted by the sleuths in cornering the assassins and those who aided and abetted this heinous crime. The dubious role of late Sri Lankan president Ranasinghe Premadasa in encouraging the LTTE to foment trouble in India also cost him dearly, suffering Rajiv Gandhi's fate two years later in 1993 at a May Day rally in Colombo.

The book is certainly worth a reading. Rajeev Sharma's account of the 'whodunit' drama of Rajiv's assassination is amazing and gripping. For those who believe that the SIT investigated everything that was to be investigated, the book is an eye-opener.

Beyond the Tigers is unputdownable. It is possible that you may not read this book from cover to cover at one go : there may be an attempted burglary in your house or you may have the prime minister as a visitor.

T R Ramachandran*

---

* *T R Ramachandran is a veteran journalist and noted television political analyst. He is the Political Editor of Newstime-Eenadu group of newspapers.*

PART I

THE HURLY BURLY

1 PROLOGUE

Several "fishing" speedboats surrounded an anchored ship in the high seas in Bay of Bengal in March 1990. Jaffna was not very far. The ship's more important cargo was transferred to the speedboats, after which the "fishermen" sped towards Jaffna.

The cargo pickers had to come back for the next round of mid-sea transfer. The *Sunbird* had sailed again, only to stop a few nautical miles away after the "fishermen" on the speedboats flashed coded signals.

Even in the high seas, the Tamil-speaking "fishermen" could not take any risk. The clandestine offloading of cargo from the 100-tonne, 80-feet-long ship could be noticed and the vessel seized under international maritime laws.

That was what happened. Malaysian authorities intercepted *Sunbird* on suspicion and found it carrying wireless sets and other communication equipment instead of the declared cargo, timber. The vessel was seized, brought to Penang and the six-member crew interrogated.

Sunbird was one of the half a dozen-odd commercial vessels of the LTTE, considered the world's deadliest and most sophisticated guerilla outfit. The ship normally transported timber, foodgrains and fertilisers, with packs of narcotics stashed in between. But this time, it had been carrying lethal explosive RDX, AK series of assault rifles, grenades, ammunition and communication equipment for the LTTE. It was the first major shipment of arms to the LTTE, which remained bogged down for over three years in armed confrontation — first with the Sri Lankan government which launched full-scale military offensive, "Operation Liberation," in January 1987 to drive out the guerilla army; then with the IPKF which moved in the Tamil-dominated areas of the island nation in August 1987, and pulled out completely in March 1990.

Kumaran Padmanathan, LTTE's most important man after Prabhakaran, had sent *Sunbird* on its clandestine mission. Padmanathan, better known as "KP" is the LTTE's lifeline, its chief arms procurer, supplier and fund-raiser. *Sunbird* had originated from Cyprus and sailed via Singapore and Malaysia.

Sunbird was kept docked at Penang harbour for six months. Following sustained grilling, the crew confessed that Sea Tigers— the LTTE's naval arm— had emptied the ship of the deadlier component of its cargo. Before they could stow away the RDX, the grenades and the arms and ammunition, and return for the wireless sets, the ship had been intercepted.

The Malaysians had informed Colombo about the *Sunbird* . The Sri Lankans had not shown much interest. They did not send any extradition request for the detained crew. As there were no adverse implications of *Sunbird* for Malaysian national security, the vessel was released and the crew freed. Within no time, in keeping with the LTTE's practice, *Sunbird* was rechristened, its registration number changed and its appearance altered beyond recognition. It still traverses international waters under a new identity.

Nobody wondered why the LTTE needed such a huge arsenal, brought by *Sunbird.* The newly installed government of president R Premadasa was negotiating peace with the LTTE and had invited it for talks. To demonstrate his good intentions, he had given the Tigers arms and ammunition—and also Rs 75 lakh in cash. Moreover, the IPKF pull-out was nearly complete.

*

Dhanu dropped the garland as she came face to face with Rajiv Gandhi.

She knelt down, ostensibly to pick up the garland, or touch Rajiv's feet. Nano-seconds later, Sriperumbudur, the birth place of saint Ramanujam, was devastated by a deafening explosion. It was the night of May 21, 1991.

Dhanu never touched Rajiv's feet. Perhaps, sparks were flying out of her cold eyes as she deliberately let the garland slip from her hands to kneel down to switch on her belt bomb. Perhaps, in the last few split seconds of his life, Rajiv felt uneasy by the steely gaze of the grotesquely dressed bespcctacled young woman. Nobody knows.

Those who were standing close to Rajiv were immediately felled by the blast ; those who were not so close could in no way see the expressions on the faces of the predator and the prey. Scores of videos and still cameras covered Rajiv's last public function, yet there was no last-minute footage of the night of the Tigers.

A fountain of orange and white light and thick smoke sprang from the blast zone. A white Ambassador sped away flashing its revolving red light. A private blue Ambassador followed seconds later. The blue car had screeched to a halt in the sterilised area at the back of the dais under a palm grove, minutes before Rajiv's arrival. Its tinted glasses were rolled up as it left the assassination site.

*

"The job is done," said a coded wireless message sent the same night from Madras to Base 14, the codename for LTTE supremo Vellupillai Prabhakaran. Base 14 also doubles up as the codename for his hideout.

The message was sent by Nero, wireless operator of the hit squad leader, Sivarasan. Scores of coded messages pertaining to Rajiv's assassination were sent from the hide-out at Kodungaiyur, Madras, where Sivarasan alias Raghuvaran's powerful wireless having a range of more than a thousand kilometres was hidden. A 60-feet-high antenna jutted out conspicuously from the hideout's rooftop.

The Indian security agencies intercepted the message but could decode it only after several days.

*

Intelligence chief M K Narayanan was a harried man the night Rajiv died.

"Are you sure that Rajiv Gandhi is dead ? Or has he been hurt?", the IB director asked N V Vatsan, IB's joint director-in charge of Tamil Nadu, who first called to break the news.

"It is not yet clear, sir. Ten or twelve policemen have also died in the blast ," Vatsan informed.

Narayanan's phone rang ceaselessly after 2225 hours that night. Tamil Nadu's inspector general of police, R K Raghvan, a seasoned former IB man supervising security arrangements for Rajiv's election meeting at Sriperumbudur that night, rang up the IB chief after Vatsan.

Chief election commissioner T N Seshan phoned to confirm whether Rajiv had indeed died in a bomb blast in Tamil Nadu. Seshan had been told about the assassination by an acquaintance who had rung up from the United States.

Prime Minister Chandra Shekhar rang up from Bhubaneswar, where he had gone for election campaigning. The DIB confirmed the "rumour" the PM had heard there. Shekhar cancelled his engagements to rush back to New Delhi.

For the next half an hour, Narayanan sat on his RAX phone. All important constitutional and government functionaries of the government had to be informed. All officers concerned were in their offices by 2300 hours.

President R Venkataraman, cabinet secretary Naresh Chandra, home secretary R K Bhargava, RAW chief Gauri Shankar Bajpai and others had been informed. The defence secretary, the three services chiefs, MI chief Lt General B M Khanna, the foreign secretary and CBI director Vijay Karan had already learnt about Rajiv's assassination.

Narayanan rang up Rajiv's top aide V George, who said he was trying to confirm the rumour. The assassination was confirmed to 10, Janpath around 2300 hours. Sonia and her daughter, Priyanka, were at home, while son Rahul was in the United States.

*

Top officials of the ministries of home, defence, external affairs, and the IB chief sat grimly in the Prime Minister's South Block office past midnight. A crisis management group (CMG) meeting was in progress. The Prime Minister was presiding.

It is rare for the CMG meeting to be held in the PM's office. Normally, such sessions are held in the office of the IB chief or home secretary. The CMG meets in situations of a national emergency or crisis, lists out the avenues available and then finally decides on the best option to set in motion the government's response mechanism.

There is no fixed time schedule for holding of the CMG . As its name indicates, the CMG meet takes place only during a national emergency . This may happen twice a day or not even once a year.

In this case, the CMG had a gruelling task at hand. The participants did not know for sure what problems they were supposed to tackle. Because they did not know anything more than that Rajiv was killed in an explosion at an election meeting in Sriperumbudur.

In police parlance, it was a blind murder. There were many theories and many suspects. Nobody had reported seeing the assassin or assassins. Nobody knew whether the killer was a male or a female. Nobody knew how the assassination took place. There was no crater on the ground, which ruled out the favourite theory of a landmine blast.

The million dollar question for the crisis managers was : did Rajiv assassination require a military response?

*

A special aircraft took off from New Delhi at around 0300 hours on May 22, 1991.

The Madras-bound eight-seater BSF plane had on board M K Narayanan, MI chief Lt General B M Khanna, RAW chief G S Bajpai and two joint directors of IB — the crack operations man Ajit Doval, who was in charge of all IB operations, and E S L Narasimhan, an expert on the LTTE.

The crisis managers were carefully picked. The emphasis was on finding out the possible involvement of a foreign power, and planning out various operations if the answer were to be a "yes".

The immediate suspicion fell on Punjab terrorists and the LTTE, in that order, though at that time there was no evidence to prove either outfit's involvement. Who killed Rajiv? How was he killed? There was no answer to these fundamental questions.

But the one big question that began intriguing India's crisis managers was whether the Sri Lankan government was in any way involved with the assassination. Did the Sri Lankan government engineer or support the assassination, or whether it had incited the assassins or connived with them?

An influential section of the Sri Lankan leadership had bitterly opposed Rajiv's foreign policy vis-a-vis Colombo. In March 1987, Prime Minister Rajiv Gandhi, visibly under pressure from the Tamil Nadu state government, had adopted aggressive postures to help Sri Lankan Tamils.

Colombo had announced an embargo against the Tamil-dominated northern and north-eastern areas of the island nation. The decision had evoked a bitter response from the Indian Tamil community. In June 1987, Rajiv sent two Coast Guard flotellas with food and medicines for the Tamils in Sri Lanka. In a rare show of defiance, the Lankan navy did not allow the flottelas entry into their waters.

Baulked by Colombo's show of strength, Rajiv sent a transport aircraft with fighter air cover to air-drop the relief material. The fighters flew over the Sri Lankan air base of Palaly near Jaffna. The Lankan air force had orders from president Junius Jayewardene not to retaliate.

The air-dropping caused an uproar in Colombo's corridors of power. Prime minister R Premadasa accused Rajiv of interfering in Sri Lanka's internal affairs and browbeating a much smaller neighbour. To drive home the point, he absented himself from the signing ceremony of Indo-Sri Lanka Peace accord in Colombo in

July 1987.

Later, when Premadasa became the Sri Lankan president, he made it clear to Rajiv's successor V P Singh that the IPKF had to pull out completely from Sri Lanka as it was an "occupational force".

V P Singh could not agree more, but the withdrawal had to be in a phased manner or else those who supported the IPKF's presence in Sri Lanka faced certain massacre at the hands of the LTTE.

Premadasa was known to be in touch with the LTTE in the fond hope of winning it over diplomatically. In fact, intelligence reports suggested that when the IPKF's phased withdrawal had begun, Premadasa, then the president, had supplied the guerillas with arms and ammunition to fight the IPKF if it were to return.

New Delhi was in a quandary. What if the Sri Lankan government's involvement in Rajiv's assassination is borne out ? What if Premadasa colluded with Prabhakaran to get rid of Rajiv who was on a come-back trail in the ongoing general elections ? What if some other country was found to be actively behind the assassination?

If answered in the affirmative, India would have had to exercise military option to salvage national honour. The entire southern coast had to be patrolled by navy and the coast guard personnel.

Troops would be needed to be redeployed. Para-military forces, like the BSF would have to be withdrawn from terrorism-hit states to back up. This would mean cancellation of elections in some states.

All these questions had to be addressed to by the expert panel, led by Narayanan. The occupants of the aircraft had animated discussions during the four-hour-long flight.

Lt Gen B M Khanna's role was crucial. Investigation was not the objective of the expert panel, but to assess the need for a military response.

*

Laxmi, the librarian at the Indian High Commission in Colombo, had received a mysterious call nearly six hours before the assassination.

"Is Rajiv Gandhi dead," the caller asked in chaste English. Laxmi, a Sri Lankan Tamil, asked the caller to identify himself, but he had already hung up. She took it as a prank and did not inform anyone about it, until the next day when she realised its importance.

Was the anonymous caller a friend or a foe ? Did he want to tip off Indian intellignece agencies about the coming event or was he a desperate conspirator or accomplice who wanted to check their secret mission's progress ?

*

Another LTTE shipment of weapons and explosives reached Jaffna. It was five months after Rajiv's assassination.

The same pattern was followed. *Golden Bird*, an LTTE ship, cast anchor in the high seas off Bay of Bengal some time in September-October, 1991. The vessel, of the same size and tonnage as *Sunbird*, had originated in Greece. This time the Tigers were more lucky. The Sea Tigers' speedboats transferred the entire cargo of RDX, ammunition and anti-aircraft guns from the ship to their speedboats and sped away to Jaffna.

It was yet again the unfailing KP at work. KP's movements are interesting and may illuminate the dark areas of the international conspiracy behind Rajiv's assassination. He was in Cyprus before the assassination, making arrangements for the *Golden Bird* shipment. But after Rajiv was killed, he shifted base to Karachi, the bustling Pakistani port city, from where he operated for quite some time.

KP has a Pakistani passport. There are reports of his hobnobbing with the Pakistani secret service, the Inter Services Intelligence (ISI).

Two months before the *Golden Bird* incident, there was another development. Another LTTE-owned vessel, *Tong Nova*, was seized in a dramatic fashion in the Bay of Bengal, about a hundred nautical miles from Rameswaram in Tamil Nadu.

The 60-feet-long vessel, larger than a trawler but smaller than a ship, with a large boat by its side, were sighted by a reconnaisance plane of the Indian navy in the evening. Rajiv Gandhi's assassination had taken place about two months ago and surveillance in the coastal areas and high seas had been stepped up. The naval plane radioed a command to *Tong Nova* to identify itself, but the crew did not respond. The reconnaisance plane then informed its base at Vizag of the two unidentified vessels and gave their latitude-longitude. The information was passed on to the nearest naval base at Rameswaram, with instructions to immediately send an armed patrol vessel to investigate.

Though an armed patrol vessel can sail at 22 nautical miles an hour, more than doube the speed of a cargo ship, it could reach the spot only the next morning. The boat had been sunk by the Tigers by that time and only a small portion of it was visible above water. *Tong Nova* was seized and brought to Rameswaram.

There was a strong suspicion that the seized vessel was carrying arms and explosives. The vessel had originated in Cyprus and had been booked by none other than KP. What is more, K P was among the crew members to have been chargesheeted in the case. KP, who owns a chain of shipping companies in different countries, and was also found to be the owner of *Tong Nova,* was charged with illegally procuring arms.

The arrested crew feigned total ignorance about the cargo they had loaded, repeatedly telling their interrogators they had no clue about what the boxes contained.

The accused were asked some searching questions. What was the size of boxes? Did they receive any specific instruction to keep some boxes in sunlight, away from fire and some wrapped in polythene and away from water? Explosives have to be kept away from fire and ammunition from water. Where were the boxes lying when they were loaded? Were they lying hidden somewhere or were these loaded mid-sea? Who supervised the loading operation?

It was only after several days' grilling could it be reasonably established that *Tong Nova* had brought an arsenal of arms which might have been transferred to the Sea Tigers' speedboats before the vessel was seized.

The LTTE's biggest arms consignment, and perhaps the biggest-ever obtained by any terrorist organisation in the world, was yet to arrive. The consignments brought by *Sunbird* and *Golden Bird* were peanuts compared to that brought by *M V Swanee* in August 1994. The vessel, which originated in the Ukrainian Black Sea port of Nikolayev, carried 50 tons of TNT and 10 tons of RDX explosives.

In keeping with the usual LTTE tactics, the vessel's name was changed by the time it approached Jaffna. The Sea Tigers swung into action, offloading the cargo mid-sea and transferring it to some of the numerous jungle bases the LTTE has for the purpose. The end-user certificate for the shipment had been purportedly signed by Bangladesh's defence secretary. The consignment, arranged by a Dhaka-based front company of the LTTE, was required by the Bangladesh military, the end-user certificate said. *M V Swanee* was actually the *Golden Bird.*

Yet another arms consignment of the LTTE was brought in the Bay of Bengal in January 1993, but it proved to be the biggest maritime disaster for the Tigers. The 80-feet-long 100-ton capacity *M V Yahata* left France in October 1992. It was flying the Honduran flag. The Tigers changed its name as it reached the Bay of Bengal. They did not undertake any elaborate method, and simply painted over the first and last alphabet of "Yahata", so it read, *M V Ahat.*

RAW received a tip-off of an LTTE ship setting sail for Jaffna with a cargo of arms and ammunition. After Rajiv Gandhi's assassination, it had begun using submarines to monitor traffic at particular ports in south-east Asia where LTTE vessels docked regularly. The day the ship left the Thai port of Phuket, RAW had point-specific intelligence about the consignment. The Indian navy intercepted it on January 13, 1993, about 700 kms off Madras harbour. LTTE's key man, Kittu alias Krishnakumar Sathasivam, the former Jafna commander and later the Tigers' London-based international spokesman, was commanding the ship.

The Tigers kept dumping explosives into the sea during the three-day journey from the high seas to Madras harbour. Indian navy personnel, who were escorting *M V Ahat*, were helpless bystanders. The Tigers threatened to explode the ship if the Indian navy were to do something drastic. *M V Ahat* was finally blown up by Kittu when it was about ten kms away from the Madras harbour There were 18 people on board. Nine of them who tried to escape just before the ship was detonated, were arrested. Three charred bodies were found on the deck of the vessel. Six bodies could not be traced at all.

More than Rs 10 crore were spent on investigation and salvage operation which yielded nothing. A Tamil Nadu court acquitted all nine accused in the case in 1996 for lack of evidence. The court also directed the authorities to bear the expenses for sending the acquitted back to Honduras at government expense.

*

Several questions arise which defy answer.

* Could there be a link between Rajiv's assassination and LTTE's multi-million dollar arms shipments.

* Was Rajiv killed by the LTTE and the LTTE alone? Was it the brain behind the assassination or just the hand ?

* Was LTTE supremo Prabhakaran so naive as to kill Rajiv Gandhi in India and risk a crackdown which was inevitable or did he do it on behalf of some individuals or powers for money?

* Were the arms shipments a remuneration of the LTTE for killing Rajiv — the *Sunbird* an advance payment and subsequent shipments the next instalments ?

* If the LTTE had paid for these, how had it arranged the money for such massive consignments, particularly after being battered by the Sri Lankan government and the IPKF for over three years?

* How were the shipments procured? For whom had the end-user certificates been obtained and by who?

* The LTTE had not received any major arms consignment since 1986. During its armed conflict with the IPKF, the LTTE had been pushed to the wall and denuded of all weaponry and ammunition. Ironically, while the IPKF was engaged in a full-scale war with the LTTE, the guerillas were using grenades made in India. A grenade manufacturing factory making supplies to the LTTE was smashed in Coimbatore, Tamil Nadu, in 1989. This clearly proved that the guerillas were not getting arms from anywhere. How they became so rich to purchase several shiploads of arms and explosives, remains a mystery. But what does not is that the stature and strength of the Tigers had increased internationally after Rajiv's assassination. Was there a connection between the murder and the emergence of the LTTE as the deadliest terrorist outfit in the world?

* Why did the LTTE need so much arsenal when the IPKF had already pulled out and the new government of president Premadasa was having peace talks with the Tigers ?

* Was there any link between the LTTE and Premadasa, who himself became a victim of a Tiger suicide bomber on May 1, 1993? If so, could it have a bearing on Rajiv's assassination?

*

Imagine this scenario.

Rajiv Gandhi is on a come-back trail. Certain vested interests within India and abroad don't want it. But they are all respectable people and are constantly under public and media gaze. So they need an expert agency which can carry out the assassination. Why not an Indian or foreign terrorist outfit which has a known enmity against Rajiv Gandhi? The LTTE fits the bill, but so do several terrorist outfits from Punjab, Kashmir and north-eastern India.

But before they strike a deal with anyone, they need cover—somebody who can negotiate with the terrorists and keep in touch with them at a regular basis. A prominent jet-setter with pretensions of being a religious figure is willing to be the middle-man between the real conspirators and executioners.

Enter international arms dealers and drug traffickers at this stage. They open their coffers in lieu of political patronage and other material benefits which come as a by-product. Secret accounts in Switzerland and dubious banks as the now-collapsed Bank of Credit and Commerce International (BCCI) are used to finance the operation. The LTTE is promised an uninterrupted weapons supply for doing the job. The LTTE is tasked. Perhaps other outfits also were, but the Tigers struck first.

This may not be pure fiction.

2 THE NIGHT OF THE TIGERS

A day before the assassination, Dhanu showed signs of nervousness.

She complained of severe headache and running nose. On May 18, just three days before the D-day, she had twisted her ankle coming down the stairs from Nalini's one-room rented accommodation near Madras High Court. Dhanu did not pay much heed to it then. But by the next day, the ankle had swollen considerably and the would-be assassin had started limping.

This threw Sivarasan into a tizzy. Everything had been planned meticulously. Minutest possible details had been taken care of. But Dhanu's ankle threatened to jeopardise all their plans.

Sivarasan had tried to make sure that the chief executor of their mission got all attention and care. The Black Tigress had come out of Jaffna for the first time in her life. This was true of most LTTE cadres. Only too aware of this, the chief of the assassination squad opened his purse strings for Dhanu. Sivarasan had given clear instructions to Nalini and Subha to fulfill all her desires for food, entertainment, dresses and cosmetics and not bother about the money. During the last twenty days of Dhanu's life, Nalini and Subha had spent as much as Rs 10,000 on her — a princely sum considering the miserly budgets of most LTTE operations.

Nalini had virtually become her alter ego since Dhanu came to Madras in early June. She used to take the Black Tigress out to the market, beach and restaurants every day. Dhanu's favourite food was chicken biryani, a luxury in the jungles of Jaffna.

The would-be assassin bought herself a few dresses, trinklets and cosmetics. Never before in her life had she used cosmetics.

She also bought a pair of spectacles—again a first-time purchase which she did not really require.

Dhanu had suddenly become fond of the cinema, seeing as many as six Tamil movies in twenty days. An introvert who betrayed no emotion, Dhanu had never told Nalini she liked watching films. But ever since she had seen her first, every second or third day she would ask Nalini to take her out for a movie.

Dhanu had, in fact, watched a movie just the day before the assassination. Nalini had taken her for a night show. Despite having a headache, Dhanu watched the movie, silently. It was a social drama.

Dhanu's injury on the penultimate day of the terrorists' mission was beginning to cast an element of doubt over the entire operation. But Dhanu was a Black Tigress, trained to kill herself to kill the target. Her's were nerves of steel. She assured Sivarasan that Subha, the standby human bomb, would not be required for the operation.

The last-minute details of the conspiracy were thrashed out at the residence of Nalini and Bhagyanathan's mother, Padma. Besides Dhanu, Sivarasan and Subha, Bhagyanathan, Nalini, Haribabu, Sriharan and Arivu were also present at the meeting. Sivarasan assigned each one of them specific tasks for the next day.

Haribabu was to buy a garland and wait for the assassination squad at (Broadway) Parrys Corner mofussil bus stand at 1700 hours. Nalini was instructed to take a half-day leave and return home by the afternoon.

The next morning, Sivarasan visited Haribabu to remind him of the evening programme. As the photographer was not at home, he asked his sister to convey the message. Haribabu bought a sandalwood garland from Poompuhar Handicrafts, Mount Road, Madras and went to see his friend, Ravi Shankar, a freelance photographer to borrow a camera. The conspirators were indeed frugal . The Chinon camera that was to photograph the assassination was borrowed. The film reel had been given to Haribabu by Arivu.

As the fateful evening approached, Sivarasan started getting ready at Vijayan's house. He changed into white kurta pyjama and hid his favourite weapon, a 9-mm pistol, inside a cloth pouch specially stitched by Vijayan's wife.

From there Sivarasan went to a hideout at Kodungaiyar where Dhanu and Subha were waiting. The two Black Tigresses dressed inside a closed room— Subha in a saree and Dhanu in a churidar-kurta.. An unusual dress in southern India, Dhanu's churidar had been stitched at a shop at Purasawalkam in Madras. It was loose enough to conceal the belt bomb. It was so garish that more than one witness remembered the woman wearing it.

That only one set of churidar had been ordered to be stiched demonstrated the level of preparedness. It also indicated that had Dhanu's fallen ill at Sriperumbudur, the assassins might have had to defer execution of their plot. Two belt bombs were ordered to be made, though the unused belt bomb has not been recovered. Sivarasan's anxiety was understandable when Dhanu sprained her ankle a day before the assassination.

He need not have worried. Dhanu was up and about the morning of May 21. After her daily chores, she applied lipstick and nail polish. (The SIT recovered a partially used vial of nail polish from Nalini's house later; Dhanu's severed arm showed her polished fingernails. The colour of her nail polish matched that found at Nalini's house. Chemical tests also proved the two samples were from the same vial. There was no doubt that Dhanu and Nalini had stayed together at least for some time.)

The four conspirators, Dhanu, Sivarasan, Nalini and Subha — went to a nearby temple and offered prayers. They then proceeded to the Broadway bus stand around 1700 hours. Haribabu was waiting for them.

The five-member squad boarded a Kancheepuram-bound bus which was to go via Sriperumbudur. They were among the first passengers to board. The conductor was later interrogated by the SIT and the stubs of the five tickets, purchased by Haribabu, recovered. (The conductor told the SIT Dhanu had sat near the window, along with Nalini. Sivarasan and Subha sat together while

Haribabu sat alone. Dhanu looked out from the window and kept silent throughout the journey. Subha and Sivarasan chatted merrily.)

They reached Sriperumbudur two hours later and entered a restaurant close to the public meeting venue for dinner.

Sivarasan asked Dhanu what she wanted. Chicken biryani, she replied immediately. Chicken biryani was ordered for all.

Dhanu ate to her heart's content. It was her last supper.

They then bought flowers from a local vendor and reached the Sriperumbudur meeting site about 30 minutes before Rajiv Gandhi's scheduled arrival.

Sivarasan walked to the meeting venue, smoking. This was deliberate; smoking, drinking and adultery are against LTTE ethos*.

Rajiv's flight from Vishakhapatnam was delayed. This did not upset the conspirators' plans. They arrived early and mingled with the crowd. Haribabu, who was well known in journalistic circles, and Nalini helped them find their bearings.

When a press photographer enquired about Sivarasan, clad in a kurta and pyjama, Haribabu introduced him as a reporter of the Madras-based English fortnightly *Aside*; a press accreditation card of the publication had been forged for the purpose. Dhanu and Subha took care not to speak too much because of their Sri Lankan accent.

Nalini was nervous right from the time the killer squad members reached the assassination site. Her anxiety increased when it was announced that Rajiv Gandhi was about to arrive. She kept biting her nails, thinking whether Sivarasan and company would succeed or not.

---

* *Sivarasan's smoking must have been an attempt to smokescreen his LTTE identity. The Tigers' chief is said to be a stickler to the puritanical rules. LTTE cadres do not attract any punishment if these rules are flouted for operational reasons.*

Not a single member of the assassination squad carried any cyanide capsule, so common with LTTE cadres. The capsule could have blown the lid off the operation had any of them got arrested during the getaway.

Haribabu was busy taking photographs of the crowd from different angles as instructed. The LTTE has a penchant for recording history of "Eelam-in-the-making"; it records every major terrorist act executed by the Tigers to motivate cadres. In fact, as many as 450 video cassettes and hundreds of photographs of various LTTE operations were seized by the SIT and the Tamil Nadu police during post-assassination raids.

Haribabu had earlier proved his usefulness for the LTTE by taking videos and photos of strategic buildings. But he was given only that much information as was necessary for a photographer.

This time, too, Haribabu was merely told to record the assassination of an important leader — it was not until a fortnight before the actual event that he realised the target was none other than Rajiv Gandhi. Even then, he was not given the complete picture. What if he were to develop cold feet?

Haribabu was told Rajiv would be gunned down from close range. He was instructed to be in the immediate vicinity to get the best shots. Presuming Sivarasan would be firing, Haribabu kept away from him and clung to Dhanu, the walking death. He had taken nine photographs already.

Sivarasan carried his 9-mm pistol, presumably to kill Dhanu if she were to be caught unawares and overpowered. In such an eventuality, he would have aimed at the beltbomb. The circuit would thus break and the bomb would explode.

Sniffer dogs had been pressed into service in the evening, some hours before Rajiv's arrival. Dhanu had gone away. Even if she had not, the sniffer dogs could not have smelt her belt bomb, made of RDX- an odourless plastic explosive. No member of the killer team had been checked or frisked. The dais was also combed, but Rajiv would never reach it.

Minutes before Rajiv's arrival, an Ambassador drove up and parked close to the sterilised zone under a palm grove. A local woman congress worker, Kumudavalli, later told the SIT that Latha Priyakumar, daughter of veteran Tamil Nadu Congress leader Margatham Chandrasekhar, alighted from the vehicle along with another woman and a young girl.

Kumudavalli said the second woman and the child— Latha Kannan and her daughter Kokila—were seen talking to Sivarasan and Dhanu. The assassins stood together with Latha and Kokila as they waited for Rajiv to come.

According to Kumudavalli, Latha Priyakumar had told the organisers that Latha Kannan wished to garland Rajiv and have her daughter read out a Hindi poem in his praise. Kannan and Kokila were then allowed to stand with other people who wanted to garland Rajiv. These people had already been checked and frisked. But Dhanu was not; she sneaked in along with Kannan and Kokila. The die was cast.

Rajiv arrived at the venue at 2210 hours. He garlanded Indira Gandhi's statue which was about two hundred yards from the dais. He spent some minutes there. It was around 2218 hours that he reached the red carpet area.

There was commotion as Rajiv arrived. He was mobbed by people wanting to garland him. Latha Kannan garlanded Rajiv and told him that her daughter had composed a poem in Hindi in his honour and asked him whether he would like to hear it.

Rajiv stopped. Kokila started reciting her poem. Dhanu lunged forward, trying to pierce through the crowd. She was stopped in her tracks by a woman police officer, Anusuya. Rajiv noticed the dark, spectacled woman struggling to reach him and the sub-inspector restraining her.

"Relax. Take it easy," he told Anusuya politely. Released from Anusuya's grip, Dhanu approached Rajiv, then she dropped the garland, and knelt as if to pick it up or touch his feet. Haribabu lifted his camera to shoot his tenth photo. As he pressed the button of his camera, Dhanu activated her belt bomb.

The explosion was deafening. Dhanu was blown away. Rajiv's upper-torso was virtually wiped out, only the back of his skull remained. His body could be recognised only through his white sports shoes. It was only after about half an hour that Rajiv's body, or whatever was left of it, could be put on a stretcher and carted to hospital.

It took the hospital staff more than eight hours to sew the body before Sonia Gandhi and Priyanka arrived by a special Indian air force plane around 0900 hours the next day.

All hell broke loose after the blast. People ran helter-skelter. A rumour that there would be more blasts spread like jungle fire. Within minutes, the ground was empty. Even the policemen fled. Only the IG, Raghavan and a few policemen hung.

Sivarasan ran to the Indira Gandhi statue. He had directed every member of the assassination squad to reach the spot immediately after the explosion. Subha and Nalini were already waiting there. Sivarasan told them not to wait for Haribabu as he too had died.

The conspirators had not brought any vehicle as it could have been identified and their escape noted. They walked briskly towards the highway. Sivarasan was feeling thirsty. They stopped near a cluster of houses. An old woman was standing in front of her house, trying to figure out the cause of the explosion.

On Sivarasan's instructions, Nalini asked for water. After quenching his thirst, Sivarasan told the old woman Rajiv Gandhi had died in a blast.

As they neared the highway, they spotted an autorickshaw. The driver was waiting for a group of Congress workers he had brought. Sivarasan told him there was no point waiting for anybody as a bomb had exploded and many people, including Rajiv Gandhi, had been killed. The driver, convinced by Sivarasan's argument and a promise of Rs 75, agreed to ferry them, but only up to Poonamallee where the municipal limits of his permit ended. It suited the squad fine.

The drive from Sriperumbudur to Poonamallee threw up one more mystery which remains unsolved till date. Worse, the mystery element was not even investigated.

A young man had also got into the auto. He had sat with the driver and did not talk to anyone. In fact, nobody talked to anybody, the auto driver recalled when questioned by the SIT.

The unidentified man got off about two kms short of Poonamallee, and without a word or looking back, just disappeared into the darkness. Did he pay? The driver gave an emphatic 'no'. "I thought that he was with them," the driver said referring to Sivarasan, Nalini and Subha.

Who was this mysterious man?

Kumudavalli said she saw a young bearded man, in shirt and a pair of trousers, hanging around Sivarasan and Dhanu, talking to both of them.

Was he Sivarasan's accomplice or his boss? Most likely, this unidentified man was his assistant. Kumudavalli did not recall seeing the man giving any orders to Sivarasan.

No search party was sent to inquire about the man who got off near Poonamallee. There is no mention about him in any chargesheet. No attempt was made to get more details of his description. No computer sketch of his was prepared. Obviously, in the absence of answers to these questions, investigators do not even know whether he is alive or dead. And yet, he could have been the key spoke in the conspiracy wheel.

On the way to Poonamallee, Sivarasan kept tearing off the pages of the notebook that he carried to pose as a reporter. Perhaps he had jotted down something. Or perhaps, he did not want even a blank notebook to fall into the hands of the police. Balls of torn pages rolled into nowhere on the wind-swept road. Nothing was left of it by the time the auto reached Poonamallee.

This was only the first leg of the journey from Sriperumbudur to Madras after the assassination. The second and third legs were rather uneventful. Sivarasan had to wake up an autorickshaw driver in Poonamallee. He was hired only up to Mount Road, where Sivarasan took a third auto rickshaw to Kondagayayur.

Sivarasan had seen police strength swelling every minute with more and more police vehicles seen after every kilometre. Some people had started stoning vehicles also.

It was 0130 hours when they reached Madras.

Nalini was too scared to stay alone in her room. When the autorickshaw stopped, she did not get off saying she wanted to be with them. Sivarasan did not argue further and beckoned the driver to drive on. This was the only conversation among the hit squad members that the autorickshaw driver recalled when interrogated by the SIT.

Sivarasan started looking for someone the moment he entered the house. He flew into a rage when he saw Santhan. Santhan was snoring away on the terrace.

The One-eyed Jack was not the type to fall apart at the drop of a hat. He performed yoga religiously every morning for half an hour. Besides keeping his body chiselled and fit like a fiddle, the yogic exercises also ensured he kept his cool under all circumstances.

It was incredible for the chief of the assassination squad to believe any member of his team could be sleeping on the night of the Tigers.

Sivarasan tried to wake up Santhan. First, he called him by name, then he shook him. When all this failed he kicked him. Santhan got up with a start.

Sivarasan told Santhan if he ever got caught it would be while he was sleeping*.

---

* *Sivarasan's joke-cum-warning came out to be true a few weeks later. Santhan was actually caught while he was asleep on the terrace of a different hideout in Madras in July. It was well past midnight when a S I T team, headed by a SP, tiptoed right up to the sleeping conspirator. The same drama was enacted. He did not get up on the calling of the policemen. A police inspector sat on him, making it difficult for him to continue sleeping. Santhan awoke only to find armed policemen ringing him. He tried to rummage under his pillow for his cyanide capsule. But it had been taken away by the police.*

Subha had shut herself in a room as soon as she reached Jaykumar's house after the kill.

The Black Tigress was upset over Dhanu's death. She had controlled her tears throughout the journey from Sriperumbudur to Madras but now she confined herself in the room for two days. Her behaviour was very human, quite unlike her Black Tigress training which makes delicate girls into walking scorpions.

On May 24 night Sivarasan sent a coded message to Pottu Amman, saying: "Subha not eating. Crying all the time. Difficult for us to control her."

Pottu Amman replied that all possible attempts be made to console Subha and added that her name would be written in letters of gold in the history of "Tamil Eelam".

*

As everybody, including the hit squad members, fled after the blast, nobody noticed Haribabu's camera. It lay on the photographer chest for quite some before a Tamil Nadu police officer, Raghavan, chanced upon it.

Raghavan immediately opened the camera, took out the reel and handed it over to a policeman to get it developed without any delay. A local photographer was woken up, but he did not have the facility to develop a coloured film. The policeman had to go to Madras to get the reel developed, but after the blast even the police vehicles had disappeared. Left with nothing, he hitch-hiked his way to Madras to get the reel developed.

At least one more murder would have been committed had Sivarasan known that Haribabu had left behind a damning evidence and that a policeman without protection was heading in the same direction as him with it.

Haribabu's photos exposed the LTTE on May 24 when Dhanu's photograph was published by *The Hindu*. Next day, other newspapers published another photograph, showing Dhanu holding a garland. By now, Dhanu was the suspected suicide bomber.

The heat turned on Sivarasan and his killer squad after the One-eyed Jack was identified as the main suspect. Then began India's most dramatic manhunt.

*

IB's chief of operations in Madras had a sleepless night on May 21. By the next day, Vatsan and his men had received an information which was to prove crucial. The Haribabu-Muthuraja-Bhagyanathan nexus had come to light. The IB had begun making discreet inquiries about Bhagyanathan, though at that time it was not known that his sister, Nalini, was a more important conspirator. Vatsan, in his early fifties made the most out of about hundred personnel under his command. Vatsan was also instrumental in steering the investigators to the right direction. "Look for the one-eyed man, Raghuvaran," was the crisp message he passed on to the investigators.

CBI chief Vijay Karan and other investigators flew to Colombo on May 23. By that time, Vatsan and his men had collected more information about the One-eyed Jack. He maintained this man could even have been involved in the Padmanabha assassination barely a year ago. Vijay Karan and company were also told by Sri Lankan officials that they would do best if they looked for Raghuvaran whose movements in the past five or six months had been suspicious.

A Special Investigation Team, the SIT, headed by D R Karthikeyan, was formed. Karthikeyan's appointment was viewed with surprise in security and media circles. Chasing murderers through magnifying glasses was not exactly his forte.

A SIT team flew to Madras from Delhi hours after the assassination. It included Vijay Karan, additional director S K Datta, DIG Amod Kanth, SP Amit Varma, DSP M Narayana (all from the CBI), eminent explosives expert Major Sabbharwal from the NSG and three of his colleagues, computer expert D Ram from the National Crime Record Bureau (NCRB) and two more of his colleagues, and the IB's Ajit Doval (joint director, Operations), ESL Narasimhan, joint director (SA) and Colonel Sundaram.

The diminutive, dark-complexioned Doval is known for dare-devil operations and brilliant methods for collecting intelligence. Col Sundaram is a walking encyclopaedia on explosives and ammunitions. Narasimhan is an expert on the LTTE and knows the terrorist outfit like the back of his palm.

RAW chief G S Bajpai and his IB counterpart, M K Narayanan, also arrived in Madras. Their efforts were supplemented by invaluable local inputs from A X Alexander (RAW), Vatsan (IB), S Ramani from the CBI who later briefly became security advisor-cum-investigator to the Jain Commission of Inquiry and IG R K Raghavan, DIG Perumal Swami, SP D Manoharan (all of the Tamil Nadu police). M Raghottaman, a DSP of CBI, Madras,worked as SIT's chief investigating officer. CBI's legal wing officer Jacob Daniel was made available to the SIT full time for his advice on tricky situations.

Initially, about thirty investigators worked on the SIT round the clock. Besides, a host of finger-print, forensic, ballistic and computer experts were roped in. A number of commandos were attached to the SIT and put under the command of a highly-motivated officer, Captain Ravi. Several squads of sniffer dogs and a helicopter were kept at the SIT's disposal. As the case became curiouser and curiouser, the SIT's strength rose steadily, peaking at over a hundred.

The SIT was equipped well to crack open a blind assassination. But initially, top investigative brains of the country did not even know for hours together whether it was a bomb or a landmine that killed Rajiv.

PART II

CAT AND MOUSE

3 THE INVESTIGATION

Theories abounded on the Sriperumbudur bomb that threatened to blow India apart.

For hours, investigators debated whether it was a bomb or a landmine that had killed Rajiv and 15 others. If it was a bomb, how had it been smuggled into the public meeting venue already sterilised? Was the explosive planted under the earth and triggered off by a remote control just when Rajiv reached the designated spot or was it concealed in a bouquet? Or was the bomb hidden in a garland — a distinct possibility considering the size of the South Indian garlands which are thick enough to conceal a stick of dynamite or a plastic explosive?

It was not until the next day when the evidence collected till then indicated that the explosive device was strapped to the body of a member of a suicide squad. This was deduced from the fact that the wounds on Rajiv's body were restricted to the upper portion. This ruled out planting of a time device on the ground under the red carpet near the dais, as otherwise, his legs would have been blown away.

According to one theory, a landmine was more probable. Knowing that security men normally search the dais for explosives, the assassins could have chosen the path connecting the dais to the main road for planting a landmine. Initial media reports indicated that a large crater was formed at the explosion site, giving credence to the landmine theory. Remote controlled devices, after all, can be activated by radiowaves from a distance of 500 metres.

But there were no craters. This confounded the investigators: how was a bomb, lethal enough to kill 16 and injure 22 without forming a crater on the ground, placed? Things were not falling in place.

A high-level police investigation team, led by Tamil Nadu's inspector general of police (crime) began pondering. Top police officials believed a Sri Lankan Tamil girl, whose mutilated body had neither been identified nor claimed by anyone till then, had possibly activated a highly sophisticated remote-control device.

This device, according to preliminary investigations, was probably placed in a bouquet to detonate what appeared to be an incendiary bomb. The girl, who apparently belonged to a suicide squad, had her head blown off in the explosion. The police did not rule out the involvement of another youth, whose body had not been identified till then.

The bouquet bomb theory received the support of noted forensic expert P Chandra Sekharan, director of the Forensic Science Laboratory in Madras.

The puzzling question was that if the bomb was indeed concealed in a bouquet, how had it escaped the metal detector test? That the girl, in her twenties, evaded detection could mean that metal detection had not been carried out on her or that she had joined the crowd at the last minute and thus avoided the test. The bouquet bomb theory, too, eventually proved to be wrong.

An earlier version said it was a parcel that blew up on Rajiv's face. A middle-aged woman, accompanied by two men, forced her way through the crowd to present the parcel to him. Despite efforts by the police to restrain her, the woman had her way and managed to hold the object aloft before Rajiv before the explosion occurred. This theory, too, eventually proved incorrect.

Another point that engaged the attention of the sleuths was the bursting of crackers when Rajiv garlanded the statue of his mother Indira Gandhi and again a few minutes later, when he himself was garlanded. Was it an attempt to camouflage the sound of the explosion? The possibility could not be ruled out. More so because in the din of cracker bursts, it took several minutes for the security men to realise that a bomb had gone off.

The type of the bomb and the "remote control" device apparently used reminded the investigators of the assassination of

Sri Lanka's minister of state for defence, Ranjan Wijeratne, in Colombo in 1990, though the Sriperumbudur explosion was much smaller.

Then began a no-holds-barred duel between the organisers of the Sriperumbudur meeting on the one hand and the police and the administration on the other. The media had a field day as the warring parties liberally leaked to the press glaring lapses on either side.

Two women Congress workers alleged that the police were not armed with metal detectors. Lakshmi Albert and Rama Devi, president and general secretary respectively of the Tamil Nadu Women Congress, issued a statement saying that Rajiv had not been provided enough security by the state police. They said they were both present at the site from 8.30 pm and that no security check had been carried out on handbags that fateful night. The police simply scanned the garlands and shawls with the naked eye, they claimed.

On the other hand, the police said it had wanted the meeting venue shifted. Mohammed Iqbal, superintendent of police (Chengalpattu West), who eventually died in the blast, was not at all satisfied with the site-a tank bed adjacent to the Sriperumbudur bypass.

The first choice of the police was a school ground on Chengalpattu Road. But Margatham Chandrasekhar, for whose election campaign Rajiv had decided to visit Sriperumbudur, opposed the idea. Alternative sites suggested by the police were rejected on one ground or the other.

There was more. After reluctantly agreeing to the tank-bed site, the police instructed Congress functionaries to provide all material to erect barricades. But till the fateful day, the material that was provided was enough only for one-side barricading.

For a week, investigators groped in the dark. Lakshmi Albert told reporters in Madras six days after the assassination that she had seen the suspected assassin hanging around at the venue for about two hours. She said the unidentified woman was the last in the reception queue, next to Rama Devi, but that she soon moved up further. Albert described the woman as being heavily made-up and 'garish looking', carrying a shoulder bag and a note book which made her resemble a journalist. With her was 'a tall, fair woman,' who did not belong to the women's wing of the state Congress.

There were reports that the suspected assassin was accompanied by two Congress women. Four women, one carrying a bouquet, stood close to Rajiv when the blast occurred.

ASSASSIN A CHEMISTRY POSTGRADUATE ?

The SIT began verifying the antecedents of a number of Sri Lankan Tamil girls in Tamil Nadu in the years age group 20-30. The suspect list was compiled on the basis of anonymous calls and letters received from the public, names furnished by educational institutions and missing persons from refugee camps besides the records available with the Q branch of Tamil Nadu police.

The Tamil Nadu police began the painstaking job of photo-identification of about 120,000 Sri Lankan refugees in the state, besides about a thousand militants.

Some time during this period, the CBI acquired photographs of the post-explosion scene at Sriperumudur. The photographs were taken by a photographer of a Tamil magazine *Junior Vikatan* of the *Ananda Vikatan* group of publications. Balasubramanian, the managing director of the *Ananda Viktan* later said the CBI had taken nearly 80 prints of the photographs.

Four days after the assassination, the SIT swung into action on a tip-off that a girl resembling the hitherto-unknown woman assassin had studied at Madras Christian College, Tambaram. There were stark similarities of build, hair and facial features. Both wore glasses. After completing her MSc, the girl, Mabel Jabashanthi was offered the M Phil course in chemistry. But she chose to return to Sri Lanka. Though the college had a post-graduate women's hostel, Jabashanthi stayed outside the college campus with a Sri Lankan Tamil family as a paying guest.

College records showed the girl hailed from an ordinary family of Jaffna. Her father was a school teacher. A Christian, she was said to be quite religious and attended prayer meetings regularly. The investigators came across an interesting information about her; she was a student of the college in 1987 when Rajiv attended its anniversary function as Prime Minister.

The sleuths took away all records pertaining to Jabashanthi.

According to statements by her acquaintances in Madras, Jabashanthi left for Colombo after post-graduation and took up teaching there. The CBI asked the Interpol to verify if Jabashanthi was indeed working in Colombo.

Jabashanthi, however, was not the breakthrough the investigators were looking for.

FIRST EVIDENCE OF FOREIGN HAND

The first breakthrough thrown up was also the first evidence of the "foreign hand". A few days after the assassination, investigators recovered from the site a foreign-made 9 volts battery with two switches for triggering off an explosion.

Going by the intensity of the blast, it was clear the conspirators must have had packed not less than half-a-kg of C1, C2, C3 combination of explosives and an equal weight of pellets together in the specially-made pockets in the suicide bomber's jacket.

The assaiants chose the "Claymore effect" to inflict maximum damage by stuffing hundreds of tiny 2-mm spherical pellets in the plastic explosive tied to the suicide bomber's waist. Investigators used a powerful magnet to collect the steel pellets strewn all around. Hundreds of pellets were recovered.

It was then that the sleuths realised the assassin had worn a vest jacket and a waist belt with the explosive charge on her back. The jacket was intended to keep the explosive intact till she triggered the detonator. She might have feared that the detonator would go off in jostling in the crowd if the precaution was not taken. The possibility of the conspirators field-testing the belt bomb using a dummy was not ruled out by the investigators at this stage.

The two on-off switches picked up from the site confirmed the police version that the assassin had initiated the high explosive with the help of a detonator, (and not a remote control as previously believed), which in turn was initiated by a battery. Using the Claymore effect, terrorists elsewhere in the world have caused considerable damage by detonating plastic explosive filled with iron fillings, nails and broken metal pieces in crude fashion. *The Hindu* reported: "This is the first time that the technique had been perfected using steel pellets of uniform size which the sleuths said raised many questions about the involvement of 'foreign hand'."

The 8-cm-wide and 65-cm-long abdominal belt, similar to the one used by patients suffering from spinal problems, had steel ribs for support. Three ribs had been removed to accommodate gelatine sticks.

The explosive used was so powerful that body organs were found far away from the blast site. Some pieces of flesh were found under the red carpet used to welcome Rajiv. One body was found on top of the pandal over the dais.

THE POST-MORTEM

Rajiv's facial bones had been badly damaged with the left portion of the trunk and the left portion of his face blasted away.

It is still not known whether doctors had taken an X-ray of the body before conducting the post-mortem to ascertain the extent of damage to the bones. As the body was consigned to flames, absence of any X-ray report on the condition of the bones may not confirm the extent of damage, the number of bones missing and the type of explosive used.

Doctors at the general hospital were unaware of any X-ray being taken before the post-mortem as they were racing against time to complete the exercise to send the body to New Delhi.

The post-mortem could be conducted only on the head and limbs of the woman assassin as this was all that was left of her.

The legs were rather masculine, leading an expert to conclude these were the limbs of a person who had done a lot of running, climbing and trekking.

The left hand which was recovered was, however, feminine. The post-mortem showed that contrary to previous assumption, the assassin was not under the influence of stereoids or a stimulant.

The woman possessed an athletic physique, the kind normally associated with military personnel.*

This indicated the assassin could be a trained militant. It was an assumption that eventually did not prove to be too off the mark.

SEARCH FOR THE MAN IN KURTA-PYJAMA

The official count of the injured persons went up to 22 two days after the explosion when Jayabalan, an amateur photographer, got himself admitted to a city hospital. He later told the SIT he remembered having clicked just before the explosion.

"I saw Haribabu, another photographer, standing on his toes and holding his camera over his head to get pictures of Rajiv Gandhi surrounded by several women. I also tried the same method from behind Haribabu and clicked once. The next moment the blast occurred. I felt a severe shock and thought for a second that there was an electric short circuit. Then something hit my leg."

As Jayabalan bolted, he was hit again, this time on the back of his head. Blood started oozing out. "I cried for help and two policemen standing by the dais came forward. But as they saw a body of a police inspector, they rushed towards him," he was quoted in the media as saying. He reached home on his own.

---

* *In fact, a neighbour of Nalini in the Villivakkam locality of Madras where the woman assassin and her gang used to go frequently told the SIT later that the suicide attacker could carry weights easily. On May 21, 1991, the woman assassin was seen leaving the Villivakkam house carrying a "big bag" — which, in retrospect, is believed to have contained the vest-jacket explosive.*

After two days when the city became calm, Jayabalan handed over the camera with the film roll and his stained clothes to the DIG at the police headquarters. He had clicked at least eight frames. The unprocessed film he returned to the police contained the very last moments of Rajiv's life.

The SIT picked up vital clues from the photographic evidence, ironically provided by the conspirators themselves. The assassination was planned so as to wipe off all trace of the killers or possible leads for investigators. But the turn of events proved otherwise.

The head of the suspected woman assassin was intact. Though Rajiv's body could not be identified by face, the head and other remains of the woman bomber were easily pieced together. Besides, the surprise recovery of photographic evidence from the scene of crime provided additional lead.

Miraculously, the camera used for the photographing the woman was not destroyed by the blast.The photographs of the woman waiting patiently to garland Rajiv along with an unidentified "fourth person" was a valuable piece of evidence, without which the SIT would have been left totally in the dark.

On May 29, 1991, *The Hindu* published the photograph of the "fourth person"—a young bespectacled man clad in white kurta-pyjama. The man carried a notepad and was seen talking to the woman assassin. Suspicion about the possible involvement of this fourth person arose as he was not found among the injured, even though he was well within the range of the explosion just before it occurred.

But even after eight days of the assassination, investigators merely had suspicion about his role on the basis of circumstantial evidence; there was nothing concrete against him. By this time, the SIT had discarded all theories about a bouquet bomb or landmine. The investigations had shown conclusively that the Sriperumbudur explosion had been triggered by a belt bomb, which experts said had an impact-radius of six metres.

The specially-prepared explosive had a built-in safety catch to ensure that the device did not go off earlier than intended. The safety catch was an additional switch. There were two switches, ensuring that the bomb would go off only when the second switch was activated to complete the circuit.

The CBI released to the newspapers three colour photographs of the suspected assassin and the bespectacled man in white kurta-pyjama, carrying a note book and a bag slung over his shoulders. A press note accompanying the photos admitted that the identity of the persons in the enclosed photographs needed to be established. The CBI announced that it would "suitably reward" anybody who provided information or clues leading to the establishment of the identity of those persons.

Nanjil Kumaran, Tamil Nadu superintendent of police in charge of VIP protection, said he had seen the kurta-pyjama clad man somewhere before. "The face is familiar," Kumaran was quoted in the newspapers as saying. The scribbling pad which the man was holding was later recovered from the scene, perforated with pellets. It was blank.

The kurta-pyjama man was suspected to be a "standby" in case the woman assassin failed.

ASSASSIN'S SMILE

Investigators got a clear hint of the nerves of steel the woman assassin had. This came after they examined several eyewitnesses. The eyewitness account given by woman constable who had earlier tried to prevent the woman assassin from nearing Rajiv, shows the cold-blooded nature of the suicide attack. Anusuya had stopped the woman assassin when she was jostling to come closer to Rajiv. Seeing this, Rajiv waved to Anusuya and said : "Relax. Take it easy."

And Rajiv's death lurked closer to him ironically on his own beckoning. According to the eyewitness account, while bending the woman assassin smiled at Anusyua. Immediately after the explosion occurred.

"The bomb took a while to splutter into life before going off, sounding like a dozon drums before the big bang,"

Neena Gopal, a Dubai-based journalist who travelled with Rajiv from Madras to Sriperumbudur on the fateful night, described the explosion.

THE VIDEO TAPE

Neena Gopal said that a video tape recording the blast was seized by the IB and the CBI a day after the assassination. Intelligence officers who interviewed her said the last scene of the tape showed Rajiv's body being thrown back and a cameraman and the camera being splattered with blood.

She said investigators were working on the two-women theory even then.

Gopal's version found an echo in the May 25, 1991 edition of *The Indian Express*, Madras which said the video tape seized by the CBI on May 24 ended with the recording of the explosion. The newspaper said the video film, shot by a Madras-based videographer engaged by Congress functionaries, contained frames of the sequence of events leading to the blast. The video tape covered the crucial part of the incident when people flanked the way to the dais as Rajiv walked towards the stage receiving garlands. It showed the suspected assassin worming her way into the queue. The CBI has this recording.

MYSTERIES GALORE

Even as the SIT was working round-the-clock to crack open the "perfect murder", a spate of mysteries were reported.

After the photographs of the suspected assassin were splashed in newspapers across the country, a mini-truck driver told the Coimbatore police he had given a lift to a woman, resembling the assassin, on May 20, 1991 from Nanjangud in Karnataka towards Ooty.

The driver said the woman got off on sighting a white Ambassador in which two fair-complexioned men were waiting.

The driver claimed the woman sat by his side during their brief journey, spoke only in English, and that too when he attempted a conversation in Tamil. When she opened her handbag to take out her spectacles he noticed a revolver in it. The woman all the while was listening to music on her tape recorder.

The driver told the police he was "absolutely certain" it was the assassin who had travelled with him in the van. He also told the police that he could even identify the two fair-complexioned persons with whom the woman had conversed.

DID SHE VISIT LTTE DETENU IN VELLORE PRISON?

Bhoopathi, an AIADMK worker, claimed to have seen the woman assassin on January 29, 1991.

Four months before Rajiv was assassinated, 162 Sri Lankan Tamil militants, most of them belonging to the LTTE, were arrested in connection with a riot inside the Police Recruits School hostel at Vellore. While most were remanded to judicial custody and lodged in the central prison at Vellore, 31 hardcore LTTE cadres were booked under the National Security Act (NSA) on January 21, 1991; they were to be detained for an year without trial.

Bhoopathi had told the CBI that he had not only seen the woman assassin but had also conversed with her at the jail as a visitor. But he could only recognise the face of the woman from the picture of her reconstructed body; he did not recognise the face of the bespectacled woman assassin.

Strangely, all application forms between January 23 and January 31, filled by visitors to the prison stating the names of the detenues they desired to meet were missing.

When quizzed on this, jail officials claimed no one had visited the jail on these days. Intelligence officials did not swallow this as they knew that more than a thousand political prisoners had been lodged at that prison between January 28, 1991 and January 31. Surely, they had visitors.

Moreover, despite what the jail authorities claimed, Bhoopathy stuck to his claim: that he had visited the jail twice during this period and filled the prescribed entry form. When shown the photograph of the woman assassin's severed head, he insisted he had spoken to this very woman for nearly three hours on January 29.

An *Indian Express* report, quoting undisclosed sources in the Vellore jail, said visitors' records were either not maintained properly or not kept at all during January 28-31 because of the large number of visitors. It was quite possible that visitors might have been allowed inside without entry petitions.

There was violation of yet another jail rule. As per the rules, a Q branch official had to be present within the earshot whenever a person talks to a LTTE prisoner. This too had not been adhered to. If it had been done, the authorities could have known the identity of the prisoner the girl had come to meet.

Bhoopathy described the woman as dark and in her mid-20s. She was wearing a full-length skirt and had her hair tied loosely with a ribbon.

THE FOURTH PERSON MYSTERY

Did the conspirators chase the ambulance carrying Rajiv's body to hospital? There were reports suggesting as much.

K Chokalingam, managing director of Devaki Hospital, Madras, gave a startling information to the investigators. A former president of the Tamil Nadu Congress Committee's medical unit, Chokalingam said he rushed in an ambulance to the general hospital on news of the assassination. He said his driver first saw a dark, stocky man at the hospital. He resembled the kurta-pyjama clad man whose photograph appeared in the newspapers. There were three people with him.

The four had come in a blue Gypsy. The vehicle was unnumbered, the number plate reading "For registration".

Some time later, Rajiv's body was transported to the airport in the Devaki Hospital ambulance. Tamil Nadu Congress president

Vazhapadi Ramamurthy accompanied the body to the airport.

The ambulance parked slightly away from the entrance of the VIP lounge after it reached the airport. When the driver hit the ignition to bring it closer to the VIP lounge entrance, the vehicle would not start. It was discovered after some time that a mango seed and other things had been stuffed into its silencer. Chokalingam brought the matter to the notice of the airport security personnel, who were standing near by.

As he was about to return to the city, Chokalingam said he saw for the first time the stocky man, this time dressed in blue shirt and trousers, ‘‘like some of the uniformed airport personnel.” With him was another man of a smaller build and a lighter complexion.

While he was almost identical in build and complexion to the "fourth person" whose pictures had been published, this man was not wearing spectacles. His hair style was also different.

The point of resemblance that struck him most was his "expressionless visage’’ and the posture. Like the man in picture, he stood with his arms clasped in front and he was totally impassive when he spoke.

This man stepped up to him and asked in Tamil which hospital the ambulance had come from, where the hospital was located and who the woman IAS officer was who were to return to the city in the ambulance. Chokalingam, by now deciding enough was enough, curtly told him to mind his own business.

Then the man’s companion butted in to ask Chokalingam for a lift to the city. This man was of medium build and wore the same blue uniform. When the request was promptly turned down, the man argued with Chokalingam that he might as well offer them a lift since he was allowing the woman * to travel in the vehicle.

** Which woman? Is it the woman IAS officer the suspected "fourth person" had inquired about from Chockalingam ? The "Indian Express" report, which has reported the incident, does not make it clear. The report has also not given the precise timing of the entire hospital-airport drama.*

Chokalingam said while the stocky man spoke Tamil in a strange and mechanical manner "like a robot", his companion was fluent in the language and had a Thanjavur accent.

This episode raises more questions than it answers. First: was the stocky person the same as the kurta-pyjama clad man whom the CBI was searching for? Who were the three others with him? What was their mission? Why were they uniformed? Why was the van tampered with?

Probably they wanted Chokalingam and party to get delayed.

Why were they interested in delaying Chokalingam? Was their conversation really meaningless? Why were they so inquisitive? Why were they so keen on travelling back to the city in Chokalingam's ambulance ?

These questions are abegging answers even now.

Another discovery was made during early investigations. There was no ambulance in Rajiv's convoy to Sriperumbudur on May 21. This, despite the fact that as part of a contingency plan two ambulances accompanied him on his tours with five or six policemen having the same blood group as Rajiv.

Two city hospitals used to supply the ambulances with a well-equipped medical team. On May 21, Rajiv's body as well as bodies of other deceased were taken in a police van from Sriperumbudur to Madras, a distance of 40 km. This lapse could have proved costly had Rajiv been alive with injuries.

In fact, published reports said the Congress dropped the proposal to provide an ambulance when a hospital sought payment for the services.

THE BELT BOMB

It was the first time when a world leader had been assassinated by a suicide attacker wearing a belt bomb. The plotters had probably lifted the idea from a Frederick Forsyth bestseller published in 1989. In this thriller, *The Negotiator*, a similar belt bomb is triggered by kidnappers of the son of the US President to kill him.

In the novel, the bomb is planted on the unsuspecting 21-year-old in a broad leather belt which his abductors had given to hold up the denim jeans. Forsyth's belt bomb was three inches wide and made of two strips of cowhide sewn together along their edges. It had a heavy and ornate brass buckle, four inches long and slightly wider than the belt. The buckle was deceptive. Though appearing solid, in fact it was hollow. The explosive was a two-ounce wafer of Semtex, composed of 45 per cent penta tetro ether nitrate (PETN), 45 per cent RDX and 10 per cent plasticiser. The wafer was three inches long and one and half inches wide. It was inserted between the two strands of leather precisely against the kidnapped youth's backbone.

The suspected woman assassin, too, had the explosives strapped in a denim belt with velcro lining. About 65-cm-long and 8-cm-broad, some of the steel ribs reinforcing it had been removed to accommodate the explosive. The bomb in the novel was triggered off by remote control, while the Sriperumbudur bomb was set off by the assassin herself.

In the novel, a miniature detonator was buried in the explosive and connected to a lithium battery of the type used in digital watches. The battery was placed inside a hollow sculpted within the thickness of the double leather as well as a pulse receiver of the size of a match box. The receiver was hidden in the buckle. From the receiver a further wire, the aerial, ran right round the belt, between the layers of leather. The bomb in the novel could have been detonated from a range of 300 yards.

The bomb that killed Rajiv was made in Madras by one Elayathamby Jayabalan, a Sri Lankan Tamil chemical engineer from Frankfurt. Tamil daily *Dinamani* quoted "highly placed sources" as saying that Jayabalan supplied specialised batteries used in improvised explosives and radio-controlled devices.

Jayabalan reportedly flew into Madras from Frankfurt on April 21—exactly a month before the assassination— and was in constant touch with the Madras-based "logistical officer" of the LTTE, Nixon. Jayabalan and Nixon made two trips —one to Porur and the other to Tiruchi— where they camped. The CBI, with the help of Interpol, flashed Jayabalan's photograph to all Indian embassies and missions across the world. He had passports of four different countries; all were fake.

K Mohan Das, a former director general of police of Tamil Nadu, was of the opinion that the bomb had been manufactured near Madras, given Tamil Nadu's history of bomb blasts. The explosive used in the Mennambakkam airport blast in 1985, in which at least 30 people were killed, was found to have been made in a Madras suburb.

The Sriperumbudur bomb was designed to eliminate a specific target. It was very much unlike the bombs exploded in Delhi and other northern Indian cities between 1985 and 1991, which invariably were weapons of indiscriminate mass killings. This was clear from the fact that the blast did not create a crater. It did not even damage the coir mat laid on the ground. So much so, that even the wooden barricades in the immediate proximity of the explosion remained intact.

Several parts of the bomb device—battery, switches, wires and belt shreds— were recovered. If the quantity of the explosive had been high enough, all these parts would have burnt or melted as was the case in a series of bomb blasts in public transport buses in Delhi in early 1991.

WHO WAS SHE ?

Even after ten days of Rajiv's assassination, the assassin had remained a Mona Lisa. She had been given at least half a dozen names and life-sketches by the media and those claiming to identify her.

Among the first names to be bandied about was "Comrade Malini", an LTTE woman leader, which was followed in quick succession by other identities: Jayanthi, Shanthi, Kamsi, Akileswari and Sundari. A common factor in all these identities was that all made her out to be an LTTE cadre from the Vavuniya area.

Non-LTTE cadres in Colombo set themselves on the onerous task of identifying the woman assassin. The People's Liberation Organisation of Tamil Eelam (PLOT) had put 20 of its cadres on the job full time. The non-LTTE groups were a valuable source of information, as the Sri Lankan intelligence agencies with little access to the north and the east had limited information about the LTTE.

With the flashing of the photographs of the belt bomb woman in Sri Lanka's media and on Rupavahini, the television network, the SIT was flooded with calls and 'information' about the identity of the woman. This only compounded the SIT's problems as a number of theories were being floated by groups which had no love lost with the LTTE.

The arrival of a special team in Colombo on May 30, 1991, fuelled speculations that the investigators had zeroed-in on the real identity of the assassin. CBI director Vijay Karan, additional director S K Datta, SIT Chief D R Karthikeyan and U N Abhyankar, a joint secretary in the ministry of external affairs, had meetings with the Sri Lankan civil and military intelligence officials soon after their arrival.

A peculiar difficulty faced by the SIT related to the differences between the photograph of the woman before the blast and her severed head recovered later. Another dimension was added by the missing studs on her ears and a new 'bindi' on her dead face. It was not immediately clear if the woman wore a bindi because the photographs taken immediately after the recovery of her body did not have the mark, but those taken by the media later had shown this in focus. How did the mark on the forehead appear if it was not there earlier?

Then there was the handbag mystery.

While the photographs of the three women —Latha Kannan and her daughter Kokila sandwiching the suspected assassin— did not show the presence of any strap or hand bag on Latha Kannan's shoulder, a photograph of her body revealed the strap on her left forearm.

Where did the handbag emerge from? Did by any chance, the woman with the belt bomb hand over her bag to a companion? What intrigued the investigators was that the assassin needed a contact in the Congress to reach a vantage point in the garlanding queue. Were the mother and daughter from Arakonam used as a front to gain that entry ? This suspicion gained credence from the fact that the main suspect, the LTTE, had a massive network in Tamil Nadu with a number of local Tamils on its payrolls.

The mysterious role of Latha Kannan and her daughter Kokila, who were seen flanking the woman assassin minutes before the blast, was unravelled after Nalini's arrest. Nalini told her interrogators that an unidentified person known to the kurta-pyjama-clad man had put the woman assassin on to the mother and daughter. In fact, without the "timely assistance" rendered by Latha Kannan, who had joined the Congress in late 1989 after a long stint in the DMK, it would have become extremely difficult for the assassin to infiltrate into the "sterile zone" and reach near Rajiv.

According to Nalini's account, she, along with the kurta-pyjama clad man, the assassin and one more woman accomplice were introduced to a person who was sitting behind the stage under the cover of darkness. The "stranger" immediately introduced the suicide bomber, who wasted no time in picking up a conversation with her. Investigations also revealed that the handbag carried by the woman assassin had been handed over to Kannan minutes before the blast.

Even three weeks after the assassination, the investigators had not been able to identity the woman assassin. This, despite the fact that they used the most advanced and scientific methods of investigation.

The woman had three of her teeth missing, two of these from early childhood. Dental experts assessed the woman's age at 25 years. She possessed "incompetent upper lip" which could not cover her protruding teeth. The odontological study was conducted by J G Kannappan and N Gnanasundaram of the Madras Medical College.

DAMP SQUIB IN THE CITY OF TAJ

While frantic efforts were on by the investigators in Madras to identify the woman assassin, intelligence officials were sent on a wild goos chase to the far-away city of the Taj.

Sleuths of the CBI, IB and RAW made a beeline for Agra. Their destination: Sarojini Naidu Medical College where a woman with severe burn injuries was being treated. The woman, who said her name was Nasreen, had attracted suspicion because she had come from Madras.

Nasreen had sustained extensive burn injuries above her waist. Police found it rather intriguing that the woman travelled in such a condition all the way from Madras to Agra, where she did not have any relatives.

Nasreen had been admitted to the hospital on May 26, five days after Rajiv's assassination. She told the police her husband, Vicky, a Tamil, had tried to burn her. She aroused all the more suspicion with contradictory statements, Agra range DIG S P Singh said. Sometimes she said she hailed from Ludhiana, and at other times she said she was from Jalandhar.

Nasreen told the police that she was travelling from Madras to Ludhiana and wanted to take some help from a friend in Delhi. But since she was in great pain during the journey, her co-travellers persuaded her to alight at Agra for treatment. A local shopkeeper had been giving medicines and other help to her. Apart from the woman, the shopkeeper was also questioned by civil and police authorities.

The woman was X-rayed in the hospital. Experts also conducted chemical tests to establish the nature of burns.

The high drama ended on an anti-climatic note when Rahul Sahay, the attending doctor, said the wounds suffered by Nasreen appeared to have been caused three weeks prior to May 26.

"MISSING" FROM HOSPITAL

Even as the investigators were trying to put together various pieces of the jigsaw puzzle, the mystery shrouding the assassination deepened further when two of the Sriperumbudur blast injured admitted to the Kilpauk Medical College hospital were reported missing from May 22 afternoon.

Three persons including Congress leader Margatham Chandrashekhar's son, Lalith, were admitted to the hospital. While Lalith was officially discharged and admitted to the Apollo Hospital the next day, the two others were missing from May 22.

Then there were other small but significant developments. The blue Ambassador in which the woman assassin was suspected to have had travelled was found at a tourist taxi service in Madras. The car was seen in the video film of the Sriperumbudur public meeting, and its driver and owner were questioned.

On May 31, the CBI got cracking on another lead. A Sri Lankan woman resembling the suspected assassin had exchanged travellers' cheques worth $200 on May 5 and 10 at the State Bank of India branch at Menambakkam Kamraj domestic airport. She said her name was Jebarani and told the counter staff she was staying at a hotel in Pallavaram and would be proceeding to Kancheepuram. While exchanging the money at the counter, she was not wearing spectacles.

A desperate SIT on June 5 doubled the reward money to Rs 1 million to anyone providing clues to the identity of the suspects involved. The investigators believed that there had to be people injured in the Sriperumbudur blast who did not report to any hospital. Knowing their whereabouts would provide a breakthrough, it believed.

The first vital clue about the identity of the kurta-pyjama-clad man came in the first week of June with the arrest of an LTTE militant from Nagapattinam. The militant, whose identity was not disclosed, told his interrogators that the man being hunted was none other than the "One-eyed Jack", a hardcore LTTE cadre. The man on the run had lost one eye in an armed confrontation with the Sri Lankan military and now had an artificial eye, concealed by the spectacles.

"WE HAVE BROKEN OPEN THE CASE"

The first breakthrough for the SIT came on June 11 when a 49-year-old nurse and her 25-year-old son were arrested for sheltering the assassin. The interrogation of Padma and her son Bhagyanathan also revealed that the assassin's name was Dhanu and the kurta-pyjama clad man was Sivarasan.

A gang of nine was found to have been involved in the conspiracy behind Rajiv's assassination. There were even reports of one of the key figures in the assassination having been killed at the behest of the assassins' "apex command" to blot out evidence.

Things started falling in place with the arrest of Padma and Bhagyanathan. The identity of the other members of the killer squad —Padma's daughter Nalini, Murugan and Subha— was established.

Bhagyanathan owned a press—BPL All Round Stationers— in Royapettah, central Madras. The press was a *benami* venture registered under the name of Baby alias Subramaniam, who published and printed literature on the activities of the LTTE. Subramaniam was also closely associated with Haribabu.

Padma, Bhagyanathan and Nalini had sheltered Dhanu, Sivarasan, Subha and one Dass alias Murugan at a place in Villivakkam and in their house at Royapettah under instructions from Muthuraja, an LTTE militant. Mother and son had accompanied Sivarasan, Murugan and Subha to Tirupati on May 25, four days after the assassination.

With their arrests, the "inner ring" of the comspirators had been identified. An indicator to the significance of the two arrests was that CBI director Vijay Karan airdashed to Madras immediately after hearing the news.

Meanwhile, the SIT recovered from Haribabu's residence the bill for the sandalwood garland which the suicide bomber had presented to Rajiv. The bill, dated May 21, showed that the garland, costing Rs 65, had been purchased from Poompuhar Handicrafts, a showroom on Mount Road in Madras.

On June 11, the SIT released the photographs of the two wanted women, Nalini and Subha. It also gave a description of the two women and Murugan.

Nalini, described as being about 27 years old, fair and slim with long black hair with parting on the left side, was about 5 ft 2 inches tall, with slightly protruding teeth and sunken cheeks.

Subha, according to the SIT, was about 5 ft tall, dark, stocky and had curly black hair, slightly sunken cheeks, with her lower lip slightly protruding.

Murugan alias Dass was 5 ft 6 inches tall, had a round face, uneven teeth and sparse moustache, luxurious black hair with no parting, and spoke Tamil like a typical Jaffna Tamilian.

The arrests of Padma and Bhagyanathan infused new blood in the SIT. The CBI chief announced on June 13: "We have broken open the case."

He said the air dropping of pamphlets containing the pictures of Dhanu in North Eastern province of Sri Lanka was not a futile exercise. One significant remark made by Karan at this stage was: "We have not yet arrived at any conclusion and I do not rule out the possibility of involvement of various external forces in the assassination."

PEEPING TOMS

After the identities of Sivarasan, Subha, Nalini and Murugan were established, the SIT started receiving information from residents of localities they stayed in.

A neighbour of Nalini, who had taken a two-room tenement at Villivakkam, told the investigators that Sivarasan, Subha and Dhanu had stayed in a house in the area for some days. She said she could make very little of the conversation the trio had as they would speak only occasionally, in hushed tones, often using the sign language.

Another neighbour said the conspirators never addressed each other by name and that they discovered their identities only from newspaper reports. The neighbours said Nalini and her accomplices had stayed there only for four days after the assassination. Nalini had moved into the Villivakkam house in November and returned only on the evening of May 24—three days after the assassination.

The neighbour told the SIT that whenever Dhanu and the kurta-clad man came to Nalini's residence, the lights would be on till late in the night. The only window of the single-room would remain closed all the time.

Nalini was reported to be reserved, seldom speaking to her neighbours. She was a private secretary to the managing director in an adhesive manufacturing company in Adyar in the city. An efficient worker, Nalini was drawing a monthly salary of Rs 2,000 plus. She continued to attend office till June 6—a fortnight after the assassination.

Nalini resigned on June 9, a Sunday. Early that morning, she entered the office using a duplicate key and left a note stating that she was resigning "due to unavoidable circumstances".

A tea stall owner near her office later said Nalini had come alone in an auto rickshaw at 5 am and walked straight to her office. She returned to the waiting auto rickshaw within minutes and left. Incidentally, she had attended office on the day of the assassination. Her former colleagues were shocked when they saw her photograph released by the SIT.

A witness to the assassination, she had not disclosed to her colleagues that she had been to the meeting venue, though she talked about the assassination at the lunch table.

Nalini was seen last on June 7 when she attended office. There were repeated telephone calls for her after 5.30 pm that day. The callers did not reveal their identity.

According to a near-by tea stall owner, some four or five well-dressed men climbed the wall of the company, two days later and were seen peeping inside around 4 am. He said he was not sure whether they entered.

Nalini's company management received a telephone call on May 27, six days after the assassination, enquiring whether they had seen near their office the susspected assassin and her accomplices whose photographs had appeared in the press. The caller claimed to be a CBI official investigating the Rajiv assassination case.

On June 10 morning, the CBI men stormed the office and took away papers and photographs related to Nalini. Each and every person of the 25-member staff, including women, were interrogated by the CBI. The search continued till next day evening and Nalini's pictures were released to the press and the Doordarshan.

NALINI WANTED TO BE A FILM ACTRESS

Nalini had a psychologically scarred childhood. But despite this she did not go into a shell. A deprived child of an alcoholic ex-policeman's second wife, she was gutsy and ambitious. Her father used to beat her mercilessly on the slightest pretext, and over the years she developed a violent hatred for him.

Those who knew Nalini from her childhood described her as an extrovert. She preferred to befriend the rich among her classmates at school and was a close friend of a student who later became a starlet in the Kodambakkam film world.

Born on May 26, 1964, Nalini displayed a rare streak of independence at an early age. She knew what she wanted and nothing could stop her from getting it, no matter what the risks were. The head of her school recalled her taking part in various games. Her brother Bhagyanathan and younger sister Kalyani also studied in the same institution.

A former teacher of Nalini recalled her as having an uncanny knack for making friends and influencing teachers. "She was such a nice girl that I went out of my way to help the child" the teacher said.

Nalini graduated in Economics from a city college and joined a correspondence post-graduate course in Economics at the Madras University. She had completed secretarial courses in typewriting, shorthand, accountancy, office management, business correspondence, telex operation and word processing.

A born exhibitionist, Nalini used to visit her school to show off the progress she made in life.

Her brother Bhagyanathan was a total misfit in the elite institution in which he studied along with his two sisters. He was a constant source of trouble for his mother and eventually dropped out before he could complete the fifth standard. Later, the school principal got him admitted to a school in Ettayapuram near Tirunelveli at Padma's request. He soon ran away from that school too and was brought back to Madras where he was admitted to another school in Mylapore.

Bhagyanathan was variously described by his schoolmates and teachers as a 'bully', 'an odd man out', 'a misfit' and even a 'juvenile delinquent'. Padma lived with her three children in the nursing home quarters till late 1990. Bhagyanathan was a source of constant trouble to neighbours before the family moved out to a house in Muthiah Mudali Street, Royapettah. Bhagyanathan by now had acquired links with anti-social elements. He was shunned by his former classmates who were scared by his notoriety.

Nalini's younger sister Kalyani was described as a 'low-profile girl' . She studied upto tenth standard and did a nurse aid course at VHS, Adayar before joining her mother's profession.

Investigations revealed that Subha, whose photograph was made public on June 11, had visited Nalini's office only once. That was about three or four months before the assassination. The other alleged accomplice, Doss, had met Nalini a number of times in the past few months. Whenever either of them came to her office, they did so just before the closing time and left with her.

Nine days before the assassination, Murugan had told his gang that he was going to Jaffna.

On hearing this, Bhagyanathan asked him to carry the letter which he had written to Baby Subramanian. Dhanu and Subha, who too had written letters to Akila and Pottu Amman respectively, also asked him to personally hand over the letters since he was going to Jaffna. All the letters were in Tamil.

The letters were virtual status reports of the progress of the plot and the preparations. Every conspirator had talked of his or her high morale and expressed their 'do-or-die' attitude for the operation. The letters, recovered by the SIT later, indicate that Akila is the chief of the Black Tigresses and are the only documentary evidence against her.

Murugan was playing a double game; he took the letters, read the contents, went to Kodiakkarai, stowed them in a safe place, met some people, including Shanmugham, and returned to Madras after a few days. He told his gang members he could not lay hands on a get-away boat clandestinely. What he did not say was he had never attempted to go to Jaffna.

Why did he lie to his own people? Why did he open the letters meant to be opened by people above him in the LTTE hierarchy ?

Murugan, it later turned out, was a counter-intelligence man of the LTTE. His job was to keep an eye on all hit squad members, including Sivarasan, and if necessary, report to Prabhakaran through his own independent wireless set which operated on a different frequency and needed a separate code sheet.

Mystery shrouds the whereabouts of Murugan on the assassination night. Murugan himself and other witnesses like Nalini and Padma, have told the SIT that he was sleeping at Padma's house that night. But his record shows he was not a guerilla who would have slept at home while his outfit's most important terrorist act was being enacted.

The master interrogator had participated in the LTTE's two dry-runs, attending the April 18 public meeting of Rajiv Gandhi and Jayalalitha at Marina beach, Madras, and V P Singh's May 7 meeting at Nandanam, south Madras. That the guerilla who was present at the two crucial dry-runs just before Rajiv's eventual assassination was not there at the actual event is indeed baffling.

Murugan was on an equal footing with Sivarasan. He never took orders from the One-eyed Jack. He was not dependent on Sivarasan for money either. He had brought with him one and a half kg of gold biscuits when he came to Madras from Jaffna in February-March—a typical mode of LTTE guerillas to finance their activities abroad.

Murugan was the chief of LTTE's counter-intelligence for Rajiv's assassination. He had met Prabhakaran alone in his highly fortified chamber in Jaffna five to six times between 1988 and 1991 — a rare honour for an LTTE cadre, though a fairly senior one who enlisted eight years ago and participated in several important operations. Apparently, Murugan had caught Prabhakaran's fancy wlth his incisive and extremely useful interrogation of LTTE traitors and cadres belonging to the EPRLF, and PLOT among others.

But the tough LTTE hut had softened.

Murugan had undergone a metamorphosis since he came in contact with Nalini. The professional killer, who tortured to death captured Indian soldiers and is reported to have wrenched necks of wild animals in the jungles of Jaffna, had lost the LTTE cadres' missionary zeal. He was in love.

Sivarasan was unaware of all this. The lovers had hidden it from every other member of the hit squad, even the fact that Nalini was pregnant.

After the assassination, Murugan, whose real name was Sriharan, visited the holy shrine of Tirupati on May 25 along with Nalini, Sivarasan, Subha and Bhagyanathan. The conspirators' one-day Tirupati visit was a thanksgiving exercise. Murugan shaved off his hair and Nalini did 'angapradakshinam'—rolling around the temple periphery on belly— despite her pregnancy. She had taken a vow to perform the ritual if the mission were to succeed.

After they returned from Tirupati, Murugan and Nalini married in a temple. By now, they were on the run.

On May 26, Sivarasan took Subha from Vijayan's house to Parrys Corner Bus Stand where Ravichandran alias Ravi, and Suseendran alias Mahesh met them. From there, Sivarasan and Suseendran took Subha to a safe house at Pollachi. The daring nature of the LTTE guerillas is reflected from this as the LTTE safe house at Pollachi, where Subha and Suseendran stayed for several days, was near to the ancestral house of S I T chief Karthikeyan. Sivarasan returned to Madras the same day. Between June 2 and 4, Suseendran took Subha to Trichur, Cochin, Thirunelveli and Madurai and returned to Pollachi on June 4.

Sivarasan went back to Pollachi on June 5 after learning that Subha was not well. The next day he brought Subha back to Vijayan's house at Kodungayur in Madras. Sivarasan informed Murugan about Subha's illness. On June 7, Sivarasan took Subha to Ashtalakshmi Temple at Besant Nagar in Madras where Murugan and Nalini were waiting for them. A temple was a perfect meeting point for the fugitives, particularly when Nalini had to take Subha to a nursing home in the same colony. Subha was given some medicines and she became alright some days later.

Nalini and Murugan had to find refuge. They had come to Madurai from Madras, and when Murugan asked her where they could go, Nalini suggested the name of her former employer.

Nalini was not a stunning beauty, but she was fairly good-looking and in the prime of her youth. Till recently, the very mention of her employer repelled her. A lecherous man, he had made several passes at Nalini.

But, now she needed his help. Twenty days had passed since Rajiv's assassination and everyday newspapers—vernaculars and national dailies—were replete with stories of SIT on hot trail of the conspirators. The photos of Murugan and Nalini had so far not been published as none still knew that they too were involved. After all, Murugan was with her and her ex-boss would not be able to take any liberties with her. She decided to go to the house of the man.

This proved to be the undoing of the newly-married couple.

The ex-boss was only too happy to see her, but he viewed her uncouth-looking diminutive companion having a recently shaved pate with suspicion. Nalini told him that she had come to Villupuram for some work and inquired whether she could live in his house till her job was over. She introduced Murugan as her distant cousin.

His imagination fired, the man sent Murugan out of the house on some errand and tried to caress Nalini. But Murugan returned sooner than expected, much to the discomfiture of the house owner. At night, once again he made overtures in an inebriated state in front of Murugan, whom he considered as nothing more than a domestic servant. Nalini decided enough was enough.

Early next morning, Nalini told her former boss that she was leaving. He asked her where she was going. Without thinking, she disclosed the actual destination.

A girl of Nalini's age, Bharathi, had been sharing the Madras house of Padma with Nalini and Bhagyanathan like a family member. Bharathi's mother lived at Villupuram. The couple decided to go there.

Nalini and Murugan had not seen the morning's newspapers as they had set out for Villupuram quite early. If they had, they would have done something with their faces. Every single newspaper had splashed the fugitive duo's photographs on the front pages.

When they reached the house of Bharathi's mother, they found it locked. She had read the morning newspapers and set out for Madras immediately after learning that the family with whom her daughter was staying in the state capital was wanted in the Rajiv Gandhi assassination case.

Nalini inquired about her friend's mother from the neighbours. They told her that she had gone to Madras. Before leaving, Nalini told the neighbours to tell Bharathi's mother that she was going back to Madras.

Nalini's former boss had gone back to sleep after seeing her off. The newspapers had been delivered by the time he got up. His morning tea nearly spilled when he picked up the paper: the previous night's guests were main suspects in Rajiv Gandhi assassination case. The time was around 10.00 am. He quickly picked up his telephone and called up the SIT in Madras.

The SP on the line quietly listened to his story and despatched a team to Villupuram. He knew where his team had to go in Villupuram. The interrogation of Bhagyanathan had been useful.

The team leader at Villupuram called back to inform that the wanted couple did land at the house of Bharathi's mother and Nalini had left a message that she was going back to Madras. The

SIT team had gone to the Villupuram bus stand only to find that a coach had just left for Madras.

There was enough time to catch the fugitives as the bus would reach Madras only after six hours. But there was a difficulty. Within Madras city, there were five stands. SIT formed five teams and deployed them in plainclothes at every bus stand. The Villupuram team had done a good job. The team leader had even told the SP that Murugan was wearing a cap.

The couple got off at the very first stand in Madras. They could be identified without any problem. It was raining heavily. They talked to an autorickshaw driver and sat in the vehicle.

An inspector quietly came and sat beside Murugan. A sub-inspector sat beside Nalini. The cop flashed his identity card and ordered the driver to head to the SIT headquarters.

Neither Murugan nor Nalini offered even the feeblest resistance. They were not carrying any cyanide capsules or weapons. Murugan later boasted before his interrogators he could have killed the two policemen with his bare hands, but he had not as he did not want to leave his wife in a lurch. It was not an empty boast as Murugan was trained to kill.

RAW officers intercepted and decoded a wireless message from Jaffna the next day. Papa Oscar* wanted to know who this Murugan was? "We never had any Murugan," Pottu Amman barked over the wireless.

Even Sriharan's bosses in Jaffna did not know his new assumed identity. Papa Oscar* was told who Murugan was. He shouted back: "Why was he not carrying cyanide." The wireless operator had no answer to this.

But probably there is an answer. Murugan had come to India to brainwash the likes of Nalini. But he himself was brainwashed, falling for the charms of a woman who was a couple of years elder to him. And his passion knew no bounds when Nalini reciprocated.

---

* *Papa Oscar is the LTTE's wireless code name for Pottu Amman, their intelligence chief at the time of Rajiv's assassination.*

Nalini and Murugan told the CBI their intimacy had grown in the past three months, resulting in her pregnancy.

Murugan often broke down while referring to his association with the LTTE and Prabhakaran. It was against his organisation's code of conduct that he developed a relationship with Nalini and her family whom he had assiduously cultivated for carrying out the killing as ordered by the LTTE high command, Murugan told the SIT.

He said he feared physical annihilation by the LTTE for violating Prabhakaran's order to return to Jaffna a fortnight before Rajiv's killing.

Murugan confessed that after receiving Prabhakaran's fiat, he had even gone to the coastal tip of Mandapam near Rameswaram and waited for one of the LTTE's plastic boats frequenting the Indian coast to ferry him back to Sri Lanka. But his strong attachment to Nalini prompted him to change his mind.

Murugan had brainwashed Nalini into believing that the IPKF had committed atrocities in Sri Lanka and that Rajiv Gandhi was to be blamed for this.

Nalini said in her confession to the SIT that Dhanu had convinced her that the IPKF men had raped her and killed her two brothers. Nalini started firmly believing that if the IPKF could commit such atrocities aginst Sri Lankan Tamils, they could do the same to Tamils in India.

She said to avoid detection of her secret relationship with Murugan, she shifted to a rented single room accommodation in suburban Villivakkam in Madras. The Villivakkam residence also came in handy for providing shelter to Dhanu, Subha and Sivarasan. She confessed that the suicide bomber and her standby, Subha, were brought by Sivarasan to her new rented house just a fortnight before the assassination.

The interrogation of Nalini and Murugan revealed that Sivarasan was ready with a pistol in Sriperumbudur on the assassination night and would have shot Rajiv if the belt bomb had failed to explode. Nothing was left to chance by the killer squad.

The back-up plans were also ready in case the Sriperumbudur operation failed. They would have killed Rajiv either at Pondicherry or Krishnagiri the next day where the former prime minister was scheduled to address public meetings if they had failed at Sriperumbudur.

Murugan also said Sivarasan was among the top rung leaders of the LTTE. He enjoyed many privileges, such as unlimited flow of money and personal vehicles. In the LTTE hierarchy, only top leaders are allowed own vehicles.

The importance of Murugan was amply reflected when the SIT produced him before the court of Chief Judicial Magistrate, Chingleput for extension of his remand on July 12, exactly a month after his arrest. It produced a tonsured look-alike of Murugan as a decoy following information that the LTTE could attempt a rescue. The court complex resembled a battle zone as AK-47-toting uniformed men were deployed.

The SIT stated in its affidavit that Murugan had been assigned by the LTTE to assassinate Rajiv Gandhi. He was described as a key member of the LTTE and coordinator of the plot. The SIT said one Muthurajah, who masterminded the operation and later attempted to cross over to Sri Lanka, might have escaped to Jaffna.

A few days after the arrests of Nalini and Murugan, two more important LTTE cadres fell into the SIT dragnet: Robert Payas, 25, a native of Jaffna and G Perarivalan alias Arivu from Jolarpet in Tamil Nadu. Payas, a Sri Lankan Tamil, had sheltered Sivarasan, Dhanu and Subha. Arivu had been staying with Bhagyanathan and Padma.

A provision store in Porur, near Madras used to be the conspirators' "drop" point for messages from Jaffna, Italy, Denmark and Canada till the assassination. There was only one call for Payas after the assassination about a week later. It was a local call and Payas spoke in hushed tones, the provision store owner told the SIT. An Omni was seen outside Payas' house for several days until a day before the assassination. It was used for transporting people, particularly women.

Another harbourer of the killer squad, Jaikumar, was arrested on June 26. Jaikumar, a Sri Lankan Tamil from Jaffna, had provided shelter to Sivarasan and Subha in Madras. Jaikumar was found to be related to Robert Payas.

The vigil on Sivarasan and Subha continued. Huge posters announcing reward to anyone leading to the arrest of the two absconders were displayed at all public places in Tamil Nadu, particularly the areas like Thondi, Sayalgudi, Keelakkarai, Rameswaram, Ramanathapuram and the coastal areas. The reward posters were affixed even on buses and walls of schools.

In the last week of June, the investigators identified the sandals worn by Dhanu from among the 60 pairs of footwear found strewn around the explosion site. Experts had taken Dhanu's foot impression and matched it with the footwear pairs found at the spot. A silver anklet worn by the suicide attacker was also recovered from the spot. The investigators made a blow-up of the picture of the sandals and were trying to find the shop which had sold these. Some pictures of the chappals were sent to Sri Lanka to find out if these were sold there.

TADA REVIVED

For trial of the accused, the government revived the controversial Terrorist and Disruptive Activities (Prevention) Act (TADA) with retrospective effect from May 23, 1991 by an ordinance. A CBI counsel told the Madras High Court on June 28 that it was wrong to presume that the Act had expired on May 23. And even if assuming that the Act was not in force then, all arrests in the Rajiv murder case were valid since the assassination had occurred a day before TADA's expiry.

DHANU WAS A PEEPING TOM

The suicide bomber and her standby at times displayed traits of ordinary people. These insights into their behaviour came to light when they lived with Nalini for a week before the assassination.

A neighbour said Nalini used to come frequently to her house to leave her keys. Their interaction was limited to this as Nalini never spoke much. About a month before the assassination, a short, stocky man—whom she later identified as the wanted kurta-pyjama man— used to come to Nalini's house and stay there off and on. The neighbours never heard this man (Sivarasan) speak. A few days later, a dark woman (Subha) too came to live with Nalini.

Another neighbour, who lived on the other side of Nalini's one-room tenement, said : "Only Dhanu would walk up and down, peeping into our houses, but she too never spoke to us. Subha never came out. For three days in the week, she just stayed indoors. When we peeped in we saw her lying down. She used to frequently apply sandalwood paste and lime on her face."

On May 21, the departure of the group at about 4.30 p.m. raised the curiosity of the neighbours, though none of them asked where they were going. "I saw the short man and the three girls leaving after handing over the keys to me. Subha was wearing a blue silk saree with a black border and Nalini a red saree. Dhanu was wearing an orange kameez, green salwar and dupatta and high-heeled shoes. She wore a tight chain around her neck. The chain was not of gold. I think it was an imitation piece.* She did not have any bindi but was wearing spectacles." None noticed what Sivarasan was wearing at that time.

After that the neighbours saw Nalini and other members were seen only on May 23 night when she came to pick up the keys. They again left on May 25.

Bhagyanathan's press, acquired just about a month before the assassination, was another meeting point for the conspirators. He was somehow very secretive about his 'letter press'. He never allowed anyone near the press.

The neighbours did not see any work done in the press, but the lights used to be on during nights. When the house owner told

* *Obviously it was not an imitation piece. It was a real cyanide capsule.*

him that the Madras Electricity Services might object to this, Bhagyanathan assured him that he would take care of this. The neighbours also said that they used to see jeans-lad women coming to the place in auto-rickshaws and spending considerable time inside the press.

There was no evidence of any printing activity. Thick layers of dust had settled on the articles inside when the SIT raided it after Bhagyanathan's arrest.

AN ARRESTING PERFORMANCE

Twenty four hours after the assassination, the CBI called on the National Crime Records Bureau, a newly created police information service which wields an electronic truncheon to prove that crime does not pay. The CBI's request: could the NCRB computers be used to track the killers ?

A two-man, one-software team of the NCRB left for Madras immediately.

By sifting through the information filtering in about the prime suspects, Sivarasan and Subha, portraits were 'painted' bit-by-bit —and flashed across the country.

The arrest of Murugan was a major victory for scientific investigations — a key factor in tracking down today's space-age criminals. Days later, the NCRB team won kudos again when their portrait of Sivarasan turned out to be uncannily similar to the photo on his driving license recovered later.

It was the Facial Analysis and Criminal Identification System (FACIS) developed in-house that turned the heat on the fugitives. Based on a PC/XT, all that the menu-based system needs is an EGA card to "paint" portraits according to eye-witness specifications. This system is much superior to the computer-based sketching systems. In fact, FACIS can offer up to 640 million portraits. With this system, up to 80 to 85 per cent likeness of the fugitive can be achieved.

The creation is done by recalling from the computer's memory the near likeness of various parts of the face as described by the witness. The facial characteristics are then put together to get a rough picture. The final picture requires some expertise involving touching up of the portrait with a computer mouse.

After the arrest of Bhagyanathan, Padma, Nalini and Murugan, the SIT had cracked open the Rajiv Gandhi assassination case as far as the modus operandi of the killer squad was concerned. But Sivarasan and Subha were still on the run. The SIT went on a media blitz to track them down.

The Coast Guard had been alerted to eliminate the possibility of their escaping by sea.

The SIT was flooded with telephone calls and letters, each claiming to be providing a valuable lead. But most calls were crank. The SIT could not afford to ignore any, though verifying all leads was no different from locating a needle in a haystack on a moonless night.

One such letter was received by the Indian High Commission in Colombo. It "identified" a Colombo-based Indian correspondent as the 'One-eyed Jack'. The letter was accompanied by a newspaper clipping with photograph of the LTTE delegation on their arrival for peace talks in the island nation's capital in 1989. The photograph of a bearded Indian correspondent interviewing the LTTE delegation was marked with an arrow by the letter's author to "identify" Sivarasan. The letter writer gave his code name as Jackal and wanted the Indian High Commission to insert advertisements in local papers giving details how the reward money of one million rupees be passed on to him.

*

The SIT issued a press release on the updated descriptions of Sivarasan and Subha after it arrested from New Delhi important LTTE cadres— Kanak Sabhapathy, in his seventies, and teenager Athirai. The two were intercepted at the Indira Gandhi International Airport when they were trying to take a flight to London on forged passports.

The old man and the young girl were close to Sivarasan and Subha and had been meeting them often since before the assassination. They had come to Madras from Jaffna a few weeks before Rajiv's assassination. Their mission was to smuggle Sivarasan and Subha first to Kathmandu and then eventually to Singapore or some other south-east Asian country where the LTTE has a large number of sympathisers. Sabhapathy and Athirai had planned to bring Sivarasan and Subha to New Delhi and then arrange their escape. Sabhapathy and Athirai knew in advance the plot to kill Rajiv by employing a woman suicide bomber.

Security was toned up in the Kakinada port town of Andhra Pradesh in the first week of July following a CBI alert that the fugitives may attempt to flee the country through the Andhra coast. The Trawlers' Association was also cautioned that the wanted criminals may try to hire trawlers.

VIDEO TAPE ON 'DRY RUNS'

More came to be known about Sivarasan when a video tape on the assassination squad's "dry run" on another former prime minister, V P Singh, was handed over to the SIT on July 17. The video clip shows Sivarasan seated in the front row of the press enclosure barely five to six metres from the dais at Singh's election rally at Nandanam in the heart of Madras city on May 8.

Whenever the camera panned from the stage to the audience, it caught Sivarasan in different moods. But he is never seen taking notes unlike other reporters present. As the camera pans cross Sivarasan, he is either fidgety, looking around or even flashing a smile.

Shot by the Jhanabanu visual media unit, the video footage is the only known video recording of Sivarasan. The clip was obtained by the English fortnightly *Frontline*. It confirmed reports that the killer squad had carried out "dry runs" to check the efficacy of security arrangements at VIP functions.

The killer squad had carried out another 'dry run' the following night at Perambur in the city. The target this time was AIADMK leader J Jayalalitha.

Interrogation of Nalini and others that followed the surfacing of the video tape, revealed that the squad that assassinated Rajiv was present at all dry runs. Dhanu had even garlanded V P Singh soon after his arrival at the venue well past midnight.

Those present at the Nandnam meeting included Subha, Sivarasan, Murugan, Nalini and Haribabu. But the others were not seen in the video tape that showed Sivarasan. This was probably because they could not find seats at the centre and took corner seats on the left which was not covered by the video camera. Two faces with Sri Lankan features, one of a man in a checked shirt and the other a woman with protruded teeth, could not be identified immediately.

The dry runs served several purposes. First, the killer squad members familiarised themselves with the security arrangements for VIPs, and its loopholes. Second, it also made their faces familiar with security personnel. They hoped to get accepted as journalists covering all VIP public meetings.

Nalini was initially told by the LTTE strike group that their task was to establish a rapport with all the Indian leaders so that whoever emerged as Prime Minister, they could seek India's help to find a lasting solution to the ethnic strife in Sri Lanka.

THE WIDER CONSPIRACY

Even as the tape of the dry run was being studied by the investigators, a statement made by home minister S B Chavan in Parliament on July 25 came as a shocking pointer to a wider conspiracy behind Rajiv's assassination. Chavan said the LTTE could have been an "instrument or tool" to execute the plot to kill Rajiv Gandhi. In other words, there could be another set of people using the LTTE.

What set the Indian government thinking was the sudden surfacing of anti-aircraft guns and surface-to-air missiles in the LTTE armoury. Though the Tigers did not face any paucity of funds, procuring and shipping such sophisticated weapons to Jaffna was not an easy task. The LTTE could not have done this without assistance from some international agency or supplier. Indian intelligence agencies began wondering who could this be.

Though Sivarasan came to Tamil Nadu much earlier, he had returned to Jaffna some time in April 1991 to brief the LTTE leadership about the arrangements he had made. He returned to Tamil Nadu by the end of April with Subha, Dhanu and Murugan.

It was then that the team stayed with Shanmugham at Kodiakadu before proceeding to Madras.

SHANMUGHAM

The very name of Shanmugham, a smuggler and LTTE sympathiser, makes those who are familiar with the Rajiv Gandhi assassination case smile cryptically. Several leads were instantly closed with the mysterious death of this 35-year-old harbourer of Rajiv's assassins.

A few days after he was arrested and remanded to SIT custody for 30 days in the third week of July, 1991, Shanmugham's body was found hanging from a tree branch which was too low for him to hang from.

Shanmugham was the most important catch the SIT had made — perhaps even more important than Nalini and Murugan in many ways. He had admitted before his interrogators that he knew Sivarasan quite well. Long before he landed in India with Dhanu, Sivarasan had already paid him several visits. But he had always introduced him as Raghuvaran or Raghuappa. Shanmugham told the SIT he had no idea about the assassination plot and had learnt about Sivarasan's involvement only from newspapers.

A SIT team had brought Shanmugham to his hometown, Vedaranyam, from Madras on July 18 in a helicopter. On the basis of his information, the SIT had seized huge quantities of explosives, powerful Japanese wireless sets and more than 3,200 litres of petrol buried on the coast near his native village Kodiakadu, 10 km off Vedaranyam. In Thanjavur district of Tamil Nadu, Vedaranyam is the nearest point on the Indian coast to Jaffna peninsula and Velvettiturai, the hometown of LTTE chief Prabhakaran.

Vedaranyam, an overblown fishing village; is known to have been the favourite infiltration/exfiltration point for LTTE militants. Its location is such that before Rajiv's killing, residents of Jaffna routinely made the 30-minute boat ride to Vedaranyan to see the latest Tamil movies.

Though security agencies spread their net in this village soon after the assassination, Shanmugham evaded the SIT for almost three weeks. A rich overlord, who was rolling in money courtesy the LTTE after years of penury, Shanmugham had the reputation of having on his payrolls most of the local police and politicians.

Shanmugham was under intense interrogation at the Highways Department Inspection Bungalow near the Vedaranyam police station since July 18. The official version was that he had his dinner around 9 pm. Then, on the pretext of washing his hands, he went to the backyard and suddenly disappeared, giving a slip to the security men. Apparently, he had scaled the compound wall leaving behind his dhoti and shirt.

At dinner, his uncle, Seetharaman, had visited Shanmugham and castigated him for being a "traitor". Shanmugham appeared depressed after his uncle left.

A search was launched on the night of July 19, but Shamugham was not to be found. The next morning, he was found hanging from a tree which was just a few hundred yards from the inspection bungalow.

People thronged Gandhi Park in Vedaranyam where Shanmugham's body was found hanging. They allowed the body to be taken to Nagapattinam only after the intervention of senior police officers. Such was his clout that all shops and business establishments remained closed as a mark of respect. His widow, Bhavani Ammal, sent telegrams to the President and Prime Minister stating that the CBI had killed her husband.

Shanmugham was in "friendly" custody. The SIT maintained he had cooperated fully during interrogation. It was surprising that Shanmugham should have made an escape attempt as he had feared for his life and had opened up to his interrogators only after he was assured of protection. Moreover, he had made no attempt to escape from the forest area where digging operations went on for four hours to unearth the explosives and other things.

The next day the Madras Doordarshan telecast footage of Shanmugham identifying the arms, ammunition and communication equipment he had stashed away at his forest hide-out. He was not handcuffed either during the forest seizure or during his interrogation at the inspection bungalow as he had cooperated willingly.

Residents of Vedaranyam believe Shanmugham was lured out with the promise of a safe passage by his accomplices. Angry at his betrayal, they murdered him and hung his body from a tree to make it appear like a suicide.

Enquiries with these people revealed that Shanmugham had fallen out with a local politician, a notorious smuggler enjoying close contacts with the LTTE. They dismissed the official version of his "escape" as a cock-and-bull story.

Then came the post-mortem report which further fuelled the suicide-or-murder controversy.

The CBI claimed the post-mortem report showed signs of a "classical hanging". The victim had semen and stool discharge and saliva dribbling from his mouth. There were litigature marks around the neck and the body did not bear any sign of injury. The saliva was fresh and the victim's stomach empty, indicating the victim had committed "suicide" shortly before his body was found at dawn.

But was it suicide? Could he have actually hanged himself from a branch which was so near the ground? The hyoid bone in the neck was unbroken.

Did Shanmugham visit someone before he hanged himself? A blue lungi was found under him. But he had been wearing a white dhoti earlier which he had left at the inspection bungalow.

The post-mortem was conducted at the Nagapattinam Hospital the same evening the body was recovered. Questions were raised as Thanjavur or Madras General Hospital were better equipped. But the counter view was that the SIT hurried because of the suspicion that Shanmugham might have died of cyanide poisoning which necessitated the examination at the earliest.

Shanmugham's death under suspicious circumstances remains one of the puzzles in the Rajiv Gandhi assassination case.

His body was cremated at Vedaranyam on July 21. The man knew too much.

DIXON

Even as Sivarasan and Subha continued to elude one of the biggest-ever dragnets in the crime history of the country, the raids by security agencies had brought to light the vast and complex network the LTTE had established in Tamil Nadu. The unearthing of a grenade manufacturing unit in Coimbatore and seizure of sophisticated wirelesss communication sets in Tiruchirapalli and a huge cache of explosives in the coastal Kodiakadu in Thanjavur district revealed that the state had become a virtual operational base for the Tigers.

The LTTE militants, who had earlier confined their activities to the Thanjavur coastline areas and parts of Coimbatore district, had extended their base to Ramanathapuram, Pudukottai, Tiruchirapalli, Madurai, North Arcot and Periyar districts over the past few years.

The very high frequency wireless communication set recovered from Dixon's house in Dr Munusamy Colony in Coimbatore was used by the dead militant to keep in touch with Sivarasan and the LTTE high command in Jaffna. Police seized three very high frequency walkie-talkies, with Dixon's name engraved on one of these, from the house of Dr Gopalakrishnan, a local homoeopathic physician. A huge haul of explosives was seized from the house of the physician who had let out his "clinic" to the LTTE to store the material before taking it to Jaffna. The seizure included 100,000 detonators, 5,600 pen torch cells, army shoes, slippers, lungis, blue lamps, metal spare parts and tins of red phosphorus.

It was during these investigations that the role of Dixon came to light.

Dixon was the Tigers' communication expert who was deployed by the LTTE to maintain information links between the militant groups and the leadership in Jaffna as well as the LTTE's leaders in other countries.

Dixon was in constant touch with his bosses, using powerful wireless sets and public telephones provided for international communication. Frequent international calls made at odd hours by young men aroused the suspicion of the telephone booth owner who reported the matter to the police. Investigation revealed that the militants spoke to their leaders in London and other places.

The arrest on July 27 of two hardcore LTTE cadres, Vikki alias Vigneswaran and Raghu, a former aide to Prabhakaran, came as a breakthrough. It helped in unearthing of the LTTE's arms manufacturing units in Coimbatore where the locals were also involved.

Investigations brought to light the operation of two different groups sent by the LTTE to carry out two specific assignments — eliminate political adversaries and establish a strong base for the manufacture and supply of arms and ammunition to carry on the fight for a separate Eelam in Sri Lanka.

It was a timely tip-off by a carpenter that helped the SIT to crack the communication network of the LTTE and unearth its grenade factory in Coimbatore in August.

The carpenter was glued to his radio listening to film music at his native village, Thudiyalur, five kms off Coimbatore. Irritated by a spell of transmission disturbance, he was about to switch off the radio in disgust when he heard a creaky voice in Tamil enquiring about arms supplies.

Stunned for a moment, he quickly recovered composure when he remembered the SIT's appeal to the people to report to the nearest police station if they came across transmission disturbance over radio and television. He rushed to the Thudiyalur police station and reported the conversation he had heard.

Even as the police personnel were trying to pass on the tip-off to their officers in Coimbatore, a traffic constable stumbled on two men moving about suspiciously, and when questioned, answering incoherently. They were fisked, and a cyanide capsule was found hidden in one's pocket. The were later identified as Raghu and Vicky.

Convinced that they were militants, the constable herded them to the police station. Raghu and Vicky's arrest helped the SIT close in on Guna, a close associate of Prabhakaran, and Dixon. When their safehouse in Coimbatore was stormed on July 28, both committed suicide.

The interrogation of Raghu and Vicky revealed that Dixon, had gone with Raghu alias Sivaraj to a late night film show in Coimbatore even as the SIT was on his trail and his photos just published in the newspapers. Moreover, he had gone on a sightseeing visit to the popular hill resort Ooty a few weeks ago along with Vicky and others.

The 'Q' branch of Tamil Nadu police probed the Ooty visit in mid-July. The nephew of a Tamil film actress had accompanied him on the "pleasure trip" in an airconditioned Fiat. The choice of a Fiat, hired in Bangalore, was deliberate as the police were checking Marutis and Gypsys.

The Ooty angle was significant in view of the statement of the van driver who had given a lift to Dhanu from Nanjangudu in Karnataka near Ooty. The van driver had said that the woman (Dhanu) asked him to stop the van on seeing two youngsters waiting with a car on the roaside in the forest area about 12 km from Nanjangudu. Then she left with them. This was on May 20 evening, a day before the assassination. The police were obviously looking for any connection between what the van driver had told them and Dixon's visit to Ooty.

500-MEMBER LTTE KILLER SQUAD

The security agencies made another important arrest during this period. Twenty-year-old Varadan alias Shankar, a Sri Lankan

Tamil who was arrested from a LTTE hideout at Chittipalyam near Karur in Tamil Nadu on August 17 night, made a sensational confession. He said he was one of the 500-member killer squad the LTTE had sent to India in the first week of May to eliminate people opposed to it.

Varadan said in a written statement that he was in Tiruchi on May 21, the day Rajiv was assassinated, and was exulted when he heard the news over radio. But he also said he did not know whether Sivarasan and Subha belonged to the LTTE. Nor did he know of their whereabouts. He claimed he was closely associated with Dixon.

Varadan said the killer squad arrived by boats at Vedaranyam on May 10. He had gone to Bangalore with Arasan and stayed at Indira Nagar. Arasan had committed suicide a few days ago. He underwent four months' arms training at Mullaitheevu in northern Sri Lanka and had fought against the IPKF.

SIVARASAN

Sivarasan continues to be an enigma till date. Not much is authentically known about him. The arrested LTTE cadres too, divulged little to the SIT about the One-eyed-Jack. Believed to be the son of a Jaffna-based school teacher, Sivarasan's real name is said to be Bhagyachandran (also spelt as Pakyachandran).

He joined the LTTE in 1984 and was soon hailed as the terrorist outfit's one of the leading experts in handling rocket-propelled grenade launchers. It was while handling explosives a few years ago that he had lost his left eye.

What else can one call it but a quirk of fate that Sivarasan had narrowly escaped the IPKF's dragnet in the Jaffna peninsula. This escape proved too costly for India. A man of several aliases, Sivarasan was later shifted from the LTTE military wing in the eastern Batticaloa district to the Udupiddy area in Jaffna area as a political organiser.

Santhan, who had assisted him in Rajiv's assassination and in the murder of Padmanabha, told the SIT he had been asked by

Pottu Amman in Jaffna in April 1991 to accompany Sivarasan, Subha and Dhanu and follow Sivarasan's instructions. He said he did not know of the plan to assassinate Rajiv until much later.

Murugan, the first LTTE man to be arrested in connection with the case, could not throw much light either. All that could be extracted from Murugan was that because of the privileges Sivarasan enjoyed, such as unlimited flow of money and vehicles, he believed that the one-eyed Jack was a top-rung LTTE man.

Shanmugham told investigators he knew the one-eyed man as Raghuvaran and remained unaware for several days that 'Raghuvaran' and 'Sivarasan' were the same. Shanmugham was the person who had received Sivarasan and other members of the killer squad at his house in Thanjavur district in March 1991.

Equally uninformative were other arrested LTTE cadres like Jaykumar, Vijayan and Bhaskaran who did not make their interrogators any wiser about Sivarasan. This despite the fact that they had been brought to India by Sivarasan. They told the SIT that their function was merely to provide him with hideouts in various places.

The LTTE made several attempts to rescue the holed-up Sivarasan but each mission flopped for some reason or the other. The most dramatic attempt was by David, a senior LTTE functionary and leader of the LTTE's sea wing, the "Sea Tigers". The boat carrying the rescue party met with an accident on the high seas in June 1991 and the entire rescue team, including David, perished.

David was senior to Sivarasan in the LTTE hierarchy and had, in fact, led the LTTE killer squad in the assassination of EPRLF leader K Padmanabha in Madras in June 1990. Sivarasan had acted as David's deputy.

The inability of the LTTE in rescuing him was in sharp contrast to the ease with which Sivarasan and others had shuttled between the two countries up to May 1991. Sivarasan had made three trips since December 1990, bringing with him members of the killer squad and gold biscuits.

But he was not so lucky this time. The nation-wide red alert by Indian security agencies after the assassination had Sivarasan trapped.

4 THE MANHUNT

By now, the SIT had launched the biggest-ever manhunt in the history of India. It got as many as 300,000 colour posters of Sivarasan and Subha printed which were put up at vantage points in a number of cities, particularly down south.

Sivarasan became a much-sighted man. Not unlike an UFO. In June 1991, within a span of 24 hours, Sivarasan was reported to have been sighted at four different places, as far apart as Porur, a Madras suburb, and Attrikal, a village in Kerala. Each time he was "sighted", there was high drama.

SIT chief D R Karthikeyan sought the assistance of the public in tracking down the One-eyed Jack as he could be easily identified by his facial features and eyes. Sivarasan's left eye was smaller. He had an artificial glass eye which was implanted by a Madras opthalmologist about two years ago. This could be recognised even when he was wearing glasses.

Due to this defect, Sivarasan developed peculiar mannerisms, like raising his chin to have a clear vision. Karthikeyan said Sivarasan would be seen straining to see with his right eye. One definite point of identification was his missing left eyeball and closed eyelids which could be in the absence of the glass eye. Even when he was wearing the artificial eye, the difference between the two eyes was perceptible as the left eye looked smaller.

On June 17, Karthikeyan appealed to opthalmologists in Madras to go through their records and find if at any point of time in the past two years they had given a glass eye to a man of Sivarasan's description.

The SIT managed to obtain a second photograph of Sivarasan from his driving licence application, filed on April 4, 1991. It was not a recent photograph and was found to have been touched up.

Sivarasan was known to have moved around in the suburbs of Madras like Porur, Villivakkam, Gunnidipoondi and Neelankarai and in Besant Nagar and Parrys corner of the city, using motorcycles, autorickshaws and even cycles.

On June 29 morning, a Broadway-bound bus from Thiruvanmiyur halted at Royapetta in Madras to pick up a 30-year-old man carrying a parcel. The passenger, who had a startling resemblance to Sivarasan, left the parcel under the conductor's seat at the rear and moved up. Passengers scrambled out of the bus fearing a blast.

The previous night, the Madurai police had combed the city following a tip-off that a couple resembling Sivarasan and Subha were spotted hiring a three-wheeler near Vaigai river. Patrolling in the coastal district of Ramanathapuram was intensified.

Police intercepted a Tambaram-bound bus to question a Subha look-alike. The woman was identified as Arpuda Mary, who was going to appear for a job interview.

In the last week of June, Sivarasan was "spotted" at suburban Porur. Residents said "Sivarasan", dressed in trousers and shirt, was seen on two successive evenings walking towards a house in the Porur locality along with two Sri Lankan Tamils.

Robert Payas and his cousin Jaykumar, both Sri Lankan Tamils arrested in connection with the assassination, also had houses in Porur area. Neighbours said the person they had seen on thsoe two days had a shoddy appearance, a blackened face, and wore dirty clothes. His nose and lower jaw bore an acute resemblance to the wanted kurta-pyjama clad man.

More spice was added when a charred body, suspected to be that of a Sri Lankan Tamil, was found at New Kalpakkam in Chengai Anna district of Tamil Nadu on June 30. The youth had been stabbed to death, and his body bore more than 80 per cent burn injuries. His face was mutilated.

This was the second body to have been found in three days in the district after the SIT launched its hunt for Sivarasan and Subha. On June 27, the police had fished out the body of a 30-year-old Sri

Lankan Tamil with gunshot injuries on his left eyebrow from a pond near Fuzhal. These incidents gave rise to rumours that the one-eyed Jack had been killed to blot out crucial evidence in the case.

Then there were reports of Sivarasan having been sighted in the Pulicat-Ennore coastal belt and interception of a wireless message allegedly sent by him seeking help from Jaffna.

A combing operation was launched in the Pulicat lake area on July 3. The house-to-house search was conducted by inspector general of police (law and order) W I Dawaram . All land and sea escape routes were sealed before the operation. The Nellore district police were put on alert following specific tip-offs about the fugitives.

In far-away Raipur in Madhya Pradesh, disciplinary action was taken against an assistant sub-inspector of the railway police and five constables in the last week of July. They were charged with failing to inform the authorities about the interrogation of a train passenger resembling Sivarasan. The Raipur railway police had received information from Bilaspur that a Sivarasan look-alike was travelling by the Howrah-Ahmedabad Express. The informant had even given the coach number (S-4) in which the man was travelling.

By the first week of July, investigators were exploring all possibilities, including the possibility of Sivarasan having already sneaked out of Tamil Nadu. If he had, his most likely destination could either be Bangalore or Bombay.

There were rumours of Sivarasan escaping to the Bombay underworld. With Bangalore no more a safe haven, Dharavi in Bombay was likely to be *the* place. This view was bolstered by press reports that the late Vardaraja, don of the Bombay underworld in the eighties, had made a huge cash donation to the LTTE. If organised crime was sheltering Sivarasan, it was bad news as penetrating the Bombay underworld had always been a tough proposition.

*

THE WILD GOOSE CHASE

On July 11, the SIT issued a press release giving personal details of the fugitives on the basis of updated information. It said Sivarasan, Subha and another person, Nehru alias Gokul, had been sighted during the past ten days and were seen moving around with large bags. The SIT alerted the authorities to set up road blocks and look out for the three accused.

The Sivarasan trail in several states led the police on a wild goose chase.

Intensive combing operations were launched in Bangalore and Vishakhapatnam to check autorickshaws following tip-offs that Sivarasan and Subha were seen travelling in a three-wheeler scooter. More than 100 trawlers were searched at Vishakapatnam harbour, and a close watch kept at the Bhimilipatnam port, about 20 kms away. All hotels and lodges in the city were searched thoroughly.

In the Gulbarga district of Karnataka, police searched the Bombay-bound Minar Express on the night of July 9 following an information from the Secunderabad railway superintendent of police that Sivarasan and Subha had boarded the train in Hyderabad.

Police combed the Kuridi hills on Tamil Nadu-Kerala border on July 9 night following a tip-off that Sivarasan and Subha were holed up there. Expectations of a major breakthrough heightened when the police recovered cooking utensils, a blood-stained shirt and four dhotis from a hide-out. The man, living in the hide-out along with a woman, had coerced a local boy into buying provisions and cooking utensils for them. The boy told the police that the man had a "lot of hundred rupee notes". Further investigation showed the man was a petty criminal on the run.

The Gujarat police swung into action on July 19 following reports that Sivarasan was sighted in the temple town of Dwarka in Jamnagar district. The informant told the police a "suspicious-looking" south Indian man had travelled with him in a bus on Rajkot-Okha route. and had alighted at Dwarka. The police raided hotels and lodges in Dwarka, Mithapur and Okha, and even checked the boats and ships anchored at the Okha jetty.

The Hubli police conducted widespread searches of the passing vehicles and lodges on July 24 following a "tip-off" that Sivarasan and Subha had disembarked from a Bangalore-bound bus.

On August 10, the Indian Navy and the Tamil Nadu Police launched a massive hunt for the fugitives on the Rameswaram coast. There was a tip-off that they were planning to escape to Jaffna with the help of seven LTTE militants who had landed the previous day on a powerful speedboat.

A house-to-house search was carried out in Rameswaram and Dhanushkodi. All possible routes and several commercial jetties in and around these areas were sealed off and a unit of the SIT rushed to Rameswaram.

A flat-bottomed plastic speedboat with three outboard engines was first spotted off Dhanushkodi island on the morning of August 9 by a naval ship which chased it. The boat with seven militants on board entered shallow waters when a helicopter from Uchipuli naval detatchment in Thanjavur coast picked it up. The boat *Karainagar*, was speeding in the direction of a casurina grove, three kms from Rameswaram. It was found abandoned near the grove, but there was no sign of the militants.

Police found a passport size photo of Sivarasan and a note about Mahendran, strengthening suspicion that the *Karainagar* was on a rescue mission. The police alerted local fishermen as Sivarasan and Subha could easily melt away in the huge crowds gathered for Adi-Amavasya.

Then there was a report of Sivarasan having been sighted in Mysore city in Karnataka.

Two college lecturers waited for two hours early on August 12 at the residence of a senior police official to report about a man resembling Sivarasan. He was alone and bore marks of injuries on his face.

The police took the information seriously, especially in the wake of a LTTE threat to blow up the Krishanaraja Sagar reservoir on August 13 night. Police immediately mounted a vigil on the villages in and around the Krishnaraja Sagar reservoir, which houses the world famous Brindavan gardens. Tourist entry into the gardens was stopped.

The Calcutta police, too, were put on alert after Sivarasan and Subha were reported to be hiding in a south Indian pocket in the city. Colour posters of the two fugitives were put up at public places and the Calcutta airport authorities alerted.

It was not just the Rs 15 lakh reward for information leading to the arrest of Sivarasan and Subha which was the prime motivation for informants. Some people used the opportunity to settle personal scores.

The case of a SIT team being led to a house in suburban Tambaram in Madras by the parents of a teenaged girl to teach a lesson to an eve-teaser is just one of them.

The Sivarasan trail had also put the sleuths in many an embarrassing situation. Anyone closely resembling the One-eyed Jack and Subha was picked up and taken to Malligai, SIT's fortress-like headquarters.

Among those mistaken for Sivarasan and detained was Tamil Nadu assembly speaker Sedapatti Muthia's bodyguard.

Another person fitting Sivarasan's description was detained at the Madras airport as he disembarked from an Indian Airlines plane coming from Bangalore on the night of June 24. He was let off when he was identified as Mahendran, an officer in a nationalised bank in Madras.

There was panic among the passengers and staff at the domestic departure terminal at New Delhi airport on July 18 when security agencies made a passenger for Bangalore to disembark just before the take-off. Suspicion about the Tamil-speaking Sivarasan look-alike was fuelled further when his ticket was found to have some discrepancy. The passenger was let off after being identified as Mohammad Daoud, a bona-fide businessman.

A woman resembling Subha was surrounded by hundreds of villagers in Tiruvanmalai in Tamil Nadu on August 5. She had entered the residence of the Thandaramattu MLA, Sundar, at Chinniyambettai village. Her "crime" was to have given disjointed answers when forced with a barrage of questions.

In yet another instance of a goof-up, a mathematics lecturer of the Jagadguru Murugharajendrra Institute at Chitradurga near Mysore was detained on August 14. M K Mehboob Sab, with a missing eye, matched Sivarasan's features perfectly. He had arrived in Mysore four days before on one of his annual trips to the city to evaluate answer scripts of an engineering examination.

As on previous occasions, Mehboob Sab had checked into his favourite lodge with one of his fellow lecturers, M N Nanjappa. Soon after the pot-bellied Mehboob Sab had returned from his morning walk, he was picked up by plain clothed policemen and taken to Mysore police commissioner V V Bhaskar for questioning, and then to Karnataka IG (law and order). When the IG learnt of Sab's identity, he apologised profusely.

Ye another suspect was reported the next day from Coimbatore. A 30-year-old bearded man with an artificial eye was picked up from a bus stop at Ramanathapuram in the city. The man was eventually identified as Jose Jerome, an electrician by profession. The damage to his left eye was cogential and he had fixed an artificial lens.

One call led a SIT team and commandos of the crack National Security Guards to a house in the Madras suburbs. After surrounding the house, the officers called out to the inmates to come out. Even after 15 minutes, there was little response, save for the occasional opening and closing of windows. This "confirmed" the presence of LTTE militants in the house. Just when the Black Cat commandos were preparing to storm the house, an elderly lady cautiously opened the door, ready to face the armed men whom she mistook for dacoits. The elderly couple had been busy for the past 15 minutes in hiding their jewels and valuables in a shoe before deciding to face the "dacoits".

And then there was the case of an anonymous phone call from a man who claimed to have a vital information and an equipment that would lead to the arrest of Sivarasan. It turned out that the man, who was wearing eight shirts under which he claimed the "equipment" was concealed, was demented.

*

SOMETHING CONCRETE AT LAST

The old man saw a woman of ripe years advancing towards his house in Kodungayur, a newly developed Madras colony. The colony was thinly populated.

An irritated Bhaskaran blocked the woman's path and asked her what she wanted. She said that she wanted to see his daughter. While replying, the woman tried to peep into the unlit room. Bhaskaran could not control his anger. He yelled at the woman, and slammed the door, muttering to himself.

Sivarasan overheard the heated exchange between his harbourer and the neighbour. He and Subha realised that it was not the police but some silly neighbour who wanted to chat her evening away with the lady of the house.

But the Mantels were not silly at all. It was the second week of June, 1996 and the nation was following the investigation with rapt attention. The elderly Anglo-Indian couple had become suspicious about strange goings-on in the house of Bhaskaran and his son, Vijayan. They had also sighted a man they thought resembled Sivarasan. Every morning before daybreak, the man took a bath at a borewell in the backyard. He was also seen on the terrace in early mornings or evenings, doing yoga. On another occasion the Mantels spotted a couple : who resembled Sivarasan and Subha. It was an amateurish recce that old lady Mantel had conducted.

The Mantels had a niggling suspicion that their neighbours were Rajiv's assassins and had already spent several sleepless nights. On several occasions in the past, Mantel, a retired railway employee, had toyed with the idea of informing the SIT about his suspicions. He had gone to the SIT headquarters, but had developed cold feet. But this time, it was not just a suspicion. Bhaskaran's unprovoked hostility had confirmed their worst fears. The Mantel family had to do something.

Mustering courage, Mantel's wife walked up to a restaurant to make a telephone call to the SIT control room. The nervous woman looked around before lifting the receiver from the cradle, then quickly dialled the number. She did not identify herself.

"I can tell you where Sivarasan is. Send me a vehicle and an escort," She whispered into the mouthpiece, which she had carefully cupped with her hands.

"Who are you ? Where are you calling from," the SIT DIG who received her call asked gruffly.

She gave the name of the restaurant, but did not divulge her identity or residential address. Then she hung up. Her heart was pounding.

The DIG asked for a vehicle to fetch her, but was told after some time that no vehicle was available. He told his boss about the telephone call and that there was no vehicle to fetch the caller. The SIT received hundreds of calls; most were misleading or a hoax.

The woman went back home after waiting at the restaurant for about half an hour. No SIT team turned up. After this, the Mantels could never gather courage to contact the investigators the second time. Sivarasan and Subha, alongwith their wireless operater Nero, stayed in the same locality for more than a fortnight after this incident.

*

"I still don't see the reason why you want an entire house to yourself," said the host, while fixing yet another drink for Bhaskaran. "And who will pay the rent?"

Bhaskaran had come to his friend on June 27 and said he had to take a house on rent. His friend did not take him seriously. He was not convinced by Bhaskaran's story that he wanted to live away from his quarrelsome son.

Bhaskaran was quite tipsy. He had lost count of the number of pegs he had gulped. "I have enough money," the old man said cockily.

To prove that he was flush with cash, Bhaskaran took out a hundred rupee note and asked his host to get roasted chicken. Then taking another swig from his glass a whisky soaked Bhaskaran leaned over and whispered he wanted the house not for himself but for Sivarasan.

If the two men were drinking in a pub, all eyes would have turned to them because the host jumped, as if stung by a scorpion.

"Sivarasan who ?" his startled host asked in disbelief.

"The same fellow whose photographs appear in newspapers every day. He is living with me," Bhaskaran said proudly, as if he owned a tiger. Then he said it was more than a month since Sivarasan had been staying with him and that he was desperate to change hide-out.

It took some time for the host before what the drunken Bhaskaran just blurted out sank in. Suddenly alert, he suggested the old man spent the night at his house as it was past midnight. Bhaskaran readily agreed. His house was at least five kilometres away and he was far too drunk to walk the distance. The host then quietly dropped a suggestion: why not get Sivarasan arrested and collect the huge reward? Bhaskaran replied he would let him know the next day.

Bhaskaran's mind was made up the following morning; he was game. Both men went to the SIT headquarters with their story. A SIT team immediately went with them to Kodungaiyur. But the birds had already flown.

Vijayan was at the house when Sivarasan and the others left. He told the investigators that Sivarasan picked up an air bag and walked out with Subha and Nero. He had not seen anybody waiting for the hit squad outside his house or any vehicle. But he did see Sivarasan digging up their kitchen and burying something. Vijayan proved right. A kitchen tile had been removed and several articles squirrelled away in the hole. Sivarasan's diaries (in which he had jotted down his daily expenses), his artificial eye, wireless parts, several live 9 mm cartridges, and a Tamil-English pocket dictionary were found. The dictionary had a cavity in it in which Sivarasan used to keep his pistol.

Bhaskaran's family was taken to the SIT headquarters and grilled for hours. They maintained they were kept virtual hostages by Sivarasan at gun point. Bhaskaran's friend, whose help he had sought in hiring a house for Sivarasan was also interrogated. The SIT found gaping loopholes in Bhaskaran's story. The entire family was arrested on charges of habouring the hit squad members. Bhaskaran's friend was let off.

*

Nobody noticed the edible oil tanker as it chugged into life on the night of June 28 in the sleepy colony of Kodungaiyur. Minutes later, Dhanasekharan swung the massive vehicle on the Madras-Bangalore national highway. The fuel needle showed "Full" .

The tanker was empty of oil, but it was worth its weight in gold, both for the LTTE and the SIT — Sivarasan, Subha and Nero were hiding inside. Several border checkposts came. But an empty oil tanker, with its lid open obviously did not attract anybody's attention.

Sivarasan had not told Vijayan and his family where they were going. They were not even told that the three were finally leaving their house, Madras, and even Tamil Nadu.

The tanker had been thoroughly washed and a big mattress thrown inside. Nobody witnessed the tanker's cargo loading operation. In any case, there was no street light and it was pitch dark.

Sivarasan was carrying his favourite T-56 assault rifle which he had used for killing EPRLF leader Padmanabha an year ago. He had given his loaded Austria-made Steyer pistol to Subha. Nero was without a weapon. The driver, Dhanasekharan, was accompanied by two other LTTE cadres, Vicky and Amman.

The fugitives hit upon the idea of escaping in an oil tanker after Pottu Amman informed Sivarasan that considering the stepped-up surveillance on coasts, there was no chance of a rescue boat and that they would have to remain in hiding in India till the manhunt slackened somewhat.

Had the tanker been stopped by the police, Vicky was to tap the vehicle twice. This would be the signal for Sivarasan and Subha to take combat-ready positions. If the securitymen insisted on checking the inside of the tanker, Vicky was to tap four times, and the guerillas would open fire.

In the end, the contingency plan was not required at all. The great escape was quite uneventful. Except for routine border checkposts, the getaway vehicle was not stopped during its six and a half hour-long journey to Bangalore. A lot of edible oil tankers move between Madras and Bangalore; another one did not raise any suspicion.

The tanker, registered in the name of D K Transport, Mettur, rolled into Bangalore before daybreak. All three hidden passengers had sustained cuts and bruises on their elbows and knees, despite a mattress laid on the floor.

The tanker's destination was Domalur, a developing Bangalore suburb near Indira Nagar. The cargo was offloaded and bundled into a waiting Premier Padmini and taken to an LTTE safehouse in Indira Nagar.

Vicky and Amman parked the tanker near a roadside eating joint, came down whistling, took bath and had breakfast. They were like any other ordinary driver-cleaner pair present at the stall.

The fugitives found the Indira Nagar safehouse, to be a virtual mini-hospital. At least 15 injured LTTE cadres were there, some of them in serious condition. Somebody's arm had been blown off, somebody's leg was plastered, while some had gunshot wounds. Sivarasan, Subha and Nero immediately attended to their cuts and bruises and settled down in the single-storeyed rented house where they were to stay for a few days. Rangan, Amman, Vicky, Irumborai, Suresh Master and Kirthi—all LTTE cadres— used to live in Bangalore and kept visiting them.

*

Two youths on a moped were enjoying their ride in Coimbatore on July 26 evening, till they jumped a traffic signal. Unluckily for Vicky and Raghu, the minor offence triggered off an avalanche of events.

They were spotted by an alert traffic constable, who chased them till they were caught. Neither Vicky nor Raghu had a drivers' licence. The two were taken to the police station. The Superintendent of police suspected them to be LTTE activists. Their accent was Sri Lankan, their answers evasive. Vicky and Raghu were interrogated for hours, till broken. Vicky gave his residential address.

Next day, the Coimbatore police surrounded his house. Superintendent of police (rural Coimbaotre) Mutthu Karuppan himself supervised the raid. He was certain the house they had surrounded was an LTTE safe-house and that Sivarasan was holed up inside. RAW had already passed an information that Sivarasan was nowhere near the coast. The surrounded house was a typical LTTE safehouse— a single-storeyed house in a new thinly-populated colony.

Karuppan made an anouncement from a public address system, asking all those inside the house to come out and surrender. Dixon and Guna were trapped. Dixon opened a window and peeped out. He warned against storming of the house. Karuppan said all that he wanted was a surrender and promised no force and third degree measures would be used after their surrender. Dixon said he wanted some time to think and then ran to the wireless set to contact Pottu Amman. RAW intercepted the message. Dixon was heard telling Pottu Amman that he and Guna had been surrounded by the police and that Vicky was missing since the previous afternoon. Papa Oscar directed him to destroy the wireless set and consume cyanide. Some time had already passed and the trapped Tigers were anticipating commando action any time.

Dixon lit a stove and placed the wireless on it. Dixon and Guna stood in the middle of the room and bit into their glass capsules containing cyanide. To make sure that they are not captured and administered any antidote, Guna activated a hand-grenade and hurled it on the ground between them.

The police stormed the house on hearing the explosion. Apart from the two bodies, the police also recovered a note scribbled by Dixon, thanking SIT chief Karthikeyan on behalf of the LTTE for his "good work".

On August 2 the S I T and Black Cat commandos of NSG surrounded the Indira Nagar safehouse at Bangalore. There were intelligence reports of suspicious movements in the Indira Nagar house. All that the S I T got was the bodies of two LTTE cadres who happened to be inside the house. They had consumed cyanide. Sivarasan and his hit squad members had already been transferred to another safehouse in town.

*

The young couple were quarreling that evening. The heated argument was audible to Sivarasan, Subha and Nero in the adjacent room. This was not the first time when Mridula had fought with her husband J Ranganath.

Sivarasan and company had been living in Ranganath's two-room tenement in the congested Bangalore locality of Pottan Halli for a week. Ranganath was unemployed and in debt. But instead of paying for their lodging, the unwanted guests used to threaten Mridula from time to time. This was precisely her grouse.

Mridula used to watch television with interest. Whenever the Doordarshan flashed the pictures of Sivarasan and the other absconders in the Rajiv assassination case soliciting information from the public for their capture, her excitement would be too apparent. After a point, Nero began to switch off the TV everytime the announcement was made. Before storming out of the room, he would give her a hard stare.

Mridula was not the type who could be cowed down so easily. She argued with her husband about the rationale behind harbouring the hit squad members. Several times she suggested contacting the police and picking up the reward. But Ranganath would shudder at the very thought. He had once received a favour from the LTTE cadre and now it was his turn to return it.

But at what cost, Mridula often asked her husband. One day or the other, Sivarasan was bound to be arrested. The fact that they gave shelter to the One-eyed Jack and his accomplices would come to the knowledge of the police. And they would be arrested for sheltering the country's most wanted terrorists.

But, Ranganath was scared to incur the LTTE's wrath. What if they tipped off the police and the Tigers come to know of it. The LTTE would never forgive them, Ranganath would counter argue. Mridula would have no answer to this.

The couple was trapped. They were virtual hostages in their own house. Mridula chided her husband day in and day out for inviting trouble to their house. But even this she could have endured had the fugitives not lived on them like parasites.

As the subsequent events were to show, Sivarasan's miserly attitude ultimately proved too costly.

Mridula was piqued, but Sivarasan had no choice. He and his accomplices had to live in a house which did not fulfill even a single criterion of a LTTE safehouse. Pottan Halli was a thickly populated and congested colony. The privacy they had enjoyed in the Kodungaiyur and Indira Nagar hide-outs was not there.

Sivarasan had dumped his wireless set on instructions from Jaffna. He could not move out and was confined inside the four walls, totally dependent on whatever support he was getting from the LTTE's political wing. The political wing cadres were looking for a better safehouse, and Sivarasan had been pressing Ranganath virtually everyday to look for a new house.

The LTTE had recently rented two houses in Beroota and Mutathi reserve forest areas in the nearby Mandya district. But the injured LTTE cadres, who had been shifted from Madras some weeks ago, had to be lodged in these houses.

Ranganath's efforts finally paid dividends and a suitable house was found at Konanakunte, about six kilometres from Pottan Halli. Four LTTE cadres— Suresh Master, Amman, Keerthi and

Jamila alias Jamuna, whose one leg was amputated shifted to their new residence on August 4. Sivarasan, Subha and Nero moved into this house on Independence Day, before day break.

Sivarasan was carrying his T-56 rifle wrapped in a bed sheet, before he sat in the waiting Gypsy. He wore a golf cap and walked with his head down and finger on the trigger of the concealed rifle. Before leaving, Sivarasan directed Ranganath to immediately shift to the Konanakunte house along with his wife.

Ranganath set about meekly to implement Sivarasan's orders. It was around 9 am when he fetched a tempo, and loaded on it whatever meagre luggage he had not yet pawned. Mridula was furious. She put her foot down and made it clear she was not going to get herself entangled with Sivarasan any longer.

Mridula's brother was a clergyman in a nearby church. She told her husband that if he did not give up his idea, she would go to live with her brother. Ranganath said nothing, and an exasperated Mridula got down in front of the church.

*

The Beroota police had been tipped off about some suspected poachers trading in animal skins. When Vicky's Gypsy passed the checkpost on August 14, they followed it.

The Beroota police had no idea they were unwittingly homing in on an LTTE hideout. As a precautionary measure, the police carried firearms as poachers normally carried guns. A quick appraisal of the house confirmed their suspicions. It was an old-fashioned tiled roof house. Located in the midst of a reserve forest area, it was ideal for wildlife traders.

The inmates of the house sensed some movement outside. When they saw policemen, they panicked and consumed cyanide. Most died, but two survived. The cyanide was a give-away clue: poachers do not commit suicide.

Shortly afterwards, the Mandya checkpost in-charge heard of another house where suspicious movements were noticed. This house was in Mutathi. But this time, the police were more cautious. They knew it was LTTE cadres and not poachers they were dealing with. The young sub-inspector in-charge of the operation made more elaborate preparations, and even carried kerosene in jerrycans.

The sub-inspector was a dare-devil. He had smashed the Beroota hide-out; now he was leading another operation, again all on his own. And he did not have any anti-cyanide kits.

LTTE's main weapon is the element of surprise. But this time, the sub-inspector turned the tables on it. He saw that like all other houses in the locality, the safehouse too had a tiled roof. He divided his personnel into two teams: one stormed in from the main entrance, while the other broke through the roof and jumped in simultaneously.

The injured Tigers inside the house were taken unawares. Some were overpowered before they could consume cyanide. Some were more successful. Undeterred, the sub-inspector ordered his boys to start the "funnel treatment": a funnel was forced in the mouths of those who had swallowed cyanide and kerosene was poured in. Within minutes, the Tigers vomitted out the poison before it could get absorbed in their blood. Six or seven guerillas were thus saved in the Beroota and Mutathi operations.

A search of the house was carried out immediately after this. It yielded an important document: a chit on which was scribbled, " Ranganath. Pottan Halli"

*

Ranganath spent the night in the Konanakunte house with Sivarasan and company. He narrated to Sivarasan how Mridula quarrelled and refused to come with him. He carefully deleted Mridula's reasons for fighting with him. Sivarasan told him sternly to keep his wife under control and warned that if she were to spill the beans, he would kill both of them. Ranganath heard him meekly and nodded his head in compliance.

The fugitives guarded the Konanakunte house in shifts. Sivarasan was very strict about guarding the house they were living in, howsoever safe that house might be. In Vijayan's house at Kodungaiyur, Madras, they were only three. Sivarasan, along with Subha and Nero, used to take an eight-hour guard duty shift every day. In every house they lived in, Sivarasan selected the vantage points and supervised drilling of holes in walls and windows from where his T-56 could fire. He had adopted the same system here.

*

The sub-inspector had now hit upon the address of yet another suspected LTTE hide-out. But, unfortunately, it was in an area not under his jurisdiction. He went to the assistant commissioner of police, Bangalore, who was incharge of the Pottan Halli area.

The ACP junmped when he heard the sub-inspector's story. He was busy with Independence Day arrangements, but this was definitely far more important.

The ACP immediately got into his Gypsy and drove to Pottan Halli. Enquiries led him to a man who had seen Ranganath that very morning, loading his houshold goods on to a tempo and leaving with his wife. This fuelled the ACP's suspicion. He directed his men to trace the driver of the tempo.

Next morning, the driver was produced before the ACP. He said he had transported a couple who were quarreling before the wife had got down in front of a nearby church while the husband had gone to Konanakunte. The driver offered to take the ACP to the church where he had dropped Mridula.

Mridula became nervous when she saw uniformed policemen walking briskly towards the church verandah where she was sitting.

" I know why you have come" she blurted out before even being questioned.

The ACP was confused, but he covered it up and asked whether she really knew why he had come to see her.

"Because you want to know where Sivarasan is," she shot back, still agitated.

The ACP was thunder struck. Had he really hit pay dirt? But once again, he masked his emotions.

"Yes, tell me where is Sivarasan?" the ACP asked without batting an eyelid.

"Come on, I will show you the house, " Mridula said and started walking towards the police Gypsy.

The ACP brooded a while. They quietly asked his men to keep a watch on Mridula and told her to wait till he returned in his own maruti car-an unmarked civilian vehicle.

It was a necessary precaution. Minutes later, he was back and with Mridula by his side, drove off. Mridula quietly pointed out the house where Sivarasan and others were living, and ACP drove by.

Before initiating investigations after the Beroota-Mutathi operations, the ACP had rung up Karnataka's DIG (intelligence) A K Singh. After ascertaining where Sivarasan lived, the ACP dashed to the office of his superior, the area DCP.

DCP Kempiah was itching to storm Sivarasan's hide-out. But an information of this explosive nature had to be shared with police commissioner R Ramalingam.

Ramalingam, expectedly, was excited. But unlike Kempiah, he chose to tread a cautious path. Ramalingam told Kempiah it was a case of the SIT. SIT chief Karthikeyan was Ramalingam's senior and like him, belonged to the Karnataka cadre of the IPS. So he did not want to annoy Karthikeyan. The SIT had to be brought into the picture.

Karthikeyan reacted on the lines expected. He asked Ramalingam to sit quiet and await his arrival. Karthikeyan sent a team of SIT officers and NSG commandos, led by Captain Ravi, by road. The SIT team reached Bangalore much before day-break on August 16. The team was ordered not to embark on any operation and report to the Bangalore police commissioner. But police commissioner Ramalingam had already been told to wait till the SIT chief arrived.

It was typical bureaucratese. Nothing moved for more than two days. Soon, a virtual army of top officials was to descend on the spot and botch up everything, in stark contrast to the splendid results given by a much junior officer of Mandya district a few days ago.

OPERATION BOTCH-UP

The country's biggest and most intense manhunt for assassins on the run ended in Bangalore, ironically on the birth anniversary of Rajiv Gandhi — August 20.

An observant milk woman smelt something fishy about the new occupants of a house in Konankunte. Her suspicious were aroused by the manner in which a woman took the milk every morning: the door would open in a rather surreptitious manner, the woman's hand would stretch out to take the milk and the door would be shut again. The face of the woman who received milk was never visible.

The milk woman, Muniyamma, reported the matter to the police.

As Ramalingam later said, the police were tipped off on August 18 around 7 pm, full 36 hours before the Black Cat commandos of NSG stormed the single-storyed house.

It was a tip-off that was wasted. Rangan, the LTTE man who had arranged the get-away tanker for Sivarasan and was tending injured Tigers in Bangalore, was on his way to Konankunte to see the One-eyed Jack when he noticed policemen flooding the area. Alarmed, he reversed his vehicle and sped to the house of Irumborai, another LTTE activist.

Ranganath was at Irumboari's house on an errand from Sivarasan. Rangan told Ranganath he, too, had seen the police presence outside the Sivarasan's hideout and advised him not to go back to Sivarasan. After alerting his friends, Rangan immediately left for Madras where he was arrested a week later.

Ranganath went to his empty Pottan Halli house, from where he was arrested the next day.

But if Rangan, on a flying visit, could spot the policemen a mile off, so could Sivarasan, maintaining a hawk-eyed vigil from his hideout. Escape was impossible, Sivarasan told his accomplices. LTTE is known to pull off incredible escapes. But this case was very much different. The LTTE had never admitted its hand in Rajiv's assassination. If it were to attempt rescue of any accused in the case, its involvement would have become obvious.

The hit squad leader felt handicapped without his wireless set which had been sent to Trichy and was being operated by another LTTE guerilla.

The storming of the house was delayed because a medical team was on its way from Gwalior with the antidote for cyanide poisoning. The authorities wanted to catch Sivarasan and Subha alive, believing the assassins would be oblivious to the high-voltage drama that was being enacted all around.

There was no action as hours went by. The crowd that began with a few dozen swelled with each passing hour and by the next day, the atmosphere had become festive.

Then, as luck would have it, a lorry got bogged down in mud right in front of the targeted house. It had rained a short while ago. Nearly twenty people started pushing the lorry to take it out of the slush. Almost immediately, shots rang out from inside the house as the trapped militants mistook the lorry as a smoke screen for an imminent commando operation. A traffic constable was hit on his shoulder.

The police fired back. Two militants came out of the house but ran back. And still the police waited for the anti-cyanide kit.

Ten minutes later, there was another burst of fire, this time from the rear of the house. NSG officer Jai Singh and sub-inspector Balagi Singh were injured. NSG sharpshooters returned fire. The exchange of fire continued for some time. After some time, two pistol shots were heard inside the house and then there was silence.

It was around this time that the police commissioner sent an SOS for more reinforcements. A similar message was also sent to the CRPF battalion stationed at Yellahanka.

Action had finally begun. The air was pregnant with excitement. Inside the hide-out, Sivarasan ordered everybody to assemble in the drawing room. Nero stopped firing and joined the group. The last hour had come. They wrote a one-page note, praising Prabhakaran and the LTTE.

Holding hands together, they sang a song, presumably the "national anthem" of Eelam. A single sholt rang out and the house planged into darkness.

The single shot firing and lights going out in the surrounded hide-out were recorded by a Doordarshan camera team. It was 9.30 pm, and a whole series of futile exercises began to be enacted. Four searchlights were fixed at vantage points to see the movements in and around the targeted house. Local residents were evacuated.

At 10 pm, reinforcements started arriving and an assault was planned. But it was deferred again after the CBI chief and the police commissioner decided that a special team of doctors was needed in case the militants took cyanide. Both of them left the place, probably to contact New Delhi.

At midnight, Ramalingam informed the DCP the assault would be only after a NSG team of crack commandos reached Bangalore. Their arrival was expected only around 4 am.

Half an hour later, more than 120 CRPF men arrived at the spot. At 4.30 am, a dozen NSG commandos landed at Bangalore airport. The team reached the spot 45 minutes later. CBI and SIT chiefs held last-minute discussions before the commando action.

Soon after the commandos' arrival in the early hours of August 20, nearly a thousand personnel drawn from the NSG, the CRPF, the Karnataka state reserve police and the Bangalore city police took up positions. A fleet of ambulances was kept ready.

At 6.15 am, NSG commandos started closing in on the house from three directions.

Five minutes later they climbed the nearest spot and tried in vain to jump on the top of the house. Finally, a ladder was brought from one of the fire brigade vehicles parked nearby. The commandos made a bridge with the ladder from the adjacent house. They got on to the roof top and planted plastic explosives on the rooftop door.

Simultaneously, another NSG group crawled up to the front gate of the house and planted explosives there.

The two doors were blasted and the commandos stormed in.

There was an eerie silene. It was also the moment of truth.

The Tigers did not rush out with their guns blazing. Nor did they blow up the buildings around. All that the commandos found were the bodies of two women and five men.

Sivarasan and Subha were among the dead. While everybody else had consumed cyanide, Sivarasan had taken the double precaution to ensure that he did not survive: he took cyanide first and then shot himself from close range through the temple.

Subha was found lying hugging a woman with an artificial leg in a corner of the front room. The bodies of Sivarasan and two of his bodyguards, also holding hands in a symbolic gesture, were lying alongside. The bodies of two more militants were found lying in another corner. Sivarasan was sporting a gold ring. Subha, dressed in a kameez and petticoat, was wearing silver anklets and toe rings — an indication of her marital status.

Sivarasan and Subha were identified by Murugan who was brought to Bangalore from Madras by the SIT on August 21.

The physically handicapped woman had scribbled a two-line message in Tamil on her hand. Translated it read as follows : "We will break the door of freedom. If we fail, we will break doors to achieve it."

The house had a lot of ammunition, bombs, grenades, an AK-47 rifle and another automatic weapon. There was a pile of ash under the staircase. Its freshness indicated that just before the militants committed suicide, they had burnt all records.

Tell-tale signs of their lifestyle were strewn all around.

In the kitchen, there was about half a kg of cooked rice, little brinjal curry along with fried beef. There was enough vegetable for seven of them to last three days. The kitchen was well used. The utensils, the gas stove and the gas cylinder appeared freshly bought. An old bronze tumbler was used to measure the quantity of rice for cooking.

There were several lungis, petticoats, sanitary napkins, a packet of small sized black bindis, ear buds, women's handkerchiefs and gaudy, cheap kitbags, normally sold on the pavements. But the shoes and imported stonewashed jeans appeared to be expensive.

On the pedestal of the pooja room, there were three unbroken coconuts. There were no idols or portaits of gods.

But in another room, there was crudely made mud idol, about six inches in size . There were three small strands of cotton pasted on its forehead, indicating that the militants were followers of Lord Shiva.

There were no beds or pillows in the house. The militants used only mats and sheets. The sheets doubled up as curtains.

THE BREAKFAST SHOW

When Konankunte awoke early on August 20, residents saw rifle-toting Black Cat commandos on the rooftops.

The breakfast show was on. In fact, it was a "tamasha".

There was no proper planning. Traffic police personnel had a tough time clearing the way for ambulances as more than 120 police jeeps, cars, vans and support vehicles were parked in a haphazard manner. An unnamed "top traffic police officer" was quoted in the media as saying that more than 100 litres of petrol and diesel was wasted in just moving the vehicles from one end to the other to facilitate the entry of ambulances.

Making the Konankunte operation blatantly farcical was the utter lack of coordination between CRPF and NSG personnel. Most CRPF men kept sitting in their trucks till morning. The reason: they had not been told to take up positions.

Companies of the Karnataka state reserve police were performing the drill. They were creating so much ruckus that it could be heard even two kms away.

For the immediate neighbours of the militants, it was a nightmarish experiene.

Murthy and his son and daughter-in-law had to vacate their residence for the security agencies. Wireless sets were placed in the house, with policemen not even leaving for their meals. It had bcome a guest house of sorts.

Murthy told the investigators Sivarasan had moved in just four days ago. The key to the house, vacant for more than a month, had been left by its owner, Anathamurthy, in his house.

SIVARASAN'S DIARY

Ranganathan and Mridula were taken to several places in Bangalore and its suburbs by the SIT, including their earlier residence in Pottan Halli. A diary was among the things seized from the house.

The diary became a bone of contention nearly six months later. Bhagyanathan moved the designated court in Madras in February 1991 seeking a direction to furnish him a copy of the diary of Sivarasan. Bhagyanathan alleged that the CBI men showed him a diary and asked whether it was Sivarasan's diary. When he said he did not know, the CBI showed him some pages containing references to Sivarasan's visit along with photographer Haribabu, to the house of Vazhappadi Ramamurthy, the then state Congress President, and the Congress office in Sathyamurthi Bhavan. Alleging links between Sivarasan, Haribabu and Ramamurthy, Bhagyanathan expressed apprehensions that the CBI might suppress the "facts".

Bhagyanathan alleged that an entry in the diary mentioned about Sivarasan's visit to Sathyamurthi Bhavan at 5 pm on a particular day and referred to a photograph Sivarasan had got taken with Ramamurthi. He also alleged that he had been advised by the

CBI not to reveal these "facts", but say something against the DK and the DMK.

THEY DID NOT TRY DISGUISE

Post-Konankunte investigations unravelled another of Sivarasan's facets.

Despite their photographs being splashed all over the country and beamed daily on television, Sivarasan and Subha made no attempt at disguise. SIT officials found nothing from any of their hideouts to indicate they had attempted to disguise themselves to escape the police dragnet.

When Sivarasan and Subha were found dead in their Konankunte hideout, they looked much like they did in the pictures taken before and on the day of the assassination.

Though Sivarasan's face was slightly distorted as a result of the impact of the bullet on his right temple, his moustache, hair and general appearance were almost similar to the photograph taken by Haribabu on the assassination night.

Sivarasan's only attempt at disguise was using dark sunglasses whenever he ventured out on a motorcycle in Madras after the assassination.

There appeared to be some difference between Subha's photo taken by Haribabu on May 21 and her appearance after the suicide. Forensic experts attributed this to distortions brought about by enlarging and copying of the negative and different hairstyles.

Sivarasan and Subha had relied mostly on staying indoors and moving outside under the cover of darkness. They kept touch with the world through the radio. Besides, they read every newspaper they could lay their hands on.

They ate little and kept fit doing exercises every morning. Ever since the arrests of Nalini, Murugan and others and the spate of suicides by LTTE cadres, the two had become withdrawn.

On the afternoon of August 19, hours before the mass suicide, Sivarasan refused food on learning what happened at Muttati and

Beroota. Subha and the handicapped woman wept.

Sivarasan and Subha were cremated amid tight security at Bangalore's Wilon Garden crematorium on September 3, 1991. Others had already been cremated.

A few months after Operation Botch-up, the Konankunte house was taken over by the police following reports that some people were willing to pay anything for converting the property into a sort of 'mutt' in Sivarasan's memory

THE DOUBLE GAME

Prabhakaran continued to baffle investigators.

According to a key LTTE detenue, Prabhakaran tried till the end to ensure Sivarasan reached Jaffna safely, and had made a last ditch effort just a few days before Sivarasan's death.

But there were also reports that information on Sivarasan's whereabouts was deliberately leaked to the police at Prabhakaran's behest. With the sealing of the Tamil Nadu coastline, ferrying fuel, medicine, cloth, arms and ammunition and food to the island had come to a standstill. The militants were also unable to bring the large number of wounded cadres for treatment.

Against this backdrop, according to this theory, Prabhakaran probably hoped that if Sivarasan and Subha were to die, the vigil on the coastline would slacken and the Tigers could rebuild their network in Tamil Nadu.

Moreover, official version did not quite explain the series of events which led to the Konankunte operation.

As per the official version, police got wind of the Konankunte hideout on August 18. But intelligence reports said that they got information at least three weeks ago that Sivarasan and Subha had come to Bangalore from Tamil Nadu through the Kollegall route.

Apparently, they had intercepted an LTTE short-wave transmission from Jaffna saying Sivarasan should go to Bangalore where a number of cadres, wounded in skirmishes with the Sri Lankan army, were staying in safe houses.

According to another source, it was an LTTE cadre who had squealed on the promise of safe conduct and non-disclosure of his identity. He was said to have furnished a list of five houses in Karnataka used routinely by Tamil militants as well as the names of the Tigers staying there. However, the Konankunte hideout was not on that list.

But Prabhakaran could not, at the same time, dump a man who knew so much and who had done so much. The interrogation of Varadhan, an LTTE communication expert who was arrested from near Tiruchirapalli on August 17, bore this out.

On August 15, Prabhakaran himself contacted Varadhan on wireless and ordered him to tell Sivarasan in Bangalore to move to Namakkal in Salem district of Tamil Nadu. Apparently, fresh escape plans had been chalked out. After reaching Namakkal, Sivarasan was to have received fresh instructions from Jaffna.

Prabhakaran probably chose India's independence day to contact Varadhan as the attention of the entire security brass would be diverted.

But the message could never reach Sivarasan as Varadhan was arrested two days later.

On August 16, Varadhan had established contact with the LTTE in Jaffna using his powerful communication equipment from Chettipalayam in Tiruchirapalli district of Tamil Nadu. The twenty year old wireless expert said he had used a code-sheet prepared by the LTTE for secret messages to be passed on between the LTTE headquarters in Jaffna and its men operating in Tamil Nadu and Karnataka. The investigators seized the code sheet.

Varadhan told his interrogators that he had been assigned by the LTTE to come to Tamil Nadu to assist Dixon, a top LTTE militant and a communication specialist who committed suicide at Coimbatore in Tamil Nadu on July 28.

RANGAN

The curtain on the Sivarsan-Subha drama finally rung down ten days after their suicide.

A virtual shadow of the duo, LTTE's last important man fell into the security dragnet on August 29. Rangan was overpowered and stopped from swallowing cyanide in a busy three-storey shopping arcade in Adayar in Madras after half an hour long nerve-wracking drama in broad daylight.

An expert driver, the stockily built Rangan provided cover to Sivarasan and Subha for over a month in Tamil Nadu and Bangalore. It was he who went on errands and looked after their needs.

Twice, when police raided the hideouts, an alert Rangan had shifted them to safer places a few hours ahead. However, despite having smelt a trap at Konankunte, he could not warn Sivarasan.

It was again the travel agency and the ISD booth — two vital communication links for the LTTE— that did Rangan in. The SIT had obtained information about the calls that he had made from the ISD booth at Sastri Nagar.

The drama began a little after 9 am. Rangan came to the travel agency in an autorickshaw and conversed with the staff for about 15 minutes. Then he went away, promising to return in half an hour.

The SIT was informed about Rangan's visit. Soon afterwards, a SIT team arrived in plainclothes and took up positions.

Rangan returned only around 11 am. This time he was on foot. He walked into the travel agency where a plaintclothesman was already seated. He resumed his conversation unaware of the dragnet that had been cast all around him.

As he emerged from the travel agency, the plainclothesman followed him, signalling to his colleagues. Sensing trouble, Rangan walked into a toy shop, only to be accosted by more plainclothesmen. A shopowner exclaimed, "That is him; catch him." On hearing the shout, the well-built militant smashed through a glass pane, and entered the next room. Here again, a SIT man caught him only to be thrown off by the powerful fugitive.

As Rangan ran out into the open, a large crowd had gathered wondering what was happening. A few hundred metres away from the shop, Rangan was frontally taken by another plainclothesman after his colleague had tripped the militant. Rangan was overpowered and pinned to the ground.

He tried to grab his cyanide capsule as well as his pistol, but was disarmed and the poison taken away.

Rangan showed the police nearly ten hideouts in the residential areas of Indira Nagar, Koramangala, Basavesvaranagar, Rajajinagar, J P Nagar and Konankunte.

*

PART III

BASE 14

5 The Man In The Iron Mask

When a boy was born in the lower middle class family living at Velupillai about 44 years ago, the revenue officer of Jaffna had not dreamt even in his wildest dreams that his son would control the destinies of millions of people and change the course of history of two nations.

Prabhakaran had a humble childhood. There was nothing to manifest his larger-than-life stature he was going to acquire a couple of decades later. Like any average boy, he was scared of cockroaches and detested rats. A loner as a child, he is even now not known to mix with anyone. He does not emote. Few people have seen him laughing, particularly ever since he became the undisputed LTTE leader. His marriage with Mativadani, much younger to him, was like a typical guerilla act.

Mativadani was a student leader of Jaffna University, where the Tigers had called a strike in 1986. Prabhakaran went to the campus. He did not use any threat; his presence was enough. But there was a girl who not only opposed the strike, but also took the "leader" to task for organising strikes at the drop of a hat.

This was the first time when the LTTE chief had been rebuked and that too publicly. A stunned Prabhakaran left the venue. He returned the next day, did not ask for a date or express love. He lifted Mativadani, brought her to his bunker and married her. No one knows of what she had thought then. Today, she's the mother of Prabhakaran's two children, a son and a daughter. She is also active in LTTE's affairs.

Miserly with words, Prabhakaran is known to be ruthless, even with comrades-in-arms. Between 1980 and 1990, he got killed at least 300 men of his rival cadres and several important leaders within the LTTE who posed a challenge to him.

The most shocking case was that of his military commander, Mahatya, who Prabhakaran suspected was a double agent. Word was spread Mahatya leaked information that led to the M V Ahät ship disaster. The LTTE lost hundreds of crores of rupees with the suicidal blowing up of the intercepted ship that was carrying explosives and arms.

Mahatya was "arrested", charged with "treason", kept in isolation and tortured and interrogated for an year by the very men he had been commanding for years. Prabhakaran never visited his once right hand man in his cell.

When Mahatya had nothing new to tell the LTTE, he was put before the firing squad. Thousands of LTTE cadres witnessed the execution. Prabhakaran was not there either.

Mahatya was replaced by the low-profile Baby Subramanian. The Mahatya chapter was over, but none knew whether he had actually double crossed the LTTE or whether Prabhakaran had eliminated him for becoming too powerful.

After Rajiv Gandhi's assassination, the stock of LTTE intelligence chief Pottu Amman went up. Amman was the pivotal figure and was in direct touch not only with the hit squad leader Sivarasan, who was from the intelligence wing, but also with the Tigers' counter-intelligence and political wings in Tamil Nadu. But Prabhakaran is a man who brooks no rivalry. He replaced Amman. Very few people know that the new chief of LTTE's intelligence is a little-known man called Kapil. Pottu Amman today is marginalised and put on the battlefront.

The long list of Prabhakran's victims includes Mukundan alias Uma Maheswaran of Tamil Eelam Liberation Organisation (Telo), his successor Sri Sabharatnam, Padmanabha of EPRLF and A Amrithalingam of the moderate outfit Tamil United Liberation Front (TULF), which was willing to settle for greater autonomy within the Sri Lankan constitution.

After the IPKF had pulled out from Sri Lanka and the Indo-Lanka accord became a dead letter, Prabhakaran sent several killer squads to eliminate Vardaraj Perumal, chief minister of the autonomous north-eastern council, who had fled to India. The plot surfaced only after during Rajiv Gandhi's assassination, when one member of a killer squad was arrested. Perumal is now in Ajmer, under protection of RAW.

Prabhakaran continues to control the LTTE with an iron grip. He does not delegate powers, has no second-in-command, and all LTTE wings chiefs report to him directly. A man of distrust, Prabhakaran operates through intelligence and counter-intelligence.

Under his command, the LTTE follows three big don'ts - no smoking, no drinking, no sex. What punishment he has in store for the violator of the LTTE ethos is not known, simply because not a single violation has been reported yet.

The LTTE supremo has no formal training in guerilla warfare. Arrested cadres speak of a British mercenary, who once came to Jaffna to give a few tips to the Tigers, and met Prabhakaran. The conversation soon developed into a wordy duel on shooting skills, until Prabhakaran whipped out his favourite weapon, a 9-mm pistol, and started firing. The necks of bottles placed at quite a distance away were shot off cleanly. The mercenary was left gaping.

The stockily-built Prabhakaran is aware of his short stature; he is only five feet four. He cleverly hides his diminutive stature by the simple expedient of instructing photographers to shoot from a lower angle. A Prabhakaran shot from the normal height is rare.

Equally odd is the tough man's abhorence for air travel. When he was brought from Jafina to Madras by an IAF helicopter for talks with Rajiv Gandhi in New Delhi in the late eighties, he kept throwing up during the entire journey.

Prabhakaran is not well educated. He cannot speak good English, but can understand the language. He is always in his favourite army fatigues which, incidentally, are made in Bangalore. A loaded pistol tucked in his left belt pouch, a wireless on the right side and two threads—red and black, each carrying a cyanide capsule—around his thick neck are his personality trademarks.

He has a dog-like sleep. Probably this is the only time when he can be caught alive. And he is aware of it. That is why he sleeps with his loaded pistol under his pillow and wears two cyanide capsules instead of one worn by every LTTE cadre.

He has at least five or six underground bunkers made of solid concrete and iron in jungles which can withstand the impact of a fairly lethal bomb attack. He meets people very selectively. Whosoever he decides to meet is brought to him blindfolded.

Like Saddam Hussein, the dictator guerilla also has a personal elite unit for protection. Called Base 14, it is not a very big unit. Its strength is not even in three digits. Base 14 is not just the wireless code name of Prabhakaran but also denotes his personal special task force. It comprises of highly-motivated and brainwashed commandos who are fiercely loyal to their leader.

The IPKF once had pinned down Base 14 and surrounded him. His bodyguards stood like a wall between Prabhakaran and IPKF. The Indian troops finally captured the camp, but 17 body guards of Base 14 perished to give Prabhakaran ample time to escape into the Wanni jungles. That was the first and last time when the IPKF was closest to capturing Base 14.

His cunningness, ruthlessness, military strategy and clever chess moves, which have made Prabhakaran a living legend, are reflected clearly in a tragic incident involving the IPKF.

The cat-and-mouse game was on between the IPKF and the LTTE in the late eighties. The bitter realisation that the LTTE cadres were not underdogs as they were made out to be was dawning upon the Indian military strategists and army generals. But Jaffna's Football Field Massacre of Indian army commandos brought out the ugliest face of the Tigers. For the Indian government, the obscure incident is a big tear on the cheek of time. Prabhakaran's disinformation machinery had leaked a "news" to the Indian army that the Base 14 was hiding in a particular building in the Jaffna University campus near the football ground. Further information was collected by the Military Intelligence and other Indian intelligence agencies. An action plan was prepared and the battle-scarred commandos of Sikh Li Regiment were tasked.

The commandos were to be dropped by IAF helicopters on the targeted building. Two battalions were to move towards the building (where Prabhakaran was reported to be hiding) in pincer attack formation. The tankmen would have "sanitised" the ground leading to the targeted builing, while the simultaneous commando operation would have ensured that Prabhakaran was captured alive. It was a good action plan ... on paper.

LTTE guerillas were deployed on the trees around the targeted building. The commandos jumped down from the helicopter one after another, but only their dead bodies landed on the ground. The LTTE sharp-shooters took virtual pot-shots at the descending commandos.

The guerillas also had deployed anti-aircraft guns which vomitted out shells at the IAF helicopters. One helicopter was downed, while the other one managed to get away. Thirty four Indian Army commandos were shot dead in the air. The 35th managed to land alive on the football ground. The brave Sikh knew that he had landed in the jaws of death. But a fighter to the core and a true commando, he gave the "bayonet-charge" and ran towards the building. Like the Mahabharata hero, Arjun, he saw only the eye of the bird which had to be pierced - in this case the building where Prabhakaran was reportedly in hiding.

The commandos are trained to fight to the finish with whatever weapon they are left with. If no weapon is left, fight with your legs, arms and even teeth and nails ; but do not surrender, the Indian Army commandos are taught. In this case, it was a hopeless battle. Though the courageous Sikh Li commando was surrounded by death, he fired wherever he could and after the magazine was emptied he took out his bayonet and charged towards the targetted building- a symbolic action which demonstrated that he was not going to surrender.

It was only a symbolic fight-back. A hail of bullets felled him as he ran a few yards.

The fate of the troops who were moving ahead in the pincer-formation was no different. All roads leading to the building were mined. Tanks blew up like nine-pins.

The football field massacre was complete.

But the ugliest irony was yet to come. The Indian Army later learnt that the man for whose capture the entire operation was planned was nowhere in that area at that time.

The LTTE is an amazing outfit. It is the only terrorist organisation in the world which has a fleet of ships, anti-aircraft guns, surface-to-air missiles and even a submarine. In 1992, Indian security agencies seized a submarine assembled by Shankar, a key LTTE politburo member who was once an aeronautical engineer in Canada. It's still not known whether the submarine had ever been pressed into action.

The LTTE submarine portends alarming security threats given the fact that the Tigers are master frogmen, trained by Norwegian mercenaries. The training went on clandestinely for months on an island in the Andaman Sea.

The IPKF had unearthed a factory to manufacture microlight aircraft and destroyed it. It was once again Shankar who was instrumental in developing the aircraft. The LTTE had a diabolic plan: to launch suicide attacks on key targets, including the Sri Lankan Parliament. Once it takes off, the engine of the aircraft can be swithched off to save fuel and like a glider, it can float in the air with the wind current. Upto 15 kg of plastic explosives like RDX can be loaded onto it, and its fibreglass body can be laced with more explosives.

A very thin suicide bomber, who is made to undergo dieting to further shed his weight, is entrusted with the mission. The thinner the pilot, the more explosives the plane can take. The pilot can be asked to put on the minimum possible clothes, may be just an underwear. He has to die anyway, that is the logic. Thus the microlight aircraft can be turned into a lethal flying bomb and can carry upto twenty kg of RDX, which can wreak havoc . Considering that a microlight aircraft can easily cover a distance of 500 kilometres, its lethality can be imagined.

So far, no terrorist outfit is known to have used a microlight aircraft for a suicide attack. The news of the LTTE acquiring manufacturing knowhow of microlight aircraft leaked in the early nineties, sending panic waves in New Delhi and Colombo. Both

India and Sri Lanka decided to deploy anti-aircraft guns to ward off possible aerial attacks from terrorists. The air-space over the Sri Lankan parliament was declared a no-fly zone as long as it was in session. It was around this time that an unidentified small aircraft was reportedly seen hovering over the official residence of then Tamil Nadu chief minister Jayalalitha.

The LTTE also is perhaps the only terrorist organisation which has advanced computers for storing and processing information and uses the internet for propaganda and making appeals for funds.

Prabhakaran is not just a military strategist. His international war is waged by the LTTE's powerful propaganda wing. The suave, Paris-based Lawrence Thilakar is the chief of the propaganda unit. The bespectacled Thilakar can easily be mistaken for a college lecturer or a scientist. He is fairly senior in the LTTE hierarchy. Like KP and Shankar he is a contemporary of Prabhakaran and is also on the LTTE politburo.

The LTTE has offices in about 40-odd countries with sizable Tamil population. Funds are not much of a problem with the LTTE, thanks to its vast network. The half-a-million Tamil expatriates in Canada, Germany, Switzerland, Britain, Italy, Australia, Singapore and Malaysia "contribute" at least five per cent of their salary to the LTTE. It is not exactly a voluntary contribution, they are coerced into paying for the security of their relatives back home. The LTTE raises approximately 25 to 30 million dollars every year through extortions. Such extortions are rampant in Jaffna as well, all in name of the cause.

KP is the chief of the LTTE's fund-raising and arms procurement unit and a politburo member. The master talker rarely visits Jaffna and is always on the move—negotiating an arms deal in Europe; sending raw narcotics from the infamous Golden Triangle to countries like Pakistan which offer cheap refining factories; arranging an end-user certificate for arms and explosives from an African country.

But KP is also known to have several mistresses, including a Pakistani. Prabhakaran's strict puritanical laws obviously do not apply to KP. His lifestyle is like that of a chief executive officer of a multinational. He is director of at least half a dozen shipping companies, which are actually the front companies of the LTTE.

Arresting KP is not diflicult at all. He does not lead a guerilla's life, travels extensively, mostly by air. And he is not known to keep a cyanide capsule.

*

6 The Making Of A Suicide Bomber

You should not just be happy but also be seen to be happy about your imminent self-caused death. This is the unsaid, unwritten commandment of a suicide bomber. Perhaps, this makes the suicide bomber feel himself superior to others. Perhaps, the visions of martyrdom justify his decision to end his life. Perhaps, these visions give him a kick and keep him going..., nay, gallopping to his self-inflicted death.

A suicide squad member performs only one operation in his life—and it has to be performed with his death.

There are no rehearsals, no retakes, no repeats. There is no scope for improvement. There cannot be any regrets or moments of joy or failure. They would not come to know the result of their own operation. They are dead as soon as they take the plunge, whether their mission is accomplished or not. Their first operation is the last operation.

How these terminal terrorists end their own lives in ghastly modes is an unexplored area for psychoanalysts and students of para-psychology. But the LTTE's "Black Tigers" unit is a breed apart and seems to be beyond all frontiers of human learning and psychology.

It is the elitist and the most obscure unit of the LTTE. Several terrorist outfits, particularly the Abu Nidal group of Palestinian terrorists, are known to have had suicide squads and have successfully executed suicide missions much before the LTTE emerged on international terrorism scene. But the readiness, the ease and the aplomb with which an LTTE cadre embarks on a suicide mission is unparallelled in the history of international terrorism.

LTTE's suicide squads are also known as the "nizhal" group, which literally means the "Shadow Group".

The first recorded Black Tiger operation took place on July 5, 1987 at the Nelliady Sri Lankan army camp at Vadamarchi, 30 kms off Jaffna. Once an LTTE base, it had been captured by the Sri Lankan army. The camp had been made virtually impregnable by massive deployment of soldiers. A gutsy Tiger, Miller, suggested the LTTE recapture the camp, and volunteered to conduct the operation single-handedly. It was an operation which meant certain death for Miller.

After the go-ahead signal by Prabhakaran, Miller did a reconnaissance. There were several security barricades manned round the clock by the troops. There was no way one could pierce through all these barricades and reach the destination alive. But Miller had a plan. From the point of the first barricade to the camp which was to be recaptured, the road was metalled and straight without any curves or bends.

He asked the fellow Tigers to pack a truck with explosives and then sat behind the wheel, tied to the driver's seat, his one foot tied to the accelerator and hands tied to the steering. Wooden sticks were used in such a manner that he could not move an inch even if he wanted to. The Tigers then hit the ignition.

The truck hurtled down the road piercing through barricade after barricade. Soldiers sprayed the truck with bullets and Miller was dead as soon as he crossed the very first checkpost. But the truck rolled on and finally, it rammed against the camp and exploded. The entire structure blew up into smithereens. Severed limbs of soldiers guarding the camp were found strewn several hundred metres away.

The Tigers had videographed the suicide operation which they show to trainee Black Tigers and Tigresses till date. Miller was posthumously awarded the rank of Captain and is a reverred hero among the LTTE cadres.

The Shadow Group has carried out more than fifty suicidal attacks so far. All suicide bomber operations have been conducted in Sri Lanka, the sole exception being Rajiv Gandhi's assassination which was the only operation in which three Black Tigresses were used—Dhanu, Subha and Athirai.

Athirai is an undertrial prisoner in Tamil Nadu. She is the only Black Tigress to be in custody of Indian authorities.

As in the case of general LTTE cadre, Black Tigers and Tigresses have standing orders to refrain from sex, drinks, smoking and gamble. But these things are not taboos if their mission requires any or all of these. There has not been a single recorded case so far in which the LTTE has used a Black Tigress or a girl of the general cadre as a sex bait.

History is replete with stories of killer women. There are many references in Indian history and literature to "vishkanyas" (poison girls) who lured men to bed before killing them through a mere kiss or sexual intercourse, depending upon potency of the venom in their blood. Fed on a daily but ever increasing dose of poison from a very tender age, the ultimate test of a vishakanya of the highest order was when a cobra fell dead on biting her.

The vishkanyas were picked up at a very early age and put on a special diet of poison, the potency of which was gradually increased. The advanced stage of their training would come when a cobra is made to bite the tongue of the trainee vishkanya. The trainee girl would become unconscious, perhaps for days. The very fact that the trainee does not die even after cobra bite shows that she is on way to become a vishkanya.

The exercise of cobra biting the trainee girl would be repeated a number of times. After every such bite, the impact of snake poison would show a marked decrease. From unconsciousness to semi-consciousness to mild intoxication to no-impact— that is the progress of the trainee vishkanya.

But the next snake-bite produces weird results. The cobra would not easily bite the vishkanya. It would hestitate to go anywhere near her. The snake is coaxed and finally forced to bite the vishkanya and then falls dead. This used to be the ultimate test-cum-demonstration of the skills of the most dangerous vishkanya.

The "vishkanyas" and the Black Tigresses have a parallel: both have a desire to kill and are trained to kill. But the parallel ends there—a vishkanya does not kill herself to fulfill her mission, whereas a Black Tigress may have to do so to kill the target.

How the Tigers can rope in young girls in the Shadow Group and in such large numbers remains a mystery. No other terrorist outfit has ever had such a large number of self-destroying women in their ranks. But there is an endless queue of Tamil girls to join the Shadow Group. They make the task of security forces all the more difficult as their apparent innocence and young age provide a perfect smokescreen.

There are 150 to 200 Black Tigers and Tigresses in the LTTE at any given point of time. They are under the direct command of Pottu Amman who selects, trains and assigns them their task. Every new LTTE cadre is given the option to join the Shadow group. But not all are selected by Papa Oscar. In fact, the rejection rate is quite high.

Following are the general criteria of selecting black Tigers and Tigresses :

* Candidate should not be too well known and must not have been photographed too frequently. He or she should not have travelled extensively. Travel increases contacts and exposes them to the outside world.

* He or she must have served at only one camp. Even LTTE cadres should not know Shadow Group members.

* Suicide bombers should belong to the 16-18 age group.

* Revenge is not the personality trait the LTTE looks forward to in selection of Shadow Group members. What matters most is the level of motivation.

* The candidate need not have obtained outstanding results during training, but he or she has to be a average performer.

Once selected, Black Tigers and Tigresses are segregated and taken to Tinnevelly, a small village in the thick jungles near Jaffna, which is the headquarters of the Shadow Group. During selection and training, LTTE's women wing intelligence chief Shanthi or her deputy, Akila, are always present.

The trainees have the following do's and don'ts :

* They are given a new identity by Pottu Amman.

* There is no socialising. They cannot meet their parents or relatives nor can they come to them. They are dead to the outside world as soon as they join the guerilla army. Shadow Group members cannot mingle with their own cadre except those who are in their unit.

* They cannot go on leave and have to follow the daily drill of this highly regimented unit.

* They are trained only for suicide mission and for no other purpose. "You die only once" is the hackneyed but effective line of their trainers.

* "Political classes" — as LTTE calls the brainwashing exercises — are as important a daily routine as physical exercises and arms training.

* They cannot discuss the nature of their job with anyone, not even their immediate colleagues.

Apart from Rajiv Gandhi's assassination, the major Black Tiger strikes are the assassinations of Sri Lankan defence minister Ranjan Wijeratne (March 1991) and president R Premdasa (May, 1993). Both were carried out with military precision.

Wijeratne had a set route and timing for going from home to office and back. Despite the repeated pleadings from his security to bring constant variations in his route and timing, he had never bothered. This cost him his life. An explosive-laden truck, packed with 1000 kgs of RDX, was exploded by remote control just when the truck driver brought it close to Wijeratne's cavalcade.

Premadasa's assassination was equally ingenious. The president was attending the May Day rally when his domestic help came to the venue on a bicycle. Premdasa's security men let him in as they knew that he was working in the president's house-hold. The servant switched on a concealed belt bomb as he reached Premadasa. The suicide bomber had been employed on the recommendation of the president's cook, who later turned out to be an LTTE mole.

Do Black Tigers develop cold feet at the eleventh hour? Yes, but there is only one recorded example of this.

Prabhakaran wanted the Sri Lanka's joint operations command (JOC) office in Colombo blasted in June 1991. All preparations were over. The suicide bomber Zahir, had completed the "full-dress rehearsal" and taken to Colombo. But on D-day, Zahir disappeared.

The JOC office was blasted as per schedule by Zahir's standby. But Zahir was picked up on suspicion during the post-blast raids at hotels, guest houses and tourist lodges. During interrogation, he broke down and confessed.

Zahir is the only suicide bomber who has been caught alive. He said he was trained at Papa Oscar's personal training camp at Nallur near Jaffna. The camp is strictly reserved for those who are about to embark upon an operation. Zahir was given the final training at the Nallur camp along with his alternate for a week.

Zahir has not been questioned by the SIT, though he is still in custody of Sri Lankan authorities.

He can give a wealth of information on the psychology of Black Tigers, how they are trained and how they are brainwashed.

He may give valuable information on Dhanu and Subha who also must have been imparted final training at the Nallur Camp.

7 SINS OF OMISSION

The Verma commission of inquiry threw up vital questions. The sitting Supreme Court judge, Justice Jagdish Sharan Verma, could not go into these areas as these were outside his purview. These questions are still relevant and remain unanswered.

Justice Verma's observations— on the "disturbing" silence of the then IB chief M K Narayanan, on the blurred video footage of the Sriperumbudur function, on the conduct of Latha Priyakumar (daughter of Congress candidate Margatham Chandrasekhar), on the "imperceptible erosion of the morale of the intelligence agencies as a result of politicisation", and on the withdrawal of Rajiv's SPG security cover — are all pregnant with meaning.

The most mystifying question is why the video footage was blurred.

M K Narayanan submitted a note marked "secret" to then Prime Minister Chandra Shekhar on May 22 soon after inspecting the assassination site. In that note, after mentioning the possibility of Rajiv Gandhi falling prey to an unidentified woman suicide bomber, Narayanan wrote : " It has not yet been possible to establish whether the lady made her way into the sterilised area once Rajiv Gandhi approached or whether she had previously managed to stand in line as one of those offering salutations to Rajiv Gandhi. Video pictures of this part of the meeting are presently being scanned to try and identify the lady."

Justice Verma's report said : *"This part of the report of the DIB mentioning the fact that scanning of video pictures was being done to identify the 'lady' does indicate that on 22.5.91, there were available video pictures of that part of the meeting which could reveal the identification of the suspected human bomb. No such video pictures were made available by the SIT or*

Tamil Nadu police and it was specifically stated by the SIT Chief, D R Karthikeyan that no other video cassettes were available with the SIT.

"The commission pointed out this unusual feature of the video cassette to the SIT chief D R Karthikeyan since it may have greater significance for investigation of the crime even though to the commission it amounts to absence of some useful evidence alone."

Karthikeyan later told the Verma panel that foreign experts were examing the cassettes to find out whether these had been tampered with to obliterate any part of the recording. The commission was told at its last sitting that the outcome of that inquiry was awaited.

The SIT produced four video cassettes before the Verma commission. The Tamil Nadu congress committee had got Rajiv Gandhi's visit to Sriperumbudur recorded on video from the time he landed at Meenambakkam airport. But the organisers told the commission that they did not have the cassettes and believed the police had seized them.

Justice Verma said in an extremely meaningful observation: "The commission refrains from commenting on this aspect since it can be avoided in this inquiry but may have significance in some other proceeding."

Two video cassettes had the recording of the May 21 event and the third of the next day. The May 21 cassettes were screened at an open hearing of the Verma commission. These were blurred at the crucial portions and neither showed the actual assassination taking place nor focused on the suicide bomber.

Crucial questions arise. Was Rajiv's assassination videographed till the very last second ? Did the camera focus on the hit squad members? Who all were seated or standing near Dhanu and Sivarasan ? If the cassettes were intentionally blurred, who ordered their tampering and why? Were Rajiv's assassins standing close to any prominent person? If so, who are they?

Various documents of the ministry of home affairs (MHA) and intelligence reports make it clear that the IB and the MHA did not feel comfortable over the withdrawal of SPG cover to Rajiv Gandhi even when terrrorist threat to him had increased. This had happened despite different proposals for beefing up his security. The proposals ranged from sending Rajiv's ex-SPG personnel on deputation to Delhi police or the NSG, as was done in the case of Buta Singh and Bhajan Lal.

It would be pertinent to refer to a letter written by then IB Joint Director K N Thakur to N K Singh, then Joint Secretary (Police) in the MHA, just a day before Rajiv's assassination.

Exactly a week before, Thakur had sent a circular to all directors general of police.

Narayanan told the Verma commission that it was at his instance that K N Thakur had written to the MHA seeking NSG cover for Rajiv Gandhi for the remaining period of the elections, even ignoring any possible objection by Rajiv for ostentatious security. The fact that May 20, 1991 was a holiday for the Central government, the IB recommendation for immediate NSG deployment shows the urgency attached to the matter.

It is in this context that Justice Verma observed: "The Commission is left with the impression that the DIB M K Narayanan was not satisfied with the security arrangements for Rajiv Gandhi and was apprehensive about his safety, but for some undisclosed reason he was ineffective and has chosen to maintain silence even now. If this impression of the commission be correct, such disability in the holder of a high office is disturbing and its cause needs to be discovered and eradicated for the health of the polity."

This leads to yet another set of questions. Does it mean that Narayanan saw a specific threat to the life of Rajiv Gandhi? Or that he wanted to plug the chinks in Rajiv's security arrangements and was unable to do so because of "instructions"? Who could have prevented beefing up of Rajiv's security? Who could have benefited from making him a sitting duck for terrorists? Why was the NSG cover not provided even after IB's specific recommendation?

Thakur's letter to the MHA on May 20, 1991 assumes even more significance considering Rajiv was killed the very next day.*

Had NSG deployment been given to Rajiv, could his life been saved? The answer may well be both 'yes' and 'no'.

Punjab chief minister Beant Singh had NSG cover with Black Cat commandos guarding him when he died in an explosion caused by a suicide bomber — the first-ever in the history of Sikh terrorism. Former attorney general G Ramaswamy has a point when he says the NSG is trained to meet an "open and frontal" attack and not a "skillful and surreptitious" attack which Dhanu resorted to. Despite a security ring, Rajiv could still have been killed as the suicide bomber had already sneaked in. But he would not have died had the barricading of the venue and checking and frisking of people been upto the mark. And this was not the task of the NSG.

Against this backdroop, the statement of the self-proclaimed spy, Basak, before the Jain commission of inquiry rings out ominously. Basak told the commission that the withdrawal of SPG cover in 1989 was a signal to conspirators abroad to get ready and prepare the plan for assassinating Rajiv.

But there is another view. The very presence of NSG around Rajiv could have served as a deterrent to the assassins.

There is more to it than meets the eye. N K Singh, who was then joint secretary in the MHA and in charge of all central police organisations, was continuously involved in the security arrangements of Rajiv Gandhi. Singh told the Verma commission that even prior to the recommendations of the IB made on May 20, 1991, it had been suggested that Rajiv be provided NSG cover on a permanent basis. Singh said this proposal was discussed at a meeting convened by home secretary R K Bhargava after the general elections were announced. IB chief Narayanan had also attended that meeting, Singh said.

---

* *See Annexures for KN Thakur's letter.*

Narayanan denied participating in any such meeting.

Justice Verma has made it clear that in case of a dispute, "the commission prefers the testimony of N K Singh to that of M K Narayanan or any other person deposing differently." He explained why.

N K Singh maintained he had received K N Thakur's letter in the background that the proposal could not mature earlier to the knowledge of Narayanan himself and therefore, it did not appear to him to be a serious suggestion of the IB chief.

After Narayanan's denial, Singh filed an affidavit on January 30, 1992 , giving particulars of the meetings held with the MHA which were recorded. The affidavit did not give any record of the subjects covered at those meetings. Significantly, he also did not say in his affidavit that his earlier deposition was incorrect, did not express any wish to withdraw any part of it. Therefore, his affidavit did not neutralise his deposition. When Singh was asked during his cross-examination whether his statement regarding a meeting in the MHA, which was attended by IB chief, was incorrect, he had vehemently denied it. The then attorney general G Ramaswamy argued that N K Singh's statement differed from that of Narayanan because of confusion. Singh tried to clear this confusion in a subsequent affidavit.

This difference in the depositions of senior bureaucrats is significant.

Then home secretary R K Bhargava testified that N K Singh was one of the officers who had raised the question of Rajiv's security after the elections were announced. Bhargava said the matter was discussed by Singh with the IB and other forum, including the internal security meeting conducted by the cabinet secretary.

Says Justice Verma : "This statement of R K Bhargava, prior to the examination of N K Singh, corroborates N K Singh's version and is also consistent with the probabilities. The subsequent denial by M K Narayanan of such a meeting to discuss the subject in the MHA does not inspire confidence and the best which can be said for him is that his memory does not retain this fact inconvenient to the Central government.

"N K Singh's version is more consistent with the probabilities taking into account also the IB's anxiety throughout for a suitable alternative cover to Rajiv Gandhi on withdrawal of SPG which shows the concern of the DIB himself, notwithstanding his helplessness in view of the Central government's decision."

Justice Verma has highlighted the IB's problems, deficiencies and lapses, particularly in the context of Rajiv's assassination. He observed that if the IB was found wanting in some sphere, it was more because of its failure to express its views candidly on occasions and to ensure the necessary action but not on account of lack of its calibre or quality.

The judge further said in his report that the IB also could not perform its best on occasions because of its perception (and that of the states as well) that its role is merely advisory and that it has no powers to enforce compliance.

The Verma report makes a damning observation about the country's premier intelligence agency. Dwelling on the need for giving more teeth to the IB, it says: "The imperceptible erosion of the morale of the intelligencee agencies as a result of politicisation, real or assumed, has disclosed the need of a mechanism by which the intelligence agencies and the security persons are immunised from likely political influences and the attendant apprehensions, leaving them free to perform their duties in the spirit of true professionals."

These words assume ominous overtones particularly in the context of Justice Verma's observation about M K Narayanan's "disturbing silence" on his apprehensions of Rajiv's security before Dhanu struck.

Another important question thrown up by the Verma panel pertains to Latha Priyakumar. Priyakumar broomed aside allegations that she was responsible for Kokila's presence at Sriperumbunder, just because her mother, Latha Kannan, was a Congress worker from Arakkonam in Latha Priyakumar's constituency.

It was Kumudavalli, a Congress party member, who put Latha Priyakumar in the dock. She filed an affidavit before the Verma commission stating she saw Latha Kannan and Kokila getting off from Latha Priyakumar's car at the public meeting venue at Sriperumbudur on May 21, 1991. Later, she saw Kannan and Kokila talking with Dhanu and Sivarasan, while they waited for Rajiv.

Did Latha Priyakumar actually help Kokila gain access to Rajiv? Justice Verma says this by itself might not be of much significance. In a clear indictment of Latha Priyakumar, he says: "Latha Priyakumar does not appear to be a credible witness. Her deposition does not appear to be forthright and she gave the impression of withholding some knowledge she has."

C S Vaidyanathan, counsel for officers of Tamil Nadu, blamed Latha Priyakumar for breach of access control by securing permission for Kokila to recite a poem from the queue of garlanders which took more time than the act of garlanding. This detained Rajiv increasing the risk to him, he argued.

Latha Priyakumar insisted she reached the venue only after 9 pm even though witnesses, including Lakshmi Albert, said she was present from 8.30 pm. Priyakumar admitted having left between Arakkonam at 7 pm and 7.30 pm in a taxi for Sriperumbudur. Rajiv's meeting was scheduled for 9 pm and she had to cover about 40 to 45 kilometres, she could not have taken more than an hour to reach the venue.

Says Justice Verma : " She tried to evade this question by saying that she was sleeping throughout the way even though the road was bumpy and, therefore, she did not even know the route which her taxi took . There were certain suggestions made to her which relate to matters outside the scope of this inquiry."

The Verma commission did not go deep into the alleged role of Latha Priyakumar and did not even consider the affidavit of Kumudavalli because of its terms of reference.

The Commission's task was to make an inquiry into the following matters :

(a) Whether the assassination of Rajiv Gandhi could have been averted and whether there were lapses or dereliction of duty in this regard on the part of any of the individuals responsible for his security ;

(b) The deficiencies, if any, in the security system and arrangements as prescribed or operated in practice which might have contributed to the assassination.

An uproar had erupted over the restrictive terms of reference and Rajiv loyalists wanted the commission to probe the conspiracy angle too. Justice Verma put his foot down and declined to probe the conspiracy aspects, saying that it was "outside the domain of judicial function."

It was against this backdrop that the Jain commission was appointed on August 23, 1991 to probe conspiracy behind the assassination "with all its ramifications."

Justice Verma had sent Kumudavalli's affidavit and other important documents to the MHA, noting that these pertained to matters outside the scope and purview of his inquiry. He had also clearly said in his noting that these papers could have an important bearing on the case and the needful could be done. This was in 1992. But nothing much appeared to have happened in this direction in the last six years. Kumudavalli has neither been questioned by the S I T nor the trial court. She deposed before the Jain commission as late as in July 1996. It is still not known what is the outcome of investigation into Kumudavalli's disclosures, if any investigation has been conducted, that is.

Following are the major findings and observations of the Verma commission:

* Rajiv's assassination could have been averted but for the lapses or dereliction of duty of the Tamil Nadu police which constituted the proximate cause of the assassination.

* There were lapses and dereliction of duty by the Tamil Nadu police and consequently of the state government; of the IB, the MHA and the Central government ; and of the Congress party and organisers of the meeting.

* It was a lapse of the Central government to withdraw Rajiv's SPG cover without providing him a suitable alternative cover for proximate security. This was a contributory lapse.

* The stated reasons for SPG withdrawal were tenuous. The reasons given were mainly the lack of power under the SPG Act and inadequacy of the strength of SPG , apart from a high-profile visibility inviting criticism. None of these reasons was considered an insurmountable hurdle to give SPG cover to former Prime Ministers also from September 1991 after Rajiv's assassination. There appears no reason why this could not be done earlier for Rajiv.

* The Tamil Nadu police failed to provide the required proximate security to Rajiv and prevent the human bomb from reaching close to Rajiv. It also failed to detect the explosive device concealed on the body of the suicide bomber.

* The intelligence wing of Tamil Nadu police failed to sensitize the police force and provide the necessary intelligence back-up . It also failed to keep an effective vigilance at the venue of the meeting.

* The IB failed to share fully the entire intelligence information available to it and give the required intelligence back-up to the Tamil Nadu police.

* There were differences between the state Congress and the candidate, Margatham Chandrasekhar, who excluded the former from participation in the arrangements resulting in the lack of available party infrastructure and support for the meeting.

* State Congress President K Ramamurthy was unwilling to involve himself in the arrangements for the Sriperumbudur meeting and remained away, apparently to avoid incurring displeasure. However, Ramamurthy could have intimated to the AICC that the arrangements at Sriperumbudur were not satisfactory, as he did in the case of choice of night halt for Rajiv Gandhi.

* Chandrasekhar's choice of temple land as the venue was unsuitable as compared to the available school ground from the

security angle.

* There was lack of discipline and general irresponsibility in the behaviour of the Congress party men present at the meeting venue.

* No significant contribution was made by the AICC counsel to the commission. Even the documents containing the protest lodged by P Chidambaram against reduction in the level of protective security were produced before the commission not by the AICC counsel, but by the attorney general.

* There is an imperceptible infusion of politicisation leading to erosion in the morale of the intelligence agencies and the police forces which reduced the standard of performance of even the premier intelligence agency—IB—even though the personnel are highly competent. The adverse effect on the police forces in the states and Union Territories appears to be much more.

8 What The Spies Said

On the night of March 5-6,1991, RAW intercepted a coded message from Sivarasan in Madras to Pottu Amman in Jaffna. The One-eyed Jack wanted gold to finance his mission and an Indian Tamil girl who could give company to Dhanu and Subha. And he had a query: was Rajiv to be killed in Madras or in New Delhi.

Sivarasan argued if it was New Delhi, the operation would take more time as it would require more elaborate preparations. More safe-houses would have to be got ready in New Delhi. But if Rajiv were to be assassinated in Madras, Sivarasan said, the stage was already set.

Papa Oscar mulled over the question and told him that he would talk to the "leader" and get back to him. Next day, he told Sivarasan that it was Madras.

By the time all this came to light, India's intelligence agencies had wasted their wits and Rajiv was long assassinated.

The wireless message was not decoded until six months later. Apparently, the LTTE codes are complex and the Tigers keep changing the codes and the frequencies.

This was not the only instance when raw unintelligence was at its worst.

A brief note was issued on April 6, 1990—more than a year before the assassination—by A Thiruvengadam, deputy director of subsidiary intelligence bureau (ministry of home affairs, Madras). The note, numbered 4-B/M (TS)/90/83 was addressed to S I Jaffer Ali, DIG (Intelligence), Madras and a copy was sent to IB's New Delhi-based joint director in charge of VIP security.

The note spoke of information on the LTTE planning to attack Rajiv Gandhi. It said the militants were even more emboldened by the defeat cf the Congress at the elections. Thiruvengadam also told the IB joint director that this information had come from a source "which is fairly reliable and graded `B'. Further verification is being done."

The threat posed by the LTTE to Rajiv Gandhi was conveyed to IB by RAW from time to time. The messages of RAW in 1990 and early 1991 show the Indian intelligence agencies were not at all oblivious to the dangers posed by the LTTE. These reports highlighted the LTTE's animosity towards India, particularly Rajiv Gandhi, because of his signing the July 1987 Indo-Sri Lanka agreement with then Lankan President Junius Jayewardene. On the basis of this agreement, the Indian Peacekeeping Force (IPKF) was sent to Sri Lanka which eventually fought a full-scale war with Prabhakaran's guerillas.

Then on December 8, 1990, IB joint director, New Delhi, warned director general of police, Tamil Nadu and commissioner of police, Madras that LTTE posed threats for chief minister M Karunanidhi, state Congress president V K Ramamurthi and AIADMK general secretary Jayalalitha. Then the note, No. 29/VS/89(1)-II, said: "It is further reported that threat is also held out by the LTTE to Rajiv Gandhi, Congress-I president. It is requested that this factor may be kept in mind while arranging adequate security for Rajiv Gandhi during his visits to Tamil Nadu."

The IB also sent a circular memorandum on January 23, 1991 to all DGPs, directors (Intelligence), IGPs, IGPs (Intelligence), special IGP (Intelligence), commissioners of police of all the four metropolitan cities, superintendents of police of Lakshadweep and Dadra and Nagar Haveli, SPG director and the cabinet secretariat. The circular, no. 32/VS/90 (3)-II-903-1011, listed the various terrorist outfits which posed a danger to Rajiv.

Topping the list were the Sikh extremists. Talwinder Singh Parmar, a leading Babbar Khalsa member who had asserted that Rajiv Gandhi may not live beyond 1990, was understood to have reached Delhi to carry out some "big action" and become a martyr.

The International Sikh Youth Federation (northern faction) too, plotted an attempt on the life of Rajiv Gandhi. Tarsem Singh

Pattar, general secretary of the ISYF (N), was one of the participants at a meeting convened for this purpose. Yet another outfit was the BTFK (Bhindarwala Tigers Force of Khalistan—Manochahal group). Satnam Singh Satta, a hardcore terrorist of BTFK had indicated that his gang had been directed to carry out specific annihilations, including that of Rajiv Gandhi. Then there was the Second Panthic Committee (Sohan Singh) which once again reiterated its determination to eliminate the Congress leader.

Sikh extremists were joined by United Liberation Front of Assam, which in league with the NSCN, and the PLA also planned to eliminate Rajiv Gandhi (and Hiteswar Saikia) whom they held responsible for imposition of President's rule in Assam and the ban on NSCN and ULFA .

And then there was Amanullah Khan of the Jammu and Kashmir Liberation Front, who held out a clear threat to Rajiv Gandhi, saying the former Prime Minister was behind killings of Kashmiri muslims in the valley. Finally, there was the LTTE.

On February 15, 1991, the Union Home Ministry sent a "Crash" wireless message to the chief secretaries of all States and Union Territories. The message, bearing number VI23014/57/89GPA.III, said : "The security arrangements for Rajiv Gandhi have been reviewed in the light of latest threat assessment. According to a report, the ULFA has constituted thirty suicide squads, each having a strength of eight to twelve, to hit specific targets which include Rajiv Gandhi and Hiteswar Saikia."

IB's monthly *Intelligence Digest* No. 1/91 relating to VIP security said Rajiv Gandhi continued to face the most serious threat from Sikh terrorists, with UK-based Babbar Khalsa activist Gurmeet Singh Gill being deputed specifically to eliminate him. It said that ULFA too, had constituted suicide squads to attack Rajiv, Saikia and other Congress leaders.

A copy of an *Intelligence Digest* sent to all states and Union Territories by IB's then joint director in charge of VIP security, A P Bhatnagar, a fortnight before Rajiv's assassination, featured a document (No. 48/VS/91(6)) which highlighted terrorist threat to Rajiv, particularly from Sikh terrorists.

It said Babbar Khalsa recruits owing allegiance to the gangs of Madha Singh, Dharam Singh, Kashtiwa and Sukhdev Singh Chhaba, had reportedly been assigned the task killing Rajiv during his election campaign in Delhi. "Babbar Khalsa leadership in UK was also reportedly contemplating to organise assassination attempts on the lives of Rajiv Gandhi and his son, Rahul, through use of unconventional killing methods, like using gloves contaminated with poison," the report screamed.

It was prophetic. Rajiv did die in an unconventional terrorrist attack, though instead of the Sikhs, it was the LTTE who succeeded. Almost all intelligence messages had a recurring theme: that Rajiv faced a grave threat from terrorists of all hues and ideologies. Despite this, nothing was done to beef up his security. The hunters watched the sitting duck from all directions. The LTTE struck first.

Ironically, it was Punjab terrorists, not the LTTE, who gave sleepless nights to the VIP security managers. By their acquisition of powerful weapons like assault rifles, sub-machine guns, grenades, rockets and missiles, and their skill in fabricating sophisticated explosive devices made the Sikh terrorists a dreaded lot.

An IB document of late 1990 marked "secret" dwelt on intelligence pertaining to VIP security and gave details how Punjab terrorists had acquired sophisticated weapons from Pakistan. The deadly arsenal included telescopic rifles with an effective range of two kilometers and a new weapon, AC 104, which can fire cyanide-tipped bullets,

The document also said that the Zaffarwal faction of Khalistan Commando Force (KCF), the Budhsinghwala group of Khalistan Liberation Front (KLF) and BTFK (Manochahal) were in possession of telescopic rifles. It said KCF (Zaffarwal) had acquired M2 guns, an effective weapon to use from an aircraft.

Another IB circular, dated April 8/9, 1991, sent to all DGPs/IGPs of states and Union Territories and the police commissioners of the four metros said Sikh terrorists had obtained the know-how to detonate explosives by remote radio control mechanism and warned that the threat would become greater the following month.

The IB circulated a memorandum replete with information what Sikh terrrorists were up to. It said : "Various Sikh terrorist groups are also concentrating on efforts to infiltrate into the armed forces, organise sabotage in army units and subvert the loyalties of the force personnel. Babbar Khalsa recently issued a press note to announce setting up of their unit in the Indian Army. Wassan Singh Zaffarwal, leader of the First Panthic committee, has instructed his followers to establish cells in the Indian Army and contact with the Army officers, win over young Sikh Army personnel on their visit to their homes and depute serving officers of the Army of the rank of Subedar and above to Pakistan to receive briefing. These subversive activities have serious implications for the VIP security."

A new dimension was added to threat to VIP security from Sikh terrorists when they jammed police wireless communication on March 8 and 9, 1991, when the Punjab governor was visiting Phillaur. In fact, Punjab terrorists had done it once earlier during Rajiv Gandhi's visit to the state. Following the incidents, the state police imported a sophisticated 24-frequency "frequency hopper" which automatically jumps to another frequency if a particular frequency is jammed.

After the Phillaur incident, the IB advised all states and Union Territories to examine the possibility of using wideband jammers at the site of function of VIPs and on their routes to neutralise the jamming efforts of 'pirate' transmitters. It also suggested use of separate 'communication' vehicles which operate on frequencies independent of the police/PMF channel on VIP routes and would be able to alert the security personnel if their transmission were jammed by terrorists.

RAW reports painted vivid accounts of floats deriding the IPKF being paraded at the May Day rally in Jafna in 1990 and how the LTTE was getting a book, *Satanic Force* printed in Tamil Nadu. The Force condemned the IPKF for its alleged atrocities on Sri Lankan Tamils. Raw also gave reports of activities of the LTTE in Tamil Nadu and along the coast from time to time. These reports showed that the LTTE had its base in Tamil Nadu with activities spread over several parts of the state. A RAW report of July 1990 talks of a letter containing the LTTE's hit-list, which included several prominent Indians. Then there was a report of threat to Thanjavur's superintendent of police R Sawani because of his earlier association with Rajiv's security.

The movement of several members of LTTE in Tamil Nadu, their presence in some camps, location of their hideouts, particulars of vehicles used by them, details of their criminal activities. acquisition of arms and explosives bv them, hiring of three houses by LTTE cadres in Porur and their arrival in large numbers, seizure of huge stocks of gelatine for use in explosives, list of their sympathisers and even a contact telephone number, were reported by RAW in late 1990 and early 1991.

Three Porur safe houses were used by Rajiv's assassins. On February 25, 1991, a RAW analysis was sent to the IB detailing how LTTE's resentment against India had increased after the dismissal of DMK government in Tamil Nadu on January 30,1991 and imposition of President's rule leading to crackdown on LTTE cadres.

The RAW reports also gave information from January to early May 1991 of supporters of the LTTE who included an MLA and a doctor among others. During this period, the external intelligence agency also informed about the establishment of a wireless communication facility between LTTE units in Trichy and Sri Lanka. This wireless was eventually used by Rajiv's assassins.

RAW reports regularly mentioned the hostility of the LTTE towards Rajiv Gandhi, making it the biggest threat to the security of Rajiv. As early as on December 9, 1989, RAW had reported that there was continuing need to provide effective protection to Rajiv Gandhi and his family in view of the threat from Tamil militants and others.

All these reports were regularly sent to the IB and the MHA by the cabinet secretariat. The responsibility of the MHA was even more as Tamil Nadu was under President's Rule at the material time.

It was not as if 10, Janpath was not bothered about Rajiv's security. On February 13, 1991, V George, private secretary to Rajiv Gandhi wrote a brief letter to then Delhi Lt Governor Markandey Singh. It said: "The latest intelligence report communicated by the IB gives an alarming note with regard to the security arrangements for Rajiv Gandhi and his family members. IB has recommended a certain scale of security beefing up in which action by the Delhi Administration is called for as per the enclosed note. It is, therefore, requested that you may like to instruct the concerned officials for immediate action as suggested by the IB."

The IB's secret circular memorandum no. 32\VS/90(3)-II, 7 dated January 23,1991 had stated that "Besides providing adequate static armed guards, PSOs, ring-round teams, isolation cordon, pilot and escort vehicle and other nccessary security components adequately armed with conventional and automatic weapons, it would be necessary to enforce security precautions like searching. ensuring reliability of persons employed on armed duty, purity of food etc." As per the IB's instructions, the following action was required to be taken :

* Permanently earmarked ring-round teams for anti-sabotage check of the place of function and security duties. IB's technical teams, dog squad and bomb disposal squad were to be associated in anti-sabotage check keeping in views the terrorists' use of remote control devices.

* Special arrangements for checking of food items.

* Reviewing the quality of staff posted at 10, Janpath as many were from the older age group and were bound to have slower reflexes in case of any contingency. These staff should also be provided with more frequent training in firing.

* The Ambassador cars earmarked for pilot and escort duties were to be fitted with only ISUZU engins and the maintenance work be entrusted to CRP workshop, Lodi Road. The drivers should be given training as their performance is not up to the mark which resulted in an accident of bullet proof car a few months ago while going to Rajpath.

* The communication system with security is not very effective. This may be reviewed and the wireless sets provided.

The IB also suggested that since the security had to be beefed up in view of the latest intelligence reports, Delhi police (PM security wing) should be asked to take over the work of all security arrangements connected with Rajiv Gandhi and his family.

Political uncertainty fuelled terrorism as 1991 dawned. A series of incidents occurred, the major ones being the May 17 and 19 attacks on Congress leaders Sajjan Kumar and Jagdish Tytler respectively in Delhi. This should have shaken the country's security managers out of their complacence.

They should also have become alert in the wake of developments across the Straits.

On March 2, 1991, the LTTE struck a major blow to the Sri Lankan government when it assassinated minister of State for defence Ranjan Wijeratne along with 29 others, including five commandos in a powerful bomb blast in Colombo.

It was suspected that a van carrying the bomb had been parked on the route barely five minutes before Wijeratnee was to pass through. The LTTE used C-4 plastic explosives in the bomb, which are triggered remotely by using a 'pager' system.

The LTTE executed thc assassination with perfection, despite the fact that using radio-controlled explosive device against a fast-moving target is often not accurate due to human factors. Unless the timings have been perfected to the last second, terrorists have to depend either on visual or wireless signals to detonate the device. Even a few seconds delay between the time when the target appears in the hit zone and the actual firing would mean a miss.

Another difficulty in using radio-controlled explosive devices is that both the transmitter and the receiver have relatively short battery lives and thus tend to fail in scenarios which require placing of the device much in advance. In the case of Wijeratne, the bomb-laden vehicle was parked on the minister's route just five minutes before he passed through, but the same formula could not succeed

in case of Rajiv Gandhi, as election meetings are frequently hours behind schedule. The battery of radio-controlled device would not have lasted that long.

An action-packed Hollywood thriller, *Delta Force* was released shortly before Rajiv Gandhi's assassination. There is a striking similarity between the mode of assassination of Rajiv Gandhi and that of a dignitary's shown in the first few minutes of the film.

The opening scene shows a young naked woman strapping an explosive device in the form of a belt on her torso before putting on her clothes. In the next shot, the woman bomber goes to a public function with a bouquet in hand, walks up the dais to present the bouquet to the dignitary, and then detonates the belt bomb, killing the target and herself.

A little-known fact about Prabhakaran is his passion for Hollywood thrillers, just as he likes practising with his pistol for hours together. Is there a possibility that he could have seen *Delta Force* and then conceived of the mode by which he wanted Rajiv to be assassinated?

The *Delta Force* issue was raised before the Verma commission. Justice Verma inquired from SIT chief D R Karthikeyan and IB joint director K N Thakur about the video cassette of this movie and directed them to find out when that movie was made and marketed. After inquiries, Karthikeyan informed the commission that the video cassette of *Delta Force* was released in India in August 1991. The movie had been made in 1990 and its video casseette was available in the western countries in the first quarter of 1991.

Justice Verma's observations on the issue are hard-hitting :

"It is indeed surprising that even the IB was not aware of the making of such a movie and the availability of its cassette till mentioned by the Commission on the basis of a news item in one of the newspapers.

"To anyone who sees the video cassette of *Delta Force*, it would be obvious that such a mode of assassination was visualised much earlier in the context of terrorist activity and the idea had crystallised in the form of a movie made much before the assassination of Rajiv Gandhi. Can it then be said that the mode of assassination of Rajiv Gandhi was so extraordinary and unconventional that it could not be visualised or foreseen with the available intelligence information by efficient intelligence agencies, dealing with motivated desperate terrorists, trained and highly skilled in use of unconventional methods and explosives of all kinds?

"The intelligence agencies being unaware of this fact indicates the need for improvement of their functioning to keep abreast of professional information/knowledgee available anynwhere".

There were clear messages from the available intelligence reports and successful and abortive assassination bids on top politicians, constitutional functionaries and police officials:

* A terrorist attack on Rajiv Gandhi was imminent.

* The attack could be in an unconventional manner as seen from the ingenious methods used by terrorists in operations a few months before May 21, 1991.

* Strict security cover to Rajiv Gandhi with emphasis on impregnable proximate security was essential for his protection.

* Danger to Rajiv's life was accentuated with the announcement of elections and got further aggravated with prospects of his staging a come-back being bright.

Justice Verma took a serious note of this and observed : "The assassination of Rajiv Gandhi by the mode adopted could not be unforeseeable to the IB, the premier intelligence agency, from the facts known to it. Failure of IB to fully and properly calibrate this threat, foresee the attack made and disseminate the information with the requisite further guidelines and instructions to the state agencies, was a lapse of the IB and the MHA amounting to a contributing factor.

"If this lapse of IB was due to any extraneous factor after a proper calibration of the threat, affecting its professionalism, it would be worse and would need correction for the future."

9 THE CONSPIRACY PROBE

On the sixth day after Rajiv Gandhi's assassination, the ministry of home affairs issued a notification, appointing the one-man inquiry commission headed by Supreme Court Judge J S Verma to probe certain aspects of the assassination. The notification immediately led to an uproar because the terms of reference of the Verma Commission did not include the conspiracy angle.*

This led to bitter protests from the All India Congress Committee (AICC) whose president P V Narasimha Rao wrote to then Prime Minister Chandra Shekhar urging him to revise the terms of reference which were inadequate to unravel the conspiracy behind the assassination.

Then home secretary R K Bhargava wrote to Justice Verma seeking his opinion on the AICC request for enlarging the scope and terms of his commission. But Justice Verma declined the request saying that his consent to head the inquiry commission was confined only to the existing terms of reference. Justice Verma replied: "In my opinion, the existing terms of reference alone fall within the scope of the legitimate functions of a sitting judge and by its very nature are within the scope of the functions of the investigating agencies which are engaged in the task or investigation of the crime."

It was the inadequate terms of reference of the Verma commission of inquiry and Justice Verma's refusal to have its scope enlarged that led to the setting up of another cominission of inquiry headed by retired Delhi High Court chief justice, M C Jain.

The Jain commission's terms of reference were:

---

* *The terms of reference of the Verma commission are reproduced in the chapter : Sins of Omission*

* The sequence of events leading to, and all the facts and circumstances relating to Rajiv Gandhi's assassination at Sriperumbudur (other than the matters covered by the terms of reference for the commission of inquiry headed by Justice J S Verma);

* Whether any person or persons or agencies were responsible for conceiving, preparing and planning the assasination and whether there was any conspiracy in this behalf and, if so, all its ramifications.

The question arises why the MHA could not issue a comprehensive notification in the first place, like it was done in the case of appointment of Thakkar commissicn to probe Indira Gandhi's assassination?

The confusion was compounded when the Jain commission asked for the MHA file containing the original notings regarding the appointment of the Verma commission. The Central government counsel told a shocked Justice Jain in 1995 that the file was missing. The matter rocked Parliament also and the P V Narasimha Rao government made a statement that the file could not be traced despite the efforts of a special team which searched for the file at all possible places, including the Prime Minister's Office and the MHA.

It was the Jain commission which the Central government and its agencies dreaded the most. The reason is obvious.

Never before had an investigating agency's work come under judicial scrutiny even as the trial was on. Never before had the Central government, the state government concerned and the central agencies been forced to give so many sensitive documents to a judicial commission. Little wonder that the Jain commission remained a non-starter for over a year.

It was on August 23, 1991 that the government constituted the commission. But it wasn't before 10 months elapsed that it could hold its first public hearing in June 1992. At the very first hearing, India's attorney general questioned the jurisdiction of the commission. Justice Jain asked the law officer to file written

submissions.

Justice Jain then had to cool his heels for exactly an year. Finally, in June 1993 the government filed written submissions. The Central government counsel told the commission that it had no jurisdiction over the S I T investigations and "agencies" like the LTTE which had already been covered by the SIT.

Justice Jain passed a comprehensive 60-page order the following month, saying the commission had full jurisdiction on all matters. It could oversee SIT's work, including its lapses, and investigate leads left uninvestigated. In a self-imposed restriction, the commission decided to concentrate on the first part of the first term of reference "for the time being" so as not to prejudice the trial.

The government counsel moved an application on August 16, seeking amendment of Justice Jain's order and praying for a stay on the commission's proceedings till the plea was disposed of. There is no question of a stay, the commission said.

The Tamil Nadu government, too, moved an application for revising the cut-off date for determining the sequence of events leading to the assassination. It wanted the commission to change the cut-off year from 1981 to 1987. The plea was rejected on November 17.

Some time in early 1994, the SIT, the Central govemment and the Tamil Nadu government claimed privilege for all documents filed by them.

A New Delhi lawyer, Mushtaq Ahmed, moved the Delhi High Court in June seeking quashing of the MHA notification by which the Jain commission was appointed. His argument: the panel tantamounted to a "parallel probe" which was likely to have serious repercussions on criminal investigations for all time to come because the Jain Commission is going into the same areas in which the S I T had already completed investigations and filed the chargesheet also. Besides, the functioning of the Jain Commission was likely to prejudicially affect the ongoing trial, the petitioner argued.

Ahmed filed the petition as a public interest litigation.

He did not exactly get what he had bargained for, but he came pretty close. In July, the Delhi High Court curtailed the scope and terms of the Jain commission, and restrained it from probing areas and "agencies" covered by the SIT and individuals who had already been chargesheeted.

The court directed the commission to start its probe from July 1987 onwards when the Indo-Lanka accord was signed. The commission was not heard by the court before its wings were virtually clipped.

The Dravida Munnetra Kazhagam (DMK) decided to boycott the commission's proceedings in protest against the dilution of its terms of reference, but it did not challenge the court order either.

However, the Jain commission received redresal when in November 1995, the Delhi High Court lifted all restrictions imposed in July 1994. Mushtaq Ahmed's petition was dismissed.

The same month, the Central government moved the Supreme Court challenging the dismissal of Mushtaq Ahmed's petition. The cat was out of the bag finally; instead of Mushtaq Ahmed, it was the Narasimha Rao government which emerged as the aggrieved party and moved the apex court for killing its own creation.

In December the same year, the government filed another special leave petition (SLP) before the Supreme Court, this time challenging Justice Jain's right to summon case diaries. Both SLPs were dismissed by two different benches of the Supreme Court — one headed by Chief Justice of India, Justice A M Ahmadi, and another by Justice S P Bharucha.

On May 7, 1996, Amit Varma, a DIG of Tamil Nadu cadre, was appointed as security advisor-cum-investigator to the Jain commission. The post had been lying vacant for a year.

However, it was not before another two months that Amit Varma was finally relieved by the Tamil Nadu government.

THE MUCK OOZES

Well over a hundred witnesses deposed before the Jain commission. Following are the relevant extracts from some pertinent testimonies:

Mahant Sewa Dass Singh

If the government's efforts to thwart the course of justice appears shocking, what was more so was the testimony of Mahant Sewa Dass Singh, president of Shaheed Pheruman Shiromani Akali Dal.

I went to London on December 26, 1990. Next day, I went to his (Jagjit Singh Chohan's) residence at 64, Western Court Central London. There was office of 'Khalistan' also in that very premises... Before proceeding to London, I met the then Prime Minister Chandra Shekhar... Chandra Shekhar used to call people to solve the Punjab problem. He called various small factions and groups who had connections with terrorist outfits. I informed Chandra Shekhar that I was proceeding to London. He told me to talk to Jagjit Singh Chohan who happens to be my friend. He told me to tell Chohan to stop violence in Punjab and to find out solution to Punjab problem.

.. I went to Chohan's flat (in London) and had tea with him. About ten or twelve people were already there ... Chohan took me to the Khalistan House in the basement where communication systems and gadgets were installed. He explained the functioning of the gadgets which were used for communicating with Afghanistan, Pakistan and other countries. I asked Chohan as to who were the people who had assembled upstairs, fearing that they may not be such from whom my life may be in danger when I go out. Chohan told me that they were from Babbar Khalsa, Khalistan Commando Force, LTTE... R M Pradi of LTTE was also there. I did not ask the name of other persons. ..Chohan and those who were assembled there told me that they will see to it that Chandra Shekhar continued to remain the Prime Minister... He told me that I should convey to Chandra Shekhar to withdraw CRPF from Punjab, at least for some time. I asked Chohan what benefit he will have with the withdrawal of CRPF from Punjab. The objective for withdrawal of CRPF from Punjab was to make easy entry of weapons from Afghanistan border through Pakistan and Punjab border to India.

"When I asked him as to how Chandra Shekhar *ji* would remain PM for five years, Chohan told me that he would eliminate Rajiv Gandhi. He told me that there was no other leader in the Congress and Chandra Shekhar would be acceptable to the Congress after Rajiv and Chandra Shekhar would remain in power for five years.

I asked Chohan how Rajiv would be eliminated... He informed that there were not only Sikhs, but others also who were with them. He said Haryana people and others may be available to do this job. Sardar Talwinder Singh Parmar intervened and said 'Mahant *ji*, Rajivji to gaye' (Rajiv is gone). I wanted to know the plan, but they said 'Don't ask this'. One JKLF man also intervened and said Rajiv *ji* would be eliminated and I should tell Chandra Shekhar. " Chohan told me that they had a plan to kill Rajiv *ji* at Parliament annexe at New Delhi. I told Chohan that when Indira *ji* was killed, Sikhs in huge numbers were massacred. I told him that all three crore (thirty million) Sikhs would be massacred in India and no Sikh would survive in case Rajiv *ji* is killed in New Delhi... He said that he will not leave this path as we have already decided for such an action.

"I took Chohan downstairs in the basement and impressed upon him to revise the decision. Chohan told me that he will see that Rajiv is not killed in New Delhi and it will be considered by them that the killing may take place at some other place...

Chohan told me that he had relations with Chandraswami, the tantrik. He is his good friend and has got enough of money and plans. He also, on being asked, said they had decided not to kill Rajiv in Delhi. I came back from London on January 2,1991... Chohan gave me three letters, one of which was for Chandra Shekhar... On my persuasion, Chohan told me at the time when I was leaving that Sardar Talwinder Singh Parmar had a meeting with Indian leaders—Sharad Pawar, Om Prakash Chautala,

Chandraswami and Goenka of *Indian Express*. One meeting was held at Bombay at Express Tower which is the office of *Indian Express*. The meeting was in connection with formation of "Khalistan" and elimination of Rajiv Gandhi." I narrated to Rajiv Gandhi (in Parliament House on February 10, 1991) whatever talks I had at London. I also told him what I had conveyed to Chandra Shekhar ... Rajiv Gandhi was a bit unnerved and he started sweating. He was visibly angry... I met Rajiv*ji* again on 14th or 15th Feburary, 1991 at his residence... Two Haryana constables were caught red-handed while they were spying at his residence. This was mentioned by him to me. He also said it was the same thing which I had conveyed to him...

"Chandraswami and Sharad Pawar had financed Jagjit Singh Chohan ... Chandraswami is behind the killing of Rajivji." .. I know Chandraswami for the last ten to twelve years... O P Chautala, Chandraswami and Chandra Shekhar are very good friends. Chandraswami is very much involved in politics. Chandraswami was arrested when Rajiv*ji* was the Prime Minister... Chandraswami remained outside India for a long time after Rajiv*ji* became Prime Minister. A day after the swearing in of Chandra Shekhar, Chandraswami, returned to India and Subramnian Swamy received him at the airport. In most of international arms deals, there is the hand of Chandraswami. He has a hand in other deals also... He has links with foreign terrorist groups.

"The day when two Haryana constables were apprehended during surveillance at the residence of Rajiv*ji*, O P Chautala and Chandraswami went abroad. They went together in the same plane. They got their visas at London airport. Both of them returned to India when Chandra Shekhar became the care-taker Prime Minister...

I doubted the movements of Chautala when Haryana constables were apprehended. I had some suspicions of Chautala's links with Khalistanis based in London... Goenka was also against Rajiv Gandhi ... Chandraswami has sufficient influence in the present government (of P V Narasimha Rao). Chandraswami is an American agent. Half the ministers in the ministry of the Prime

Minister go to Chandraswami and pay respects to him.

"..Subramanian Swamy has made a wrong statement (that the LTTE alone was responsible for Rajiv's killing)... Such a statement was made by him only as a cover-up. Swamy and Chandraswami form a group. Swamy, Chautala and Chandraswami are all involved in the conspiracy to assassinate Rajiv Gandhi and they are trying to divert attention by making different statements. ...Chandra Shekhar did not take my conversation with Chohan seriously in respect of plan of Rajiv's assassination."

CHANDRA SHEKHAR

The Former Prime Minister, needless to say, would not let any mud stick on him, though, to be fair to him, he did own moral responsibility as it was during his premiership that Rajiv was assassinated.

"I cautioned Karunanidhi thrice to take steps against LTTE activities, but he did not pay any heed to it and his ministry was dissolved... During the DMK regime in Tamil Nadu, murders after murders took place, including murder of Padmanabha and no arrests were effected. In those days, National Front government was at the Centre.

"I cannot answer whether any secrets were leaked out by V P Singh and Karunanidhi to the LTTE. Murders and smuggling of arms and other activities were going on not only during the regime of V P Singh, but also during the regime of Rajiv Gandhi and during my own regime because of terrorist activities which we were not able to control.

"It is true that the Tamil Nadu government of DMK was dismissed even without governor's report. Article 356 does not require governor's report as a precondition for dismissal of a government ... I did not ask the governor to submit the report, but whatever information I had about the law and order situation in Tamil Nadu was conveyed to him and I took action of dismissal of the DMK government at that very point of time so that no mischief could be played by the DMK government.

"Question : A senior officer in the Cabinet Secretariat is on oath that Yasser Arafat remarked to you that he has warned Rajiv Gandhi against a plot to assassinate him.

"Answer : No remark to me about the plot.

Question : Will you please say that this information given to the Commission by the said officer is not correct ?

"Answer : This is not correct pertaining to my talk with Yasser Arafat. And on what basis that officer has said, it is for him to explain... Our intelligence agencies did not bring to my knowledge involvement of any foreign agency till June 20, 1991... T N Seshan came to me and did tell me that there may be a foreign hand in the assasination of Rajiv Gandhi. Seshan came to me just after two or three days of the assassination... I vaguely remember that Seshan might have named some foreign agency. Even if he had mentioned any name to me, I am not going to disclose that. I will not mention the name because of foreign relations...

"Law Minister has nothing to do with the coordination of the intelligence agencies' functioning. I do not know whether he (Subramaniam Swamy, law minister in Chandra Shekhar's cabinet) was conducting any coordination meeting of the intelligence agencies. He was not assigned any such job. Any minister could have informal meeting. But it would be very unlikely that intelligence agencies could meet in such an informal way.

"I do not remember Swamy ever mentioned any danger to the life of Rajiv Gandhi from any foreign agency. Had he brought any such thing to my knowledge, steps could have been taken... I do not remember whether Swamy gave any action plan to me after the assassination of Rajiv Gandhi in connection with apprehension of the LTTE supremo V Prabhakaran.... Even if he had made such a suggestion to me, I would not have accepted it....

"The direct responsibility for containing terrorism in Tamil Nadu was of the chief secretary, home secretary, DG Police and the Governor, but the moral responsibility is owned by me as the Prime Minister and the home minister... In my opinion, only one commission could have gone into all aspects of the investigation.

"I hear for the first time that fifteen countries have sent the communication to the Government of India about the threat to life of Rajiv Gandhi... That a human bomb could be used for any VIP was not in the perception of security people. Otherwise all possible security was provided to Rajiv Gandhi, and how the human bomb appeared at the scene requires investigation.

"If SPG would have been the complete answer to save Rajiv Gandhi and if anybody would have suggested, the SPG would have been provided to Rajiv Gandhi even without amendment of the SPG Act...

"Refuelling (of American warplanes during the Gulf War) was agreed to by Rajiv Gandhi and was also agreed to by the President (R Venkataraman). This was done after consultaton with the defence. The first protest came after the gulf war by Rajiv Gandhi and some of the Congress men. I asked Rajiv Gandhi, 'Should I stop refuelling today?' Rajiv Gandhi said, 'Take your own time,' and after three days refuelling was stopped...

"In those days, Rajiv Gandhi first went to Moscow and then to Iran which was against my advice. I do not know whether American authorities liked it or not...

"I know Mahant Sewa Dass Singh... He was going to London (in late December 1990) and he told me that he has some contacts with Sikhs residing in London who can be helpful in solving the Punjab problem. I told him to talk to everybody who can be helpful in solving the Punjab problem... He returned around January 3, 1991. He brought a letter or a message of Jagjit Singh Chohan who has declared himself as the so-called president of Khalistan. I do not remember the contents of that message because it was a cryptic one... I did not attach any significance to it. There was nothing in it to solve the Punjab problem...

"This suggestion is wrong that Mahant Sewa Dass told me that when he visited the house of Jagjit Singh Chohan, there was a meeting of several terrorist outfits at the house of Chohan in London and Chohan introduced him to those who were present as a person who had brought the message from the Prime Minister of India ... (This suggestion is also wrong) that consequently in the presence of Chohan, those terrorists informed the Mahant that since they had received a message through someone else that Chandra Shekhar has agreed to the withdrawal of CRPF from Punjab, so they are interested in continuation of Chandra Shekhar as Prime Minister for full term of five years... The CRPF was never withdrawn from Punjab during my regime. No threat to Rajiv Gandhi's life was communicated to me by Mahant Sewa Dass Singh."

CHANDRASWAMI

The tantrik's marathon testimony lasting more than twenty hours spread over five sittings yielded nothing much as most of it pertained to issues other than the conspiracy behind Rajiv Gandhi's killing.

A visibly disappointed Justice Jain remarked after the conclusion of Chandraswami's testimony that not even five per cent of the deposition pertained to Rajiv Gandhi assassination. His entire deposition is punctuated by "I do not remember" or categoric denials of all accusations against him.

"I and O P Chautala never went together to London... Mahant Sewa Dass Singh is wrong when he says that I am very much involved in politics... I have not attended any such meeting (as mentioned by Mehant Sewa Singh with R N Goenka, Sharad Pawar and Talwinder Singh Parmar at any place in Bombay.

"I have no knowledge that CIA and Mossad work in conjunction. I have no relations with CIA and Mossad. It is wrong to suggest that I wanted to eliminate Rajiv Gandhi and such was the plan of CIA and Mossad.

"I visited Sri Lanka once or twice in the year 1985 or 1986 for inauguration of Ashwamedha Yagna at the request of president Jayewardene. I met Rajadurai and Premadasa. It is wrong to suggest that I went to Sri Lanka to meet LTTE people.

"I never had any relations with the LTTE people in Madras through any one or direct... It is wrong to suggest that I had the knowledge of the conspiracy to kill Rajiv Gandhi and that I was a major player in it."

SUBRAMANIAN SWAMY

(Minister for Commerce and Law and Justice in Chandra Shekhar's Cabinet)

"Chief election commissioner T N Seshan came to me on May 22, 1991 to inform me that according to his information, Israel's intelligence outfit mossad was the real mastermind behind the LTTE in Rajiv Gandhi's assassination. When I asked him for some basis for this charge, he said he would only be able to do so if made the home minister in our government.

"I was instrumental in persuading Rajiv Gandhi in making Chandra Shekhar the Prime Minister. I was proposed by Rajiv Gandhi for Prime Ministership one week before Chandra Shekhar became Prime Minister. There was a meeting between me and Rajiv Gandhi alone when he expressed reservation about Chandra Shekhar and he urged me to accept Prime Ministership. But I told him it was too late in the day and on a subsequent occasion when Seshan was also present, Rajiv Gandhi joked about my refusal. Seshan agreed that I was very right in my refusal.

"Chandra Shekhar government resigned on March 14, 1991 and according to me Rajiv Gandhi never withdrew his support, it was purely a personality clash which led to the fall of the Chandra Shekhar government. It was his stupidity.

"CIA, like other intelligence organisations, have their presence in many countries. No country in the world liked Rajiv Gandhi as he was a strong Prime Minister. No country would like a strong Prime Minister and Rajiv Gandhi was a strong Prime Minister. ...Prior to the assassination of Rajiv Gandhi, I have no knowledge about any international agency having any hostility to Rajiv Gandhi, except LTTE. I had no knowledge about any relationship between LTTE and ISI prior to the assassination of Rajiv Gandhi. Some Sikh terrorist organisations were equally interested in eliminating Rajiv Gandhi.

"...(Yasser) Arafat never mentioned before me any threat to Rajiv Gandhi. I once took a personal message of Rajiv Gandhi to Arafat, but he did not mention about any danger to the life of Rajiv Gandhi. This meeting took place in October 1990 ... I did see in the press that Arafat was attributed a fact that international agencies are involved in the assassination, but the government was not given any intimation.

"The contact of Jayalalitha with LTTE was very strong since 1987 and more close in 1989. Re-establishment of contact took place in 1992. When Rajiv Gandhi went on election trip to Sriperumbudur, Jayalalitha avoided all his programmes. It was in pursuance of LTTE's advice and the advice was to keep away from Rajiv Gandhi's programme. Jayalalitha's contact with LTTE was there till the assassination.

"...Jayalalitha had declined to address any public meeting jointly with Rajiv Gandhi despite the fact that both their parties were contesting the elections in alliance.

"Jayalalitha, finally after much persuasion by then TNCC (I) president K Ramamurthy, agreed to address a public meeting in Krishnagiri on May 22, 1991 but suddenly decided to cancel the said joint appearance on the plea that she would go somewhere else in the neighbourhood to address the meeting.

"Jayalalitha stayed in the Dharmapuri circuit house on the night of May 21,1991 and was frequently calling the Collector, one Murugan, to enquire from 6.00 pm of that fateful day whether an important phone call had come for her from Madras and that upon being repeatedly told that no such call had come, she left the circuit house in obvious annoyance and disgust which was perceived by those who watched her, including the said Collector, as strange.

"After receiving the information (of Rajiv's assassination) she abruptly decided to disappear to Bangalore instead of driving to Madras to see the last remains of the body of the assassinated leader and her alliance partner Rajiv Gandhi. She also failed to come to Delhi for his funeral even though practically all the other leaders, even those in opposition made a point to attend.

"... Jayalalitha may be summoned by the commission for two reasons: (i) clearly a systematic pattern of escape of LTTE cadres from jail since 1992 had emerged that shows connivance at the highest level; (ii) her statement that it is the CIA which is responsible for Rajiv Gandhi's assassination. This is an attempt to exonerate the LTTE.

"... I have friends who have penetrated the LTTE. I have no contact with the LTTE.

"... International conspiracy (behind Rajiv Gandhi's assassination) cannot be ruled out. The reasons why I cannot rule out are (a) Rajiv Gandhi doubled defence expenditure and modernised India's defence ; (b) he sent troops to Sri Lanka and Maldives to demonstrate that India would defend its interests abroad ; (c) he coined phrases like *Mera Bharat Mahan* (My India is great). Unless we catch Prabhakaran we will never know whether there was any international conspiracy.

"... I cannot rule out motivating or financing aspect of the intelligence agencies like CIA, Mossad and KGB.

"...I did state in my statement on July 6, 1995 that I have friends who have penetrated into LTTE. I have no contact with LTTE. What I meant by penetration was that they know people in LTTE abroad. My friends themselves are not in LTTE.

"It is my propaganda claim that the Narasimha Rao government will not survive without my support. It is a stunt, not a genuine claim...It was not a stunt when I said in my statement on July 6, 1995 that the third financial source of LTTE is Jayalalitha. It is based on solid information.

"... On March 21, 1988 Jayalalitha, general secretary of AIADMK, demanded at a press conference in Madras that India should immediately halt its military operation against LTTE. Then she said if any harm comes to Prabhakaran due to deliberate or incidental action of IPKF, it will have an adverse impact in Tamil Nadu.

"...I heard that on March 5, 1991, Rajiv Gandhi had a meeting with some representatives of the LTTE... I heard that one journalist in Tamil Nadu had arranged this meeting... This was an LTTE tactic to make Rajiv Gandhi tour Tamil Nadu... I had no chance to discuss this meeting of LTTE representatives. But I did find his guard a bit down with regard to the LTTE and he was discussing with me the possibility of his going to Tamil Nadu sometime in April."

S B CHAVAN
(Former Union Home Minister)

Chavan created a flutter when he went on record saying that a superpower was behind Rajiv's assassination. In an unprecedented move, a spokesman of the external affairs ministry denied this, but Chavan never retracted his statement.

"In my speech on 26th of July 1991, I reiterated what I said on 4th June 1991 that some foreign agencies were involved. I did not mention any foreign power.

I had also clearly stated that when these operations are undertaken they are done in such a meticulous manner, it becomes almost impossible to get any clue. In my speech I have also said that this is my suspicion and there is no evidence with me. I have been referred to the affidavit of K K Tewary. His affidavit is based on attempts made by different foreign powers to destabilise conditions in our country. But I do not think even Tewary can possibly give any clue on what basis he is saying that they must be involved in the assassination. If any clue is given, certainly the investigating agency can be asked to investigate the matter even at this stage, but general impression which K K Tewary gave is not altogether wrong because there are forces who were trying to create destabilising conditions more in Punjab and J & K and we know the foreign powers who were supplying the arms, giving them training in training camps and providing logistic support also. In a general way, this kind of impression may be there, but I do not think that any definite clue can be given by anyone.

"Mine is the same reaction as deposed by me in respect of the statement of Subramanian Swamy recorded on 20th March 1995 when he stated that T N Seshan the then chief election commissioner informed him about the involvement of Israel's Mossad which was the real mastermind behind the LTTE in Rajiv Gandhi's assassination.

"I have mentioned in my speech in the House on 4th June, 1991 regarding involvement of super power. I made a mistake while mentioning the word super power which should have been some foreign powers. There is only one super power left. Super power in my mind, might be America. But I cannot rule out the possibility of other powers also. I did not have any information regarding involvement of the powers. The SIT had been formed and this commission had been constituted to inquire into the larger conspiracy. It was the job of the SIT to investigate all aspects of the question including involvement of foreign powers. SIT is not with the home ministry. It is with the ministry of personnel. There is no control of home ministry on investigation by the SIT.

"I cannot possibily say that there is a running thread in the assassinations of Indira Gandhi and Rajiv Gandhi, but there is no denying the fact that Rajiv Gandhi was emerging as the dynamic leader of the country having a vision of taking India into the 21st century. He was very much interested in seeing that all non-aligned countries remained together and they are able to make a common cause. That is why super power or powers were interested in seeing that this situation should not be allowed to continue. Normally I give extempore speeches. I do not remember whether my speech on 26.7.1991 was an extempore one or was based on earlier briefing or preparation. (The witness was shown his speech exhibit 112 dated 26.7.1991. After seeing the sppech the witness stated that it might be a prepared one). There was no feedback from any intelligence ragarding involvement of any foreign power in Rajiv assassination.

"I made my statement on the basis of my general impression without any feedback regarding involvement of any foreign power. I can make any statement on the basis of my general impression.

It is correct that very day the American ambassador in India met the Prime Minister, the foreign minister and the foreign secretary and the spokesperson of the MEA held a press conference and contradicted my statement regarding involvement of super power.

"It is abnormal that spokesperson of the MEA held the press conference contradicting my statement. It is not a fact that I was under any pressure to make a statement the next day denying involvement of any super power. The Prime Minister did not talk to me. My statement must have created a stir in diplomatic circles. I am not aware of the conversation which the American ambassador in India held with the Prime Minister on my statement. Neither RAW nor minister of defence ever briefed me in connection with the proceedings before this commission. I had a general impression. SIT had just started investigation. So on the basis of that general impression, I made my speeches including the speech on 14.9.1991. But I made it absolutely clear that I have no evidence at my disposal. The basis of my general impression is my 40 years of public life and the political reading of what is happening in different parts of the world.

*I am still of the view that some foreign power is involved. It is not the job of the LTTE.** The general impression is that some other powers may also be involved. That possibility I do not rule out. I am very cautious in my statement. I do not want to spoil our relations with any foreign country. So I cannot be specific, unless I have some evidence at my disposal.

"I have possibly no information as to how many Third World leaders have been assassinated by the CIA. *There is very much presence of CIA in India and in all the developing countries.** Every effort is made by them to destablise these countries. There were some congressional committees inquiring into the matter of involvement of CIA. I am not aware what transpired in these committees. (The witness was asked about the Committees, namely Church committee, Pike committee and Rockfeller commission.)

"Our IB must have identified a few of CIA agents in India. This is the work of RAW but after entry in the Indian territory, it is

---

* *Emphasis added*

the job of IB. Few of them must have been identified. I am not aware of the movement of CIA agents in Tamil Nadu from January 1991 to June 1991.

"I enquired from the SIT and the SIT informed me that there is no CIA movement in Tamil Nadu from January 1991 to June 1991. Director IB must be having all the dossiers of CIA agents and Mossad agents in India. Their movement in India does not impinge on national security of India. No dossier of any CIA agents or Mossad agens was brought to my notice. Activities connected with ISI were brought to my notice. So far as their operations in India are concerned, nothing has been brought to my notice. It has not come to my notice that so far as India is concerned, whether ISI is having any connection with Mossad, but it may be having in Afghanistan. I do not have any information that ISI, CIA and Mossad are jointly gathering intelligence and sharing intelligence in South East Asia and Middle East. *I stand by the statements which I made, whether I hold the charge or not.* *

"The chief minister of Tamil Nadu has been writing to the Government of India for extradition of Prabhakaran. For extradition some documents were received which were part of the Rajiv Gandhi assassination case. Those documents could not be parted with at that time. No information could be given to Sri Lankan then as investigation was going on. This point came up for discussion. It is quite possible that the then chief minister of Tamil Nadu might have written to the Government of India for banning the LTTE. I do not recollect whether that letter was brought to my notice. It appears that she (Jayalalitha) had written to the Prime Minister. I do not recall as to what action was taken on J Jayalalitha's letter dated 22.12.1991. Action was taken on Jayalalitha's letter dated 24.9.92. Inquiries were made on the activities of the Pattali Makkal Katchi (PMK). Finally any action was taken or not, I have to see the papers for answering.

"No inquiry was ordered by me regarding involvement of any foreign agency or power. I was depending on the IB, but IB did not supply me any information on involvement of any foreign

---

* *Emphasis added*

agency or power. SIT was actually inquiring into the entire matter of Rajiv*ji's* assassination and it could investigate into the involvement of any foreign agency or power.

"Foreign secretary Muchkund Dubey's note CG/203 never came to my notice when I was home minister. I got this information about Ministry of external affairs having some knowledge only when I was briefed to appear before this commission after looking into the record. Even the telegram Ex. CG/203 was never brought to my notice. Ex. CG/202 bears the initials of the Prime Minister below the letters 'PM'

"Arafat and PLO ambassador are important people and if they supply important information, credence must be given to it. If information which had been conveyed by PLO ambassador were to be brought into my notice, I would have asked the Prime Minister to get it enquired from RAW.

"If the Prime Minister was aware of this information he should have referred the matter to RAW.

"...I did not consult any one or the Prime Minister as to how my statement was contradicted."

LT GEN (RETD) AMARJIT SINGH KALKAT

"I was appointed as commander of the IPKF in Sri Lanka in April 1988. I retired from services on 31st December, 1993.

"My Headquarters was at Madras when I was GOC, IPKF but for overseeing the conduct of operations I had to frequently visit Sri Lanka. My jurisdiction was confined only to Sri Lanka. I was GOC, IPKF in Sri Lanka. I had in the HQ, a chief of staff—a Major General. Under the Major General there were three Brigadiers, one Brigadier was in charge of operation. He looked after the operation side. That included intelligence training etc. Another looked after civil affairs, while the third Brigadier looked after administration and logistics.

"This information was passed by other Tamil parties that *Sri Lankan Army was supplying arms and ammunitions to the LTTE* *in the major part of 1989.** I got this information through my own officers who in turn got it from the other Tamil parties other than the LTTE. I took up this matter with Sri Lankan Commander who said that there was no such thing happening.

"I only got the information that Sri Lankan Army was giving arms and ammunition. What type of arms they were supplying was not informed to me.

"... My troops captured a large number of LTTE cadres. LTTE cadres were interrogated but they did not give us any such information regarding the source of arms supply to the LTTE, to the best of my knowledge."

NARESH CHANDRA

(Former Union home secretary and ex-cabinet secretary. Presently, he is India's ambassador in the US)

"I remember one report regarding Rajiv Gandhi's security regarding use of poisonous gloves. There were reports from IB regarding several events which had taken place at various places during the period 10-12-1990 to May, 1991 which also included threats to the life of Rajiv Gandhi.

"Clandestine wireless interceptions were done by the agencies regularly. Generally the agencies avoid the exact intercepts decoded by them. I do not recall any specific message was reported to me as Home Secretary and as Cabinet Secretary in respect of the assassination of Rajiv Gandhi but there were reports of various terrorist groups trying to make plans of assassination of Indian VIPs, including Rajiv Gandhi. I recollect there were intercepts with the security agencies regarding threats to the life of Rajiv Gandhi in Tamil Nadu during his lifetime.

There is a report of IB which casts aspersions on some sections of the State Government regarding giving of information to the LTTE. These allegations have been made against DMK government that killers of Padmanabha were allowed to escape.

---

* *Emphasis added.*

Reports say that there are some common accused in Padmanabha murder case and Rajiv Gandhi assassination case. I cannot say without looking into the records as to whether some ministers in the DMK government then were providing shelter and hide-outs to Padmanabha killers. I do not recall any such report that Mossad agents had visited India and moved towards Madras. I do not recall any such report coming to me showing links of Mossad with LTTE. I do not recall having received any such reports regarding warning by Arafat to Rajiv Gandhi in connection with his security in Febaruary 1991, April 1991 and a week prior to the assassination. Intelligence agencies might have enquired about these happenings, but they did not report to me.

"I am aware of the statements made to the investigating officers much later by two terrorists, Harpreet Singh Rangi and Sukhvir Singh Khanna, that two futile attempts were made by Sikh militants to kill Rajiv Gandhi at Shahdara (East Delhi) and Faridabad (on the outskirts of Delhi). According to the statements of these two militants, the attempts failed due to the alertness of the access control system. The access control system then was of State Police. Access control system includes frisking and not allowing unknown people in the vicinity of the protected person.

"... I am not in a position to comment whether there was any inkling or any intelligence reports in our unit at Madras regarding impending threats to Rajiv Gandhi from the LTTE in April/May 1991 as I was not dealing with Rajiv's security/VIP security.

M K NARAYANAN
(Former IB director)

"During my tenure as director, IB, I had no occasion to go into the record relating to any enquiry having been made within the department about IB having received any intelligence inputs. I have no knowledge whether any enquiry was conducted as to why the conspiracy to assassinate Rajiv Gandhi could not be detected. I am not in a position to recollect whether there was any intelligence report on the activities of the persons accused in Rajiv Gandhi assassination case. There are some accused common in

Padmanabha murder case and Rajiv Gandhi assassination case. I have no knowledge whether IB had intelligence regarding LTTE cadres who were common to the two cases for the period May 1990 to May 1991.

"I do expect that our field unit in Tamil Nadu should have had some inkling about the activities of the common accused. I also expect that our field unit should have had inkling about the activities of the other accused in Rajiv Gandhi assassination case. I would not call it a lapse, it was unfortunate. *IB had no intelligence about attempt made by the two Sikh militants Harpreet Singh Rangi and Sukhvinder Singh Khanna on the life of Rajiv Gandhi at Faridabad and Shahdra. IB also did not have specific intelligence about the attacks on Sajjan Kumar and Jagdish Tytler. I do not know whether IB had any intelligence reports regarding dry run in V P Singh's meeting at Madras.** I do expect that IB should have advance intelligence about such attacks or an activity like dry run, although unfortunately it is not always possible to have intelligence inputs. Skilled, professionally trained and competent persons could always be provided to a threatened person like Rajiv Gandhi."

K N THAKUR

(Thakur was a top officer of the IB at the time of Rajiv's assassination)

"The opinion of IB's bomb expert Col Sundram who visited the spot at Sriperumbudur a day or two after the blast was that in the immediate vicinity, that is 100 feet radius of the blast centre, the bomb would have killed the target irrespective of any protective apparel.

*"It had been found that frisking of Dhanu was not done.** It has been stated in the Verma commission by IB's bomb expert Col Sundaram who visited the spot and studied the matter that had the drill of frisking been followed the explosives hidden on the person of the human bomb Dhanu could have been detected. This

---

* *Emphasis added*

detection was possible by touching. I will check up whether there was any enclosure for frisking of women at the site. Col Sundaram also stated that the metal part of the improvised bomb could have been detected by a metal detector, the hand held metal detector, had it been used to check the human bomb Dhanu as prescribed. There was breach of antisabotage check. it was found that the explosive material was RDX, a plastic explosive which does not emit vapour in sufficient quantity for a dog to normally detect it.

"Till the date of assassination, I was not aware nor the VIP security wing of the IB was aware of any such message that Sivarasan had arrived in Tamil Nadu or instructions were sought to attack Rajiv Gandhi either in Delhi or in Tamil Nadu. * Subsequent to the assassination, I came to know that such messages had been received in codes. These messages were received prior to the assassination. The details of the code and how and when it was broken are not known to me."

*

More than a hundred witnesses appeared before the Jain commission and deposed. These included former prime ministers, former Union ministers and former chief ministers. Based on their testimony and over half a million of classified documents, the commission finally submitted its final report on March 7, 1988.

---

* *There is much more to the conspiracy angle than has come to light. I have dealt with this matter in details in "Epilogue".*

PART IV

WHEELS WITHIN WHEELS

10 The Foreign Hand

But for the Indian media's hawkish eye, several dark areas of the SIT's investigations in the Rajiv Gandhi assassination case would not have come to light. There are many startling gaps in the probe.

The SIT is yet to establish how the LTTE, which fought a near suicidal battle with the Indian Army for two years and was battered to a position of near-annihilation, restored its arsenal and infrastructure in just 18 months, and then muster up enough expertise to kill the former prime minister on Indian soil?

Who gave the LTTE arms and ammunition and other infrastructural support? It could not have, like the Phoenix, risen from its ashes on its own.

Sri Lankan president Ranasinghe Premadasa was one of those who had extended a friendly hand towards the Tigers. But that could not have been all. Who were the others ? Why did they, including Premadasa, help the LTTE ? These are the questions that are intimately connected with the Rajiv Gandhi assassination and are still abegging answers.

Several important leads were obtained by the SIT, but for some inexplicable reason, these were not pursued to their logical conclusions. The uninvestigated areas given below necessitate that fresh investigations be ordered by the Indian government without any further delay to get to the root of the conspiracy in the Rajiv Gandhi assassination case.

R PREMADASA

One could begin with Ranasinghe Premadasa, who himself was assassinated in 1993.

The irrepressible, Subramaniam Swamy, publicly contended Premadasa had conspired with the LTTE against India and the possibility of the Island government financing Rajiv's assassins should be looked into. Swami made a statement at a press conference about four months after Rajiv's assassination, that the possibility of Premadasa being a "co-conspirator" should be probed.

In the last week of August 1991, Sri Lankan opposition parties and several members of the ruling party handed over to the Speaker an impeachment notice and a chargesheet against Premadasa. Among other things, the chargesheet accused the Lankan president, of "*carrying on secret negotiations with and arming the LTTE*". The chargesheet decried Premadasa, a known India-baiter, for sending the IPKF back to India without due consideration of the military aspects and thus causing destruction of the Sri Lankan army.

The chargesheet said Premadasa tapped telephones and used the government machinery to intimidate his political opponents. The impeachment notice said he had more than 500 guards to protect him and he lived in "constant fear and suspicion even of his wife".

During this period, shocking facts came to light which exposed the secret understanding Premadasa had with the LTTE. His government provided financial assistance, vehicles, arms, explosives and cement to the LTTE.

Two LTTE militants—Raghu alias Sivaraj and Vikky alias Vigneswaran— who were arrested on the outskirts of the Coimbatore in July 1991 and were charged with manufacturing arms for the LTTE in the city conceded that the Sri Lankan government often provided liberal financial assistance to the Tamil militants during the IPKF's stay in the island nation.

They said the Premadasa government provided more than 30 latest-design Japanese cars to the LTTE to fight the IPKF in the Jaffna jungles. The vehicles, suitable for use in rugged jungle terrain, were released in one batch.

Raghu said the government's offer of help came when the militant group was facing a shortage of logistics. The LTTE also received from Premadasa a double-barrel rifle firing grenade-like explosives against the IPKF.

They said the LTTE had constructed bunkers in the market places in every town under its control so that people could take shelter during air raids. There were many bunkers in the jungles and Prabhakaran was staying in one of them which had all facilities. Sri Lanka had engaged foreign pilots for bombing the Tamil areas as its air force pilots were inexperienced.

The two militants told the police the LTTE had a separate research and development wing, even in the field of agriculture. So much so, this wing had developed new varieties of agricultural products, including big sized tomatoes, which would grow easily in the jungles of Jaffna.

On September 18, 1991, Premadasa admitted that Sri Lanka's security forces fought alongside the Tamil guerillas against the Tamil National Army (TNA), a provincial militia composed of rival groups. Premadasa explained to a government parliamentary group meeting that such a situation had arisen when the IPKF started withdrawing in October 1989 and the TNA went on a rampage attacking Muslims in the East. In the past, the Premadasa government had repeatedly denied that its troops had been fighting alongside the Tigers against the TNA, whose members were forced into fleeing to India.

The Sri Lankan government issued a statement on September 23, 1991 in Colombo, saying that its defence forces had "*shared equipment" with the LTTE. It said "the LTTE was made use of by our forces to confront and neutralise the TNA." The defence forces shared equipment to fight "the common enemy*". The statement said that with the help of the LTTE, it was possible to recover a large number of weapons.

More damning disclosures followed. *Ravaya*, a Sinhala weekly, reported in November, 1991 that the office of Sri Lanka's auditor general was investigating charges that the government had paid Rs 9 crore to the LTTE in 1990 while negotiating with it.

The money had been released under the "national security requirements" clause. The treasury had released this amount after a senior officer in the finance ministry had signed the voucher for payment. The voucher had been issued without the mandatory supporting documents. The Sri Lankan newspaper also alleged that the government tried to present the Auditor General's annual report from becoming public.

The Premadasa government started talks with the LTTE in March 1989 when the rebels accepted the President's offer for talks. The talks broke down in June 1990 when the LTTE attacked police stations and army camps in the north-east.

India's foreign-secretary designate , J N Dixit, who was High Commissioner to Sri Lanka, admitted that India had agreed to pay Rs 5 crore to the LTTE "for maintenance of its cadres" if the group agreed to accept the Indo-Sri Lanka accord. Officials later disclosed that two or three instalments of Rs fifty lakh each had been paid to the LTTE before the rebel group denounced the accord in October 1987.

The most damaging disclosure of Premadasa's inexplicable hobnobbing with the LTTE came in November 1991. Lt Priyalal Jagath Vishwakumara Vathiage, a member of Sri Lanka's rapid deployment force, gave graphic details of the Premadasa-LTTE nexus in his sworn statement before the Justice for the Peace.

Lt Vathiage, who later quit the army, testified that he was personally entrusted with the task of delivering large consignments of arms and ammunition to the LTTE in the summer of 1989 under instructions that the Tamil Tigers needed these to drive out the IPKF. He had made seven trips over three weeks in June-July in 1989 carrying lorry loads of weapons and ammunition from the Gajapura camp, where he was posted, to an LTTE jungle hideout, about seven miles from the Nedumkerni camp of the IPKF.

The weapons and the ammunition were carted in brand new Tata 1210 trucks, which were without any number plates. It was Lt Vathiage's task to drive these by turns to the LTTE hideout.

Earlier, he had been sent on a reconnaissance mission of the jungle location during which he had met several LTTE members, including "Major Yogi" and "Captain Justin". A few days later,

Yogi and Justin along with three or four others, were brought to the Gajapura camp in a Sri Lankan air force helicopter, apparently from Colombo. They had been invited to lunch by Lt Vatiage's commanding officer, Major Boharan. It was over lunch that the commanding officer told Yogi that the arms would be delivered soon.

The second consignment of three lorries arrived about three weeks later and, like on the earlier occasion, he drove them to the same jungle hideout. Both the consignments were handed over to Yogi, who was camping there with nearly 40 LTTE cadres in uniform.

The seven lorry loads that Lt Vathiage had carried contained large quantities of T-56 rifles, grenades, explosives, detonators and huge stocks of 7.62 mm and T-56 ammunition.

During the period spanning the two deliveries, Sri Lankan air force helicopters made several sorties over the jungle hideout. This made most of colleagues of Lt Vathiage wonder what was happening as they had often been short of helicopters even for shifting a wounded soldier.

Lt Vathiage said he had been instructed by Major Boharan to drive LTTE cadres in his official jeep on several occasions to locations "very near" to the IPKF's Nedunkerni camp. It was some time after he had delivered the full consignment that the LTTE had launched their first attack on the camp.

Lt Vathiage said his commanding officer, after swearing him into secrecy, had told him that the "highly confidential" orders had come from the very top and nobody apart from the president and the army chief knew about it.

He said he was instructed not to disclose it at any cost, and was told that "just as we fight this war on orders" he had to carry out the task on orders. Since "the LTTE did not have the arms to drive the IPKF from Sri Lanka", they were to be "equipped to do so".

Confirming the details of the sworn statement in an interview with a Colombo lawyer, which was recorded on video, Lt Vathiage said that as an officer at the time he felt he had no option but to do as ordered, though personally he knew that it was a wrong thing to do.

Lt Vathiage, in fact, felt so bad about arming the LTTE that he kept aside two T-56 rifles from the stocks he delivered to the LTTE.

Sri Lankan government spokesman and industries minister, Ranil Wickremesinghe, defended the government's arming of the LTTE, saying it was for fighting the TNA which was attacking Sinhala villagers, while the army was being deployed in the south to curb the insurgency by the southern militants, the Janatha Vimukti Peramuna.

He argued at a meeting of the United National Party at suburban Kelaniya on September 30 that if the army had been used against the TNA, there would have been a Tamil backlash.

As this controversy snowballed into a diplomatic mess, Premadasa wrote a personal letter to the Indian Prime Minister P V Narasimha Rao in October 1991, explaining the circumstances necessitating supply of arms to the LTTE. In this letter, he dismissed reports that his government had supplied weapons to the LTTE to take on the IPKF.

Rajiv's widow Sonia, and a power centre even after her husband's murder, was not unaware of the dubious conduct of Premadasa. It was clearly reflected when Premadasa sent several requests to 10, Janpath, seeking an audience with her Sonia either on October 1 or 2, 1992, but she did not oblige.

Sonia reportedly continued to harbour strong feelings about the manner in which Premadasa boycotted the official reception in honour of Rajiv when he visited Sri Lanka in 1987 as Prime Minister.

An ugly side of Premadasa was reported in the press during the investigations of the assassination of his political rival and minister of state for defence, Ranjan Wijeratne.

Wijeratne was the former chairman of the ruling United National Party, to which Premadasa also belonged. A popular figure with the military top brass, Wijeratne was entertaining hopes of replacing Premadasa.

On March 1, 1991, Wijeratne was holding an unscheduled meeting with the Chiefs of the Army, Navy and Air force when Premadasa barged in unannounced. The embarrassment writ large on the faces of the assembled men was only too vivid for Premadasa to miss. None spoke. A much worried Premadasa retreated in silence.

The following morning, when Wijeratne was driving to his office in his bullet-proof Mercedes, he was blown to bits.

Murky aspects of the hidden Premadasa-Wijeratne rift came to the fore in a crucial interview Premadasa Udugampola, former head of Sri Lanka's bureau of special operations, gave to M D Nalapat in *The Times of India*.

Udugampola, who was forcibly retired at the age of 57, by his government when he was a DIG, had incurred the wrath of the ruling establishment for demanding an independent inquiry into the circumstances surrounding the murder of Wijeratne. He was also a bitter critic of Premadasa's policies towards the LTTE, because of which he was also on the Tigers' hit list.

The veteran of 34 years in the Sri Lankan police told Nalapat at a hideout off the Lankan coast (Udugampola was leading a fugitive's life) that he was forcibly retired bcause he repeatedly pressed for an independent inquiry into Wijeratne's killing. He said Wijeratne was killed a month after he had given the defence minister information about some important businessmen in Colombo who were secretly supplying arms to the Tigers.

"These businessmen were close to the ruling party and pressure had been brought on me to drop my inquiry. I refused and instead briefed Wijeratne about what was going on. That proved to be his death warrant," Udugampola said.

Wijeratne went to the President and demanded that these businessmen be taken into custody. When they were not, he threatened to go public. This was a week before the assassination.

Udugampola dismissed the official inquiry into the assassination as a "farce". He said Premadasa was keen that the LTTE should not be implicated in the murder as he was friendly with them. He even alleged that it was only through top-level connivance that the LTTE could have got the information about Wijeratne's route and time of travel.

Nalapat's interview of Udugampola was indeed a journalistic scoop. The Sri Lankan levelled even wilder allegations.

"The Black Cats, who were supposed to combat the Janata Vimukti Peramuna, kill those who oppose the president. Or he asks his friends, the northern terrorists (the LTTE), to do the job.

"The whole of Sri Lanka knows who is behind the killings of those officers who opposed the president's soft line on the LTTE. Just weeks ago (the latter half of 1992), there were huge anti-government agitations during the funeral of Lt Gen Vijaya Vimalaratne and Maj Gen Denzil Kobbekaduwa, because the public knows who is behind the explosives that took the lives of these two soldiers."

In April 1992, Premadasa ruled out extradition of Prabhakaran to India. It was an indirect but obvious reference to the question of extradition of Prabhakaran and LTTE intelligence chief Pottu Amman. In a speech at the muslim township of Beruwala, south of Colombo, Premadasa said : "Just because the 'younger brothers' (the LTTE) did wrong at times, the 'elder brothers' will not hand them over to next door for the purpose of making them obedient."

New Delhi was aware of Premadasa's double-crossing his own people and the Indian government by colluding with the LTTE.

RAW prepared an extensive report on collusion between Sri Lankan government and the LTTE on November 24, 1989, nearly 18 months before Rajiv's assassination. What action was taken by the Indian government is not known. The report, numbered Cab. Sectt (R&AW) UO No 1/17-A/89-SLM-346-6059 and dated November 24, 1989, is reproduced below:

"Increased collusion between SLG 'Sri Lankan government' and the LTTE has been discernible ever since commencement of the third round of talks between them (September 89). Initially, both SL Government and the LTTE concentrated on securing an agreement from India on the withdrawal of IPKF. After India and Sri Lanka agreed that the IPKF would leave Sri Lanka in a phased manner by December 31, 1989, the SL government and to a greater extent LTTE, began to see in the security set up being organised by the CM NEPC for the north-east a major irritant and obstacle.

"In the recent past, LTTE has been carrying on an intensive campaign both on the ground and on the propaganda front against the so-called Tamil National Army. It has sought to achieve this by engineering defections from CVF as well as by openly exhorting CVF volunteers to desert and cross over before specified date. When the expected response did not materialise, it went to the extent of launching a major attack on two CVF camps in Amparai district on November 5, causing the death of nearly 30 cadres of the pro-agreement groups. *It is suspected that the Sri Lankan authorities facilitated this attack by giving indirect support.*

"On the ground, there have been many reports of large quantities of arms and ammunition having been handed over by SL army to LTTE. *

"(i) 300 M-16 rifles and 30,000 rounds to match it, were handed over to LTTE in October. In Pollonaruwa four weeks ago, it handed over to LTTE ammunition for AK-47 and grenades (number not known). On another occasion in an unspecified area between Vavuniya and Mannar it handed over 400 small arms to LTTE probably without the knowledge of IGP and military commander.

*"(ii) Besides arms and ammunition, the LTTE seems to be enjoying unfettered use of helicopters of SL government for the transport of arms and movement of LTTE cadres.** According to one report, immediately after the raid at Amparai district on November 5, the helicopters of Sri Lankan security forces picked up the cadres of LTTE and regrouped them in Jaffna district. The injured LTTE cadres in the November 5 operations were airlifted to Colombo for treatment in hospitals. Added to this, *Pottu Amman,*

---

* *Emphasis added*

*Jaffna in-charge of LTTE, travels in Sri Lankan helicopters ostensibly to watch the movements of rival cadres and plan out his strategies for attacking them**.

"*(iii) The security forces are regularly utilising the LTTE for collection of intelligence on rival militant groups and are using them possibly as security guards for ministers. The cadres of LTTE don uniform of Sri Lankan security forces and are often found to be checking vehicles on roads.* * Above all, SL forces are believed to have stood by and offered support fire at the time of LTTE raids on Thumbiluvil, Turikkovil camps of TELO and EPRLF on November 5.

"(iv) The Sri Lankan Government has not taken to task the LTTE for its attack on Thubiluvil and Tirukkovil camps though it has been repeatedly expressing that it was against any private armies. On the other hand, it appeared to justify the LTTE raids. When the CM NEPC reminded Gen Attygalle of the promise of going after the LTTE camp at Kaaradiyanaru forests in Amparai, the General replied that he did not have sufficient forces to attack the LTTE camp.

"(v) *The incident at Wilpattu sanctuary (on November 9) where LTTE robbed arms of SL government did not provoke even the mildest criticism in SL government.* *

"(vi) The SL government has been requesting LTTE to give a list of its cadres to be recruited in the CVF against the enhanced strength of CVF.

"(vii) *The LTTE supremo has also recently ordered his cadres not to indulge in any violence against Sri Lankan government forces.* *

"*(viii) With the help of SL government, LTTE has established camps in the east and has placed orders for import of 5,000 weapons of Chinese make.*" *

At a time when Premadasa was facing acute political crisis at home in the wake of a bitter campaign by two former ministers,

---

* *Emphasis added*

Lalith Athulathmudali and Gamini Dissanayake, he acused unnamed "external forces" of trying to resort to "political assassinations" to destabilise the country.

"Don't be surprised if these elements try to harm me," he said while addressing a large 'Triumph of Democracy' rally in the Sri Lankan temple town of Kandy on October 19, 1991. The rally was organised to mark his successful handling of the impeachment move against him.

Premadasa said 'foreign agencies' were financing the dissidents in their campaign against him and asked from where did they obtain large sums of money to organise anti-government rallies. He said though the impeachment move against him and a no-confidence motion against the parliament speaker had been defeated, the opposition conspiracy was not over. He charged that it would not be surprising if he were assassinated in the struggle as the main opposition Sri Lanka Freedom Party realised that they could not come to power through the people's vote.

And not surprisingly, the LTTE too acted as a spokesman of Premadasa. Yogaratnam Yogi, a top rung LTTE leader, acused the Indian government of being hand in glove with the SLFP to overthrow the Premadasa government. Yogi said on the LTTE's clandestine radio *Voice of the Tigers* on May 24, 1992 that after "failing to bring down the Premadasa government through Gamini Dissanayake and his clique, India was now using its ban on the LTTE to sabotage talks between the Colombo government and the LTTE."

Premdasa's words proved prophetic when in 1993 the LTTE blasted him to death.

Given this backdrop, there are two ways of looking at the Premadasa imbroglio. One, Premadasa took his political hatred towards Rajiv to the macabre conclusion of plotting the Indian leader's assassination. And once the objective of eliminating Rajiv was achieved, Premadasa himself was bumped off in a typical LTTE style of eliminating the man who knew too much. This theory seems probable with the assertion of J Ranganath, sentenced to death by the trial court for sheltering Rajiv's assassins, Sivarasan and Subha.

Ranganath, who filed an affidavit before the Jain commission accusing the CBI of holding key facts and shielding several culprits, said in an interview to *Outlook* (December 8, 1997) that Sivarasan "wanted to go abroad directly from Bangalore."

Sivarasan feared that he might be killed if he were to go back to Jaffna, Ranganath told the magazine. He also said Sivarasan, who regarded controversial tantrik Chandraswami as his "godfather", would arrange safe passage for the one-eyed Jack.

Unfortunately, the Jain commission did not launch any investigation of its own into these allegations. The Commission did not even take cognisance of Ranganath's affidavit.

The second possible theory about Premadasa's role could be that he got Rajiv assassinated through former LTTE cadres, and then blamed the Tigers. With this masterly move, according to this theory, Premadasa killed two birds with one stone : a political adversary in a much bigger neighbouring country was removed from the scene, and the all-important foreign support base (Tamil Nadu) of enemy at home (the LTTE), smashed for years to come.

This may be a good enough reason for the LTTE to eliminate Premadasa. Ironically, Premadasa died in a shockingly similar manner as Rajiv.

Now if one considers Premadasa's conduct, can the Mossad be left undiscussed ? Certainly not, going by the proximity between the highly resourceful Israeli secret service and Colombo.

THE MOSSAD ANGLE

Was the assassination squad merely a group of fall guys, who did not have the faintest clue as to who their general was? The possibility cannot be ruled out.

Such a group is cannon fodder for plotters — expendable, expected to die or be captured without any ability to identify their master. Finding them from a floating population of some 3,000 ex-LTTE guerillas does not require a massive talent hunt.

An assassination plot of this magnitude is akin to a military operation requiring months of meticulous planning. Usually, not more than four or five people monitor the operation.

One heads the task group that draws out the action plan. Another studies the ground situation and collects intelligence on the target's security arrangements. The third group hires the assassins using go-betweens, the fourth group trains them while the fifth, the logistics team, gets down to arranging finances, documents, transportation and escape routes.

Mossad has a long experience in such operations. Could it have infiltrated the LTTE?

And an LTTE-type of organisation is an ideal target for infiltration.

Palestine Liberation Organisation chairman Yasser Arafat has claimed tipping off Rajiv nearly a month before his eventual assassination about a plot to kill him.

The British newspaper *The Observer* featured Arafat's disclosure as its lead story on June 2, 1991. Prime Minister Chandra Shekhar told *The Observer* correspondent Shyam Bhatia that Arafat met him at Rajiv's funeral in New Delhi and "told me of the warning when he came to pay his condolences".

The newspaper quoted Chandra Shekhar as saying, "it is definite, not just likely, that the Tigers are involved. Whether they are used by someone else — on that point we are not clear."

What could have been the source of Arafat's information, which he has not revealed to anyone till date, including Indian diplomats who contacted him? The PLO leader himself has been on the hit list of some splinter groups which talk the language of extreme Palestinian nationalism, but which are either heavily penetrated or directly controlled by Mossad. Could he be referring to the Israeli secret service?

Not impossible if one were to go by what Victor Ostrovsky, a former Mossad agent, and Claire Hoy, a Canadian journalist, have to say in their book, *By Way of Deception*. According to the authors, Mossad has trained the LTTE and Sri Lankan armed forces at a secret Israeli base unknown to the other, just a few yards apart.

By Way of Deception strips Mossad like never before. The book is basically the story of Victor Ostrovsky's tryst with the Mossad penned by Claire Hoy. The authors narrate a bizarre incident, so typical of Mossad operations, which has a direct bearing to our context.

"One of my assignments, he says in mid-July 1984, was to escort a group of Indian nuclear scientists who were worried about the threat of the Islamic bomb (Pakistan's bomb) and had come on a secret mission to Israel to meet with Israeli nuclear experts and exchange information. As it turned out, the Israelis were happy to accept information from the Indians, but reluctant to return the favour.

"The day after they left, I was picking up my regular paperwork when Amy* called me into the office for two assignments. The first was to help get the gear and staff for a group of Israelis going to South Africa to help train that country's secret-police units. After that, I was to go to an African embassy and pick up a man who was supposed to fly back to his home country. He was to be taken to his home in Herzlia Pituah, then driven to the airport and ushered through security.

'I'll meet you at the airport,' Amy said, 'because we have a group of people coming from Sri Lanka to train here.'

"Amy was waiting for the Sri Lankans' flight from London when I joined him. 'When these guys arrive,' he said, 'don't make a face. Don't do anything.'

" 'What do you mean ?' I asked.

" 'Well, these guys are monkeylike. They come from a place that's not developed. They're not long out of the trees. So don't expect much.'

---

* *The reference is to Amy Yaar, the boss of Victor J Ostrovsky, a Mossad katsa (intelligence gathering officer). Amy Yaar was Mossad's department head of the Far East and Africa in Tevel (liaison) when Ostrovsky was recruited in Mossad in 1984.*

"Amy and I escorted the nine Sri Lankans through a back door of the airport into an air-conditioned van. These were the first arrivals from a group that would finally total nearly 50. They would then be divided into three smaller groups :

"* An anti-terror group training at the military base near Petha Tikvah called Kfar Sirkin, learning how to overtake hijacked buses and airplanes, or deal with hijackers in a building, how to descend from helicopters on a rope, and other anti-terrorist tactics. And, of course, they would be buying Uzis and other Israeli-made equipment, including bulletproof vests, special grenades, and more.

" * A purchasing team, in Israel to buy weapons on a larger scale. They bought seven or eight large PT boats , for example, called *Devora*, which they would use mainly to patrol their northern shores against Tamils.

* A group of high-ranking officers who wanted to purchase radar and other naval equipment to counter the Tamils who were still getting through from India and mining Sri Lankan waters...

"Next I was assigned to the high-ranking officers who were looking for radar equipment. I was told to take them to a manufacturer in Ashdod named Alta that could do the work. But when he saw their specifications, the Alta representative said, 'They're just going through the motions. They're not going to buy our radar.'

" ' Why ?' I said ?

" 'These specs were not written by these monkeys,' the man said. 'They were written by a British radar manufacturer called Deca, so these guys already know what they're going to buy. Give them a banana and send them home. You are wasting your time.'

" ' Okay, but how about a brochure or something to make them happy ?'

"This conversation was going on in Hebrew while we all sat together eating cookies, and drinking tea and coffee. The Alta rep said that he didn't mind giving them a lecture to make it look as if they weren't being brushed off, 'but if we're going to do that, let's have some fun.'

"With that he went into another office for a set of big transparencies of a large vacuum-cleaner system that is used to clean harbours after oil spills. He had a series of colourful schematic drawings . Everything was written in Hebrew, but he lectured in English on this 'high capability radar equipment.' I found it difficult not to laugh. He laid it on so thick, claiming this radar could locate a guy swimming in the water and practically tell his shoe size, his name and address, and his blood type. When he'd finished, the Sri Lankans thanked him, said they were surprised at this technological advancement, but that it wouldn't fit their ships. Here they were telling us about their ships. Well, we knew about their ships. We built them !

"After dropping me off at the hotel, I told Amy the Sri Lankans weren't buying the radar. 'Yes, we knew that,' he replied.

"Amy then told me to go Kfar Sirkin where the Sri Lankan special-forces group was training, get them whatever they needed, then take them into Tel Aviv for the evening. But he cautioned me to make sure it was all coordinated with Yosy, who had just been transferred to the same department that week.

"Yosy was also looking after a group being trained by the Israelis. But they weren't supposed to meet my people. *They were Tamils, bitter enemies of my Sinhalese group* . ...

"Many Sri Lankan Tamils, escaping the bloodshed, have sought refuge (in Tamil Nadu) and the Sri Lankan government has accused Indian officials of arming and training the Tamils. They should be accusing the Mossad.

"The Tamils were training at the commando naval base, learning penetration techniques, mining landings, communications, and how to sabotage ships similar to the *Devora*. There were about 28 men in each group, so it was decided that Yosy should take the Tamils to Haifa that night while I took the Sinhalese to Tel Aviv, thus avoiding any chance encounters.

"The real problem started about two weeks into the courses, when both the Tamils and Sinhalese — unknown to each other, of course — were training at Kfar Sirkin. It is a fairly large base, but even so, on one occasion the two groups passed within a few yards of each other while they were out jogging.

"After their basic training routine at Kfar Sirkin, the Sinhalese were taken to the naval base to be taught essentially how to deal with all the techniques the Israelis had just taught the Tamils. It was pretty hectic. We had to dream up punishments or night training exercises just to keep them busy, so that both groups wouldn't be in Tel Aviv at the same time. The actions of this one man (Amy) could have jeopardised the political situation in Israel if these groups had met. I'm sure (Shimon) Peres wouldn't have slept at night if he'd known this was going on. But, of course, he did not know.

"When the three weeks were just about up and the Sinhalese were preparing to go to Atlit, the top-secret naval commando base, Amy told me he wouldn't be going with them.The *Sayret Matcal* would take over their training. This was the top intelligence reconnaissance group, the one that carried out the famous Entebbe raid. (The naval commandos are the equivalent of the American Seals.)

" 'Look we have a problem," said Amy. 'We have a group of 27 SWAT team guys from India coming in.'

" 'My God,' I said. 'What is this ? We've got Sinhalese, Tamils, and now Indians. Who's next ?'

"The SWAT team was supposed to train at the same base where Yosy had the Tamils, a tricky and potentially volatile situation. And I still had my regular office work to do, along with the daily reports. In the evenings, I took the SWAT team to dinner, again making sure none of the groups ended up in the same place. Every day I had an envelope brought to me with about $ 300 in Israeli currency to spend on them."

Like Pakistan's ISI, Mossad too, has gone out of control. One of the main themes of Victor Ostrovsky's book is that Prime Minister of Israel, though ostensibly in charge, has no real authority over the Mossad's actions.

In fact, the Israeli Prime Minister is often manipulated by Mossad into approving or taking actions that may be in the best interest of those running Mossad, but not necessarily in the best interests of Israel.

Unlike other intelligence organisations which have vast manpower — the CIA has about 25,000 employees, while the KGB's total number of employees worldwide is ten times — the Mossad is a tiny organisation. The entire Mossad has barely 1,200 employees including clerks, secretaries and cleaning staff. It has just 30 to 35 *katsas* (gathering officers or case officers) operating in the world at any given time.

Its tiny size helps Mossad attain the highest level of secrecy. Even the Cuban DGI intelligence service has some 2,000 trained operatives posted under diplomatic cover worldwide.

And yet Mossad has given new dimensions to the art of intelligence collection, analysis and covert operation and is among the most feared secret organisations of the world. This is because unlike any other country, Israel taps the loyal and reliable Jewish community all over the world who operate as volunteers.

Mossad secretly supplied arms, equipment and other things to Sri Lanka since the late seventies when Colombo did not even have diplomatic relations with Tel Aviv. Why did Sri Lanka require secret arms deals in the seventies ? The LTTE shot into prominence only in the early eighties.

Actually, more than Colombo's eagerness to acquire arms from Israel, it was Mossad's gameplan to have a presence in this non-Arab region.

Victor Ostrovsky has painted Mossad as an outfit that is run like a corporate organisation and its middle-ranking officers acting in an unscrupulous manner. Says Ostrovsky:

"(Amy) Yaar's department had people positioned throughout the far east who did little real intelligence; instead they set the framework for future business and diplomatic ties.....

"Yaar's officers in Africa were also dealing in millions of dollars in arms sales. These liaison men worked in three stages. First they made contact to find out what the country needed, what it feared, whom it regarded as enemies — information gathered through their on-site activities. The idea was to build on those needs, create a stronger relationship, then make it known that Israel could supply the government in question with weapons and training — whatever they needed.

"The final step in the process, once a country's leader had been hooked on the arms, was for the Mossad man to tell him that he must take, for instance, some agricultural equipment as well. The leader was then put in the position of saying he could expand ties with Israel only if they set up formal diplomatic relations. It was essentially a way of creating those relations through the back door, although in most cases the arms deals were so lucrative, the liaison men never bothered to follow up with the next step.

"They did in Sri Lanka, however.

"Amy Yaar made the connection, then tied the country in militarily by supplying it with substantial equipment, inluding PT boats for coastal patrol. *At the same time, Yaar and company were supplying the warring Tamils with anti-PT boat equipment to use in fighting the government forces.*

"The Israelis also trained elite forces for both sides, without either side knowing about the other, and helped Sri Lanka cheat the World Bank and other investors out of millions of dollars to pay for all the arms they were buying from them.

"The Sri Lankan government was worried about unrest among the farmers — the country has a long history of economic problems— so it wanted to split them up somewhat by moving them from one side of the island to the other. But it needed an acceptable reason to do this. That's where Amy Yaar came in. He was the one who dreamed up the great 'Mahaweli Project', a massive engineering scheme to divert the Mahaweli River from its natural course to dry areas on the other side of the country. The claim was that this would double the country's hydro-electric power and open up 750,000 acres of newly irrigated land. Besides the World Bank, Sweden, Canada, Japan, Germany, the European Economic Community, and the United States all invested in the $2.5 billion (US) project.

"From the beginning it was an overly ambitious project, but the World Bank and the other investors did not understand that... Originally a 30-year project, it was suddenly escalated in 1977 when Sri Lanka's President, Junius Jayewardene, discovered that with a little help from the Mossad, it could become most significant.

"In order to convince the World Bank especially (with its $250 million commitment) that the project was feasible —and would also serve as a convenient excuse for moving the farmers from their land— the Mossad had two Israeli academics, one an economist from Jerusalem University, the other a professor of agriculture, write scholarly papers explaining its importance and its cost. A major Israeli construction company, Solel Bonah, was given a large contract for part of the job.

"Periodically, World Bank representatives would go to Sri Lanka for spot checks, but the locals had been taught how to fool these inspectors by taking them on circuitous routes—easily explained for security reasons— then back to the same, quite small area where some construction actually had been carried out for just this purpose.

"Later, when I was working in Yaar's department at Mossad headquarters, I was assigned to escort Jayewardene's daughter-in-law — a woman named Penny— on a secret visit to Israel. She knew me as 'Simon'.

"We took here wherever she wanted to go. We were talking in general terms, but she insisted on telling about the project and how money for it was financing equipment for the army. She was complaining that they weren't really getting on with it. Ironically, the project had been *invented* to get money from the World Bank to pay for those weapons.

"At that time, Israel had no diplomatic relations with Sri Lanka. In fact, they were supposedly embargoing us."

Congress leader V N Gadgil, in fact, referred to this and several other books to drive his point home that the assassination of Rajiv was "part of an international conspiracy and showed how far the CIA's hands have stretched."

Gadgil also quoted the book *Envoy to Nehru* by Reid stating that the CIA had made an effort to weaken the Congress and the nation during Pandit Nehru's time. He also referred to other such books as the *Walson Plot* and *The Spycatcher* that portrayed the CIA's role in various international conspiracies.

There is a heavy presence of Mossad in Sri Lanka with access to the latest technology used in covert operations. Mossad is known to have close connections in Pakistan's ISI and Sri Lanka's National Intelligence Bureau. With Mossad pursuing the Western interests by proxy and both ISI and NIB looking at their own national interests, the elimination of Rajiv Gandhi could be a tempting operation.

All through, the SIT pursued a single lead— the LTTE involvement in Rajiv's assassination. But was it so ?

Was LTTE so shortsighted so as to invite India's wrath and lose its only safe haven outside Sri Lanka — Tamil Nadu— as eventually happened ?

The LTTE , on the other hand, would favour a strong leader in New Delhi to provide it much needed international backing and funds. The meeting of LTTE emissaries like Kasi Anandan and London-based sympathiser, Sitambalam, with Rajiv Gandhi , viewed in this context, are not at all surprising. These two men were reportedly negotiating with Rajiv in order to solicit his support for the LTTE. There is no report to suggest that Rajiv was showing the door to the LTTE.

And the investigators took the Rajiv-LTTE parleys as a smokescreen on the part of the Tigers to hide their true intent and lull their target into a false sense of complacency.

Who gained, or could have gained, from Rajiv's murder ?

Obviously, Sri Lanka government was the direct and the immediate beneficiary.

Sri Lanka stood to gain if Rajiv, who was tipped to return to power, were to be removed from the scene. It helped to create chaos in India and kept a giant weak. It also prevented the new Prime Minister from trusting the LTTE.

Colombo had its own vested interests in the whole affair. If it could be definitely fixed that the LTTE was in some way involved, nobody would stand to benefit more than Colombo as its main adversary, the LTTE, would then lose the sanctuary in Tamil Nadu that kept it alive during the most difficult periods. And precisely this happened.

The fortuitous finding of Hari Babu's loaded camera from the assassination site with tell-tale photographs would not look all that chancy if one looks at the whole affair from this angle.

There are only a handful of countries where the Israeli presence, both diplomatic and covert, is as heavy as in Colombo. Only in South Africa (with which Tel Aviv has a secret tie up in the nuclear field) the Israeli presence surpasses that of its mission in Sri Lanka.

Colombo's dubious distinction does not end here. It is the only Third World capital where the troika of Israeli secret service—comprising the Institution of Intelligence and Special Assignments popularly known as Mossad, the Shin Bet, normally meant for internal security duties and a rival of Mossad, and AMAN, the military intelligence—is deployed.

Interestingly, it is Shin Bet's first assignment abroad in a non-Arab land and for the first time its agents are not competing with Mossad's.

Shin Beth has gained an unmatchable experience in fighting, killing and torturing the PLO and the Arabs in the occupied territories. In Sri Lanka, these "talents" have been put to use to beef up Sri Lanka's poor internal security and ferret out the LTTE.

The AMAN is deployed in the island nation to train Sri Lankan armed forces in collection, analysis and dissemination of intelligence against its foes, including those who are abroad.

But what was there for Mossad to gain out of all this.

Bombay-based tabloid *Blitz*, which ran a series of brilliant stories attacking the SIT's obsession with only-the-LTTE-did-it theory, has an answer.

The bargain for Mossad, *Blitz* argues, was helping itself to vital information which can be put to use later by the West and turn Mossad into a truly global secret service capable of secret and offensive operations abroad. Mossad has been able to convince the Sri Lankans in the wisdom contained in Charles Proteus Steinmertz's dictum : "There will come an era of small and independent nations whose first line of defence will be (secret) knowledge." Steinmetz was a German Jew who emigrated to the US.

The Israeli troika's presence in Sri Lanka is a test case for Tel Aviv to prove to its mentors in the West that its secret forces can handle "trouble spots" in the Third World thus sparing the CIA/NSA and MI6 to fish in more troubled waters elsewhere.

The secret operations to infiltrate the LTTE started long ago when Rajiv Gandhi had decided to walk out of the trap (committing IPKF in Sri Lanka) laid by President Jayewardene and his Israeli advisers.

India figures high in the West's hit list until such time a pliable, pro-West government with firm belief in free-for-all trade policy assumes power in New Delhi. Till then, India must not walk, it must limp. And Rajiv Gandhi was determined to make India sprint. Therefore he had to go.

An American magazine commented : "With one blow, the fortunes of 844 million people became hostage to terrible uncertainty."

TONG NOVA

A new dimension was added to the murky case when the Indian Navy seized an arms-laden LTTE ship off Karaikal coast in Pondicherry in the second week of November, 1991.

The sophisticated vessel "MVS Tong Nova", registered in Thailand, was coming from Singapore. It was to unload some of its deadly cargo on the Tamil Nadu coast and reach Salaiku Mutta in northern Sri Lanka. The LTTE was to arrange a rendezvous in the waters by the evening of November 6. But there was some delay. In the meantime, the Indian Navy got alerted by intelligence messages and organised the seizure.

A diary was seized from the 10 crew members who were arrested. The diary, neatly written in Tamil, listed purchase of Surface-to-Air missiles (SAM-7), rocket propelled grenades, General Purpose Machine Guns (GPMGs), 14.5 mm guns, sniper rifles, huge quantities of explosives and raw materials like potassium nitrate and aluminium powder used in manufacturing bombs, army uniforms, battle fatigues, shoes, digital synthesisers, tyres, tubes, pyromethane poisonous tablets for making cyanide capsules and large number of 1.5 volt batteries for detonating bombs and mines.

(Incidentally, Dhanu's belt-bomb was also detonated by a 1.5 volt battery.)

Naval Officer-In Charge, Madras, Commodore H Sahney told reporters in Madras on November 10 that when *Tong Nova* was traced at ten and a half miles east of Karaikal on the Thanjavur coast, the ship turned on full throttle and tried to flee to international waters along with a smaller boat. The smaller boat, into which the contraband meant for Jaffna was to have been transferred, developed a leak and sank while being towed to Madras. The ship and the smaller boat were chased by INS Saryu and captured. International maritime laws provide for capturing suspicious vessels outside territorial waters in hot pursuit.

Commodore Sahney said the vessel had a radar and good satellite navigation facilities. The deceptively oldish grey vessel was worth at least Rs twenty million and was well-equipped to sail in oceans.

There are a number of intelligence reports, available in New Delhi as well as Tamil Nadu, about LTTE's arms smuggling by sea routes. The Tigers transfer the contraband in mid-sea to smaller boats which are ferried to well-hidden lagoons in the north coast of Sri Lanka.

The most important revelation made by the LTTE diaries in the seized ship was that an arms shipment was made to the Tigers on March 21, 1991 — exactly two months before Rajiv's assassination.

The diaries were a veritable inventory of all the arms and ammunitions smuggled by the LTTE vessels between March 21 and May 28, 1991 — that is immediately before and after Rajiv's assassination. The diaries also revealed who had made the arms purchases. While one diary listed the materials carried in the ship, the other two had some names and addresses of LTTE's contacts in places like London, Switzerland, Malaysia, Singapore, Madras and Tiruchi.

The Naval Officer in Charge, Madras commented : "We have recovered some invaluable and incriminating papers, including a diary from the ship. The route is clear and the main supply line becomes obvious now. It is for the police now to investigate further. We have done our job."

Several questions arise. Why the LTTE needed arms shipments in 1991 when the IPKF had already pulled out of Sri Lanka and the LTTE was honeymooning with President Premadasa? Were the same explosives which were smuggled by Tongnova since March 21, 1991 used in assassinating Rajiv ? Who sent these explosives ? Who were the arms dealers ? Who paid for these arms and explosives ?

The most important question of all is : were these arms shipments a payment in kind for assassinating Rajiv ?

These suspicions and doubts are still haunting. The SIT has not investigated this crucial aspect.

The *Tong Nova* seizure gave a wealth of information to the Indian security agencies on the LTTE's global gun-running syndicate.

The police came to know that Kandasami and Khader were two of the organisers in charge of the arms smuggling operations.

The role of "KP" as incharge of LTTE's international arms dealings came out in a big way for the first time. The security agencies came to know that a fleet of LTTE vessels was involved in the gun-running operations. "The Golden Bird" was the major asset of the LTTE which was the feeding ship that distributed arms, ammunition and equipment acquired from different parts of the world. Plus the Tigers had smaller vessels that kept moving in the international waters, waiting for their quota.

"KP" — LTTE'S LIFELINE

The Japanese Yakuza, Chinese Triads, Medellin Cartel, Cali Cartel, American Mafia, Russian Mafia and Italian Mafia are the transnational criminal organisations that own or charter ships. There are only three insurgent groups in the world which own and operate a fleet of deep sea going ships — the PLO, the IRA and the LTTE. Today, the LTTE owns and operates at least half a dozen deep sea going ships, each ship equipped with sophisticated radar and Inmarsat for communication with the LTTE-controlled areas in Lanka.

The Tigers were able to take on the might of the Indian Army for more than 18 months. More surprisingly, the LTTE defied speculations of its imminent extinction in the post-Rajiv assassination period when southern India was no longer available to the Tigers as a sanctuary and support base. Equally baffling is their military capabilities and global presence remain virtually unaffected even after the loss of control over Jaffna in December 1995.

After Rajiv's assassination, the LTTE started looking beyond India and south Asia. In 1995, western intelligence and security agencies received information that it had established links with FARC (Revolutionary Armed Forces of Colombia), a powerful Colombian insurgent group dealing in narcotics. For the first time, the LTTE was believed to have purchased vessels that could cross the Atlantic or Pacific and reach Latin America.

What is the key to this dramatic upswing in the LTTE fortunes? And that too after a series of setbacks mentioned above.

The global security managers should blame one man: Kumaran Padmanathan alias Selvarajah, better known as "KP".

KP is the walking nightmare of every immigration official across the globe. For a decade and half, KP has been staying a jump ahead of his trackers. He is a globe-trotter. The man of medium height and build has no trappings of a guerilla organisation like the LTTE which is commonly —and wrongly— perceived as nothing more than a jungle army.

Unlike the fellow Tigers and Tigresses, who have barely set foot outside the Lankan jungles, KP is a suave man, living life in the fast lane. He is used to five-star luxuries and possesses an extraordinary gift of the gab. He is equally at ease negotiating a shipment of Chinese rocket-launchers with a South American arms-dealer at breakfast in a five-star hotel in Singapore and discussing the price of silence of a corrupt Cambodian official for a narcotic shipment at dinner in a luxury hotel in Phnom Penh.

A businessman, a banker, a smuggler, an arms procurer — KP is all these and much more. Like Prabhakaran, he is fighting a war no less important for the realisation of LTTE's goals.

KP is one of the few LTTE cadres who are militarily untrained. Significantly, he belongs to that very small tribe of hardcore LTTE cadres whose members do not carry the customary cyanide capsule. The very presence of cyanide capsule on one's person is incriminating, that's why.

He does not have to be a trained guerilla. He is the chief of the LTTE's overseas department for clandestine operations and is also responsible for managing the Tigers' highly secretive and complex shipping network. He carries forged passports of over 20 countries and has as many aliases. He has access to dozens of bank accounts around the globe. He also posseses an impressive paraphernalia for forging documents.

He has been feeding the LTTE war machine with such aplomb that the crucial weapons and explosives procurement department of the LTTE is better known as the "KP department". Like him, all LTTE cadres working for him are militarily untrained. This helps a great deal because there are virtually no records of KP's men in the files of security and intelligence agencies worldwide.

The information regarding KP's department started trickling in only after Rajiv's assassination.

KP's real name is Tharmalingam Shanmugham Kumaran. He was born in Uddipiddy on April 6, 1955. Following are his vital particulars given by Rohan Gunaratna, a noted Sri Lankan expert on the LTTE :

KP's national identity card number : 550971231V.

His Sri Lankan passport number : J0803500.

Address : No 130 KKS Road, Jaffna, Sri Lanka and No 5, Periyar Nagar, Salem-1, Tamil Nadu.

"During 1985-86," to quote Gunaratna, "KP lived in the posh neighbourhood of Adyar in Madras and had the title to the deed Eye Pearls Farm and company at Perumgal near Vellore executed in his favour in 1987. This farm was a top secret LTTE hide out for arms and ammunition storage, as well as a center for communication with the leadership in Jaffna. He developed his relations with the international shipping trade through a Bombay shipping magnate. (Name omitted.) Kumaran has established several companies for money laundering and front organisations. They range from export import firm in Malaysia where he is a director, Rani restaurant in Cambodia, Carlton company in Bangladesh and Eagle trading company in Myanmar. The latter two companies played a vital role in the Ukrainian arms shipment to the LTTE."

KP's department became super-active in the late eighties, largely due to dramatic shift in New Delhi's policy vis-a-vis the LTTE. It was at this time when the LTTE's shipping network was expanded in a big way. Till then the Tigers were dependent on West Asian and European arms dealers for procurement of arms and explosives with end-use certificates often obtained from corrupt Nigerian officials. By 1989-90, the LTTE had extended its reach to Southeast Asia and Pakistan's booming Afghan arms bazaar. LTTE operatives were received with open arms by the Pakistani officials who treated the enemy's (India) enemy (LTTE) as friends.

An important LTTE cell was established on the Andaman coast in the Thai town of Trang before it was shifted north to a front company in Phuket. But it was in Myanmar where the Tigers found their cosiest home away from home. LTTE vessels began shipping timber from Myanmar to Thailand in the late 1980s, a business that soon brought them into contact with the Myanmar military. Sometime after mid-1990, the contacts resulted in the establishment of an LTTE base at the small town of Twantay, south of Yangon. The Tigers had to close down the facility in 1995 following protests from Colombo.

KP's singular achievement has been to make the LTTE truly a global outfit and send arms shipments to north and north-east Sri Lanka from virtually every nook and corner of the world when the Tigers needed these most. It was the unfailing efforts of KP that the LTTE strengthened its anti-aircraft capability. The Tigers had been trying to lay their hands on surface-to-air missiles since the late eighties, but had been unsuccessful.

The resourceful KP gave them the formidable SA-7s in late 1994. The missiles, sold by corrupt Cambodian generals and transported across the Thai border, were used in downing Sri Lanka's two Avro transport planes on April 28 and 29, 1995, immediately after the Tigers resumed hostilities against the government troops.

The SAMs, like most of LTTE's weaponry and explosives, were purchased through the slush money generated by narcotics smuggling. The LTTE is believed to have paid US $ 1 million a piece.

The largest single consignment to arrive in Sri Lanka came even as the LTTE was ostensibly talking peace with the government in mid-1994. The consignment of 50 tons of TNT and 10 tons of RDX explosives, arranged by a Dhaka front company, reached the LTTE in August 1994. The carrier was an LTTE vessel M V Swanee. The explosives cargo originated from the Ukrainian Black Sea port of Nikolayev. KP had managed an end-user certificate purportedly signed by Bangladesh's secretary for defence which indicated the Bangla military as the approved recipient. The Ukrainian explosives have already wreaked havoc in Sri Lanka, killing hundreds and destroying property worth millions of US dollars. And not even one ton of these explosives have been used yet.

Today, a bulk of LTTE shipping activity is carried out of South East Asia. Says Gunaratna : "The LTTE will always need a naval base in South Asia or South East Asia for its operations in the Central Indian Ocean Region."

The importance of the south-east Asian region for the LTTE is borne out by the fact that the Tigers' deep sea going operations began way back in 1984 when they purchased "Cholan" from Singapore. To finalise the Cholan purchase, Prabhakaran personally visited Singapore and Malaysia — an unusual happening because the LTTE supremo rarely goes out of Lanka.

Was KP involved in the Rajiv assassination case? It is a matter of record that some material used in Dhanu's belt bomb had originated from Singapore. The 2 mm-diameter pellets used in the belt bomb were special and found to have been manufactured in the city state.

There were intelligence reports about KP's movements in Singapore in the relevant period. After Rajiv's assassination, KP was reported to be in Pakistan where he remained for quite some time. It is highly unlikely that KP would have no involvement with the case. His actual role is in the realm of speculations only because the Singapore trail has not been investigated to the hilt.

The Jain Commission of Inquiry wanted to pursue this particular angle. This could have thrown up some valuable clues. But the Indian Government sat on the Jain Commission's request and with the abrupt closure of the commission in March 1998, the matter seems to have died its natural death.

A string of suicides by key accused put brakes on the SIT's investigations. Each suicide extinguished a flame of breakthrough. The result was islands of light surrounded by a sea of darkness.

The suicides put the SIT in the dock.

*

Members cutting across the party lines took the SIT to task in Indian Parliament. CPIM members said Home Minister S B Chavan had referred to a "foreign" hand behind Rajiv's assassination, but the main suspects were being "eliminated" one by one. Geeta Mukherjee of CPI wanted to know if Chavan had told the United States Amabassador in India that it was a case of "slip of tongue" when he had referred to a "foreign hand" in the assassination. Manoranjan Bhakta of the Congress I was concerned about the failure of intelligence agencies and the danger that LTTE activities posed to India. George Fernandes, then a Janata Dal member and now President of the Samta Party, felt that the SIT had totally failed in its task.

L K Advani, Leader of Opposition in the Tenth Lok Sabha and BJP President, said the mystery had deepened with the spate of suicides of key acused and the Government should take the House into confidence to share information about the events relating to Rajiv's assassination. Later, talking to reporters, Advani said the SIT probe was messed up and the Government should fix the responsibility for the circumstances leading to the suicide by Sivarasan and others.

Advani said it was doubtful if the Government would be able to unearth the conspiracy behind the assassination in all its essential details. He said three months after the murder, the SIT investigations seemed to have been totally messed up. This, he said, was evident from the death of the two prime suspects —Sivarasan and Subha — and a number of others who were allowed to die before them. Advani went to the extent of saying that the handling of the Indira Gandhi assassination case, too, was unsatisfactory as the SIT and the Thakkar Commission (that probed the assassination of Rajiv's mother) came out with different reports. Advani said the P V Narasimha Rao Government had failed to take the people and the Parliament into confidence in the Rajiv Gandhi assassination case and even the statement by the Home Minister regarding the death of Shanmugham was highly unsatisfactory.

Congress-I's official spokesman C P Thakur issued a statement on the matter on August 21, 1991 and said his party was deeply worried about the elimination of key sources of evidence. He said the death of prime suspects in the case "shows how deep-rooted has been this conspiracy."

The Congress said that it "would like the Government to apply abundant caution and care in the process of investigating the assassination. The party is anxious to see that the investigation uncovers the whole conspiracy and the culprits are brought to book at the earliest."

While his own party had said this in a statement, Chavan's deputy, Minister of State for Home M M Jacob, gave a clean chit to the SIT three days later. He said the Home Ministry was satisfied with the SIT's role in "Operation Sivarasan" at Konankunte. After going round the hideout in which Sivarasan and Subha committed suicide, Jacob disagreed with the perception that the investigations had reached a dead-end with the suicides. "Actually, getting Sivarasan alive would have helped to get more teeth for the investigations. It was difficult to get him alive. But Sivarasan has not fled from the country," Jacob was reported in the media as saying.

*

A rush of suicides by key LTTE cadres during investigations unsettled the SIT. In fact, a couple of Tigers committed suicides even after the Operation Sivarasan fiasco.

The investigators were confronted with a suicide right at the very beginning — that of Dhanu. But for the Hari Babu photos, the investigators would have found it extremely difficult to even identify the killers. The mysterious death of Shanmugham put the first question mark over the SIT's ability to unravel the complete conspiracy behind the assassination. The next shock was the suicide of key LTTE man and Sivarasan's close associate, Dixon in Coimbatore on July 28, 1991. Dixon, who told the police who had laid siege to his house that his name was Kishore, killed himself to evade arrest, as did one one of his associates, Guna. Only a few days before, the SIT had released photographs of Dixon and Kanthan and said that they were helping Sivarasan to continue to evade arrest.

The loss of Dixon made a material difference to the SIT, especially as it was felt that Sivarasan could be somewhere nearby and Dixon was taking care of his needs. Had Dixon been taken alive, it would have thrown light on the whereabouts of Sivarasan and a plan chalked out to arrest him.

The death of Peria Santhan, a senior LTTE militant, in an encounter with the police and the CBI in Tiruchirapalli on November 13, 1991, dealt another serious blow to the investigators' efforts to put together the pieces of zig saw puzzle in the Rajiv assassination case. Respected newspapers like *The Times of India* and *The Statesman* reported the sensational contents of Peria Santhan's letter to Prabhakaran. Santhan's undelivered letter, dated September 7, 1991, was seized from Irumborai who was arrested in October while trying to escape to Jaffna.

The letter mentions that a personal courier was chosen as all wireless sets of the LTTE in India had been seized by the police and there was no means of contacting Prabhakaran. The intercepted letter indicates that it was he, and not Sivarasan, who pulled the strings in the LTTE set-up in India. The three-page, hand-written letter in Tamil, says the wrong choice of "intelligence" men like Chinna Santhan and Murugan by Pottu Amman led to the exposure of the LTTE involvement in Rajiv's assassination.

The letter also condemned the Murugan-Nalini affair,which, according to Santhan, gave a "bad name" to the LTTE. Surprisingly, Santhan made this comment even though his own conduct in such matters was not above board. His woman accomplice, Vasuki, who was arrested from Santhan's hideout, admitted to police that she had "intimate relationship" with Peria Santhan.

The letter makes a startling revelation that as many as 27 LTTE cadres, including Sivarasan and Subha, were holed up in the Konankunte hideout in Bangalore which was stormed by the Black Cat commandos of the NSG on August 20. The police had recovered only seven bodies. What happened to the rest of the 20 Tigers. Santhan himself was among these 20 cadres.

Santhan said in his letter that he had ordered Sivarasan and Subha and others to commit suicide and administered them cyanide. After that he escaped undetected.

"When Raghuvaran (Sivarasan's LTTE name) was trapped by police in Bangalore, I directed him, Subha and 25 others staying there to end their lives and administered them cyanide. I got away. This I had done without your prior consent. Please forgive me," Santhan wrote in his letter which never reached its destination.

But how could he escape from the security forces who had laid a seige to the house for the past two days and the entire area was floodlit ? This question remains unanswered.

Peria Santhan's suicide came as a big blow to Pottu Amman who was very keen on seeing Santhan back in Jaffna. This was revealed by another LTTE cadre, Ravi, who managed to escape to Jaffna along with another mysterious character, Kanthan, despite the red alert by Indian security agencies. Ravi brazenly returned to India after some time and was arrested.

These suicides, apart from pointing accusing fingers at the SIT, also prevented flow of vital information to the investigators on the conspiracy aspects of Rajiv's assassination.

11 THE DARK AREAS

It is not the purpose of this book to find faults with the SIT, which did a reasonably good job. But the SIT was in an unseemly hurry to complete the investigation. There is no reason why the entire investigations had to be completed in one year and only one chargesheet filed. In a case, like this one, where the SIT conducted investigations in as many as 14 countries and sent questionnaires to several more, investigations could have continued even after filing of the chargesheet and additional chargesheets filed with each new breakthrough. In the case of the March 12, 1993 serial bomb blasts in Bombay— for which another special investigation team was formed— as many as 13 supplementary chargesheets have been filed so far after the main chargesheet.

In the Rajiv Gandhi assassination case, SIT chief Karthikeyan repeatedly said in media interviews that there was no need for a supplementary chargesheet and that the investigation was complete. This is rather peculiar.

The SIT is sitting on enough material which could establish the involvement of individuals it has not even named in its chargesheet. One major lead that has not been followed up are the undeciphered wireless messages.

THE UNBROKEN CODE

Between late 1989 and the first half of 1991, several Indian security agencies like the Navy, RAW and IB intercepted thousands of coded wireless messages between Tamil Nadu and Jaffna. About half of them are still to be decoded.

One crucial message was from Sivarasan on March 20-21, 1991, asking the LTTE leadership whether the assassination had to be carried out in Tamil Nadu or in New Delhi. This could be decoded only after six months. One reason for the delay was that a key decoding official of RAW had gone on a month's earned leave at a time he was needed most.

It is true that the LTTE wireless codes are extremely complex and decoding them is like trying to find a needle in a haystack on a dark night. No other terrorist organisation in the world uses such complex codes and highly sophisticated communication equipment as the LTTE. The Tigers' wireless sets are such that they automatically hop from one frequency to other within seconds. So what the interceptors record is a few unintelligible, incoherent sounds like "aa", "ee", "oo". This is a highly advanced technique to prevent jamming of the clandestine wireless and making the interception virtually impossible. Even if the message is still intercepted, decoding it is a tedious job which takes weeks, sometimes even months.

RAW is well aware of this tactic of LTTE terrorists. It has installed a state-of-the-art interception equipment in Madras which performs many functions at a time. This equipment has a channel surfer which quickly finds out the frequency the illegal wireless set is working on and latches onto that frequency. The moment the frequency is changed it latches onto the new frequency within split seconds.

The possibility of the undeciphered wireless messages unmasking important persons, inluding politicians, who colluded or connived with the LTTE, is immense.

Baby Subramaniam, a top-notch Tiger, was in Tamil Nadu between 1988 and 1990 before returning to Jaffna. He was quite active during his stay in Tamil Nadu. It would be interesting to find out who he used to visit and whether he had been trasmitting wireless messages to Jaffna.

In 1990, Tamil Nadu chief minister M Karunanidhi sent his home secretary R Nagarajan for discussions with the cabinet secretary and other top officials on certain sensitive issues . The cabinet secretary asked Nagarajan to prepare an action plan to tackle criminal elements among the Sri Lankan Tamil refugees in Tamil

Nadu.

Some days later, Indian security agencies intercepted a message referring to the tip-off on the imminent crackdown on the LTTE in Tamil Nadu. The raids on the LTTE hide-outs in Tamil Nadu did take place after some days as planned and some Tigers rounded up. But it was all stage-managed; those picked up during the raids, were offered on a platter to allay suspicions.

The incident still remains shrouded in mystery and complete details are yet to emerge. No action has been taken to identify LTTE moles in the Indian set-up.

With the assassination of Rajiv Gandhi, the LTTE was propelled on to the international terrorism radar.

But the SIT did not investigate how this happened, how this could turn out to be intrinsically involved with Rajiv.

It did not investigate how the Tigers acquired technology to assemble a submarine and manufacture microlight aircraft; to acquire surface-to-air missiles, anti-aircraft guns and a fleet of ships; to go hi-tech with computers, propagate its ideology and even seek donations through Internet ; to run a quasi-governmental set-up ; to run a parallel diplomatic set- up in more than 40 countries; to have a full-fledged naval wing and a unit of suicide bombers of males and females ; to have a vast network of drug-pushing, gun-running, front shipping companies, underground banking channels, and to possess sophisticated communication equipment and complicated wireless codes.

This did not happen overnight. But most of these developments took place just before or after Rajiv's assassination.

The SIT ought to have probed these dark areas, It should have tried to find out how at least five shipments of arms, ammunition and explosives reached the LTTE during 1990-91. The organisation, which had been virtually denuded of all arms, ammunition, explosives and equipment as no major supplies had come between 1986 and 1990, suddenly became a darling of international arms dealers not known for delivering arms shipments on credit.

The SIT's lethargy is all the more flummoxing when one takes into account the inevitable process of frauds and forgeries preceding an arms-laden ship setting sail. To give it a legal facade, arms suppliers and receivers "arrange" an "end user certificate" specifying the purchaser and the purpose. Understandably, the LTTE cannot get an end-user certificate issued against its name, so it has to procure one.

Enter jet-setting power-brokers. There is no dearth of corrupt government officials and unscrupulous defence personnel the world over who can issue genuine end-user certificates for arms and explosives. In most cases, these certificates are procured from officials of small countries in West Asia, Africa and Latin America. There are instances where end-user certificates have been obtained from the defence ministries of India's neighbours. Involvement of "respected" Indians cannot be ruled out.

The role of the then Tamil Nadu home secretary R Nagarajan too was not investigated. Nagarajan is one of the 16 accused in the Padmanabha case and has been chargesheeted and arrested in this connection. The SIT has not even questioned him in connection with Rajiv's assassination.

This brings us to the crucial question whether some arms dealers were behind the entire conspiracy to kill Rajiv — a theory that should not have been ignored after the Bofors episode and the assassination of Swedish prime minister Olof Palme in Stockholme before Rajiv's murder. Rajiv and Palme were at the two ends of the same deal — Bofors — and both were assassinated. Is there a link between the two assassinations?

The SIT has been able to get only the fourth rung of conspirators behind Rajiv Gandhi's killing. Prabhakaran, Pottu Amman and Akila, who are in the top rung, are absconding. LTTE claims Akila "died" in action in 1996, but this is believed to be apocryphal. Akila may have been given a new identity to be used in another secret operation of the Tigers. The SIT does not know much either about Shanthi, the chief of the LTTE women's intelligence wing or Akila, her deputy.

Sivarasan alias Raghuvaran, who commanded the killer gang of nine, occupies the second rung. But he perished in the bungled Bangalore operation on August 18, 1991.

The suicide bomber, Dhanu, and the alternate human bomb, Subha, who fall in the third rung are also dead. Murugan alias Sriharan, Nalini and Santhan are the fourth rung conspirators. Prabhakaran maintained such a level of secrecy that even though the LTTE launched their deadliest and biggest terrorist attack on foreign soil, he did not hold face-to-face meetings with the hit squad members. Prabhakaran only met Sivarasan and Murugan a few times and that too separately.

THE SINGAPORE TRAIL

One pertinent question that SIT seems to be in no mood to answer pertains to Dhanu's belt bomb. Despite being small, how was it so lethal that it killed 18 people?

Though SIT denies it, the belt bomb actually had three Singapore-made grenades in it. Explosives expert Major Sabharwal of the National Security Guards (NSG) , who was among the first to have conducted an on-the-spot investigation at the blast site, speaks clearly of the grenade-component of the belt bomb.

He was made to change his report by the SIT, though the original report is still available with the NSG.

An SIT officer did go to Singapore. He visited the factory where the grenades were manufactured. His findings showed that the grenade, called SFG-87 (self fragmentation grenade), was a very advanced type. Developed in 1987 by Chartered Industry, Singapore, the SFG-87 grenade is of the size of a small orange. It has a plastic coating and a filling of RDX, pellets and traces of TNT to give direction to the blast. The SFG-87 grenade has a lethal range of eight feet radius. Each grenade has 250 grams of RDX and pellets. Its total weight is just 350 grams.

Normally, two SFG-87 grenades are thrown at the target simultaneously. If one does not explode, the second will. The second one would set off the explosion of the first grenade too, as a chain reaction. The SFG-37 grenades have an immense operational superiority over the normal H E-36 type, which is normally thrown at the target one at a time. If one does not explode, it gives away the location of the thrower and makes the user of this grenade more vulnerable .

The samples of grenades and pellets brought by the SIT officer from Singapore were tested by explosives and other experts. One sample grenade was exploded in a pit at NSG headquarters in Manesar, Haryana, near New Delhi. Spectographical analysis was conducted on the sample pellets .

The results vindicated Major Sabharwal's findings: the same grenades and pellets were used in Rajiv's assassination. Yet, the SIT would have none of this.

The tests also brought to light linkages between Rajiv's assassination and the murder of EPRLF leader K Padmanabha.

When Padmanabha was murdered in his Madras apartment in broad daylight on June 19, 1990, scores of empties of bullets were recovered, forensic tests conducted and finger-prints lifted.

On August 20, 1991, the day Sivarasan, Subha and their accomplices committed mass suicide a T-56 rifle was recovered from the side of the One-eyed Jack. Several empties of this rifle were also picked up.

The pellets used in the two assassinations were common, as was the RDX The fingerprints, matched. So much so, the spectographical analyses of the pellets recovered from the sites of Padmanabha's and Rajiv's murders were the same .

The link between the two political murders was unmistakable. The pellets recovered from Sriperumbudur had a striking resemblance to the samples of pellets brought by S I T officer from Singapore as well as to those recovered from the Padmanabha murder site.

The pellets were rather unusual. Each was quite small, having a diameter of two mm. The S I T sent questionnaires to a dozen major arms manufacturing countries to identify the manufactures. No country, except Singapore , manufactured such pellets . And even in Singapore, only one company, Chartered Industry, manufactured these.

In other words, had the killers of Padmanabha been arrested, Rajiv Gandhi's murder could have been averted. The Singapore trail was vital to unravel the truth behind Rajiv' s assassination.

Why did the SIT suppress the grenade belt bomb line of investigation? Why were the linkages between Rajiv's assassination and Padmanabha's murder not investigated in depth?

Has the SIT maintained a record of the entire investigation conducted by its officers in Singapore ?

The relevance of the Singapore trail becomes even more acute as the international operations of the LTTE started from Singapore only in 1984. The LTTE's first ship *M V Cholan* was purchased then. And in keeping with the LTTE's camouflaging tactics, *M V Ahat* was registered in the name of a Singapore company, an LTTE front.

According to RAW reports and Sri Lankan intelligence, all arms and ammunition smuggling the LTTE between 1984 and 1990 was conducted through Singapore and Malaysia.

Singapore remains an important LTTE base. A lot of LTTE money, proceeds of shady deals and drug-trafficking, changes hands here through underground banking system, better known in India as *hawala.* Indian customs authorities have registered cases of gold and arms smuggling by the LTTE men through Singapore.

But the chargesheet does not mention the Singapore angle at all. The Singapore chapter is as good as closed.

THE VITAL WITNESS

A young Tamil woman, Kumudavelli, posed a big question mark on the SIT's conduct. This eyewitness created ripples in late 1991 when she filed a rather explosive affidavit before the Verma commission of inquiry.

Kumudavelli said she had seen a mother-daughter duo, Latha Kanan and Kokila — who had come in the car of Latha Priyakumar in the company of the killer squad members , Dhanu and Sivarasan.

Justice J S Verma made a damning observation about Latha Priyakumar in his report. The report said Latha Priyakumar's conduct and demeanour suggested that she had something to hide.

Kumudavelli, a Congress worker, also complained of threats and demanded security. What the SIT did was rather interesting. It made Kumudavelli a coded prosecution witness in the chargesheet. Ostensibly to ensure that she cannot depose before the Jain Commission. The Jain Commission was told that the case diary nowhere mentions that Kumudavelli was the first one to see the assassination squad.

Despite the sensational nature of her allegations, Kumudavelli has neither deposed before the Verma commission nor the trial court. It was only in July 1996 that her statement was recorded by Jain commission after the Commission summoned her.

THE SHANMUGHAM ENIGMA

For the 32-year-old don of Kodiakkarai — a strategic coastal area of Tamil Nadu for the LTTE — life was an extended sweet dream. Until a month after Rajiv's assassination when it turned into a nightmare .

Shanmugham was the uncrowned king of Kodiakkarai. He had earned his millions through smuggling — mainly petrol, diesel and kerosene — to LTTE stronghold in Jaffna. He wielded enormous clout because of his wealth, his political connections, his links with the dreaded LTTE and his influential uncle Seetharaman. His sister even married a hardcore Tiger, Yogaratnam.

Seetharaman was one of those few persons who had direct access to the Prabhakaran . In 1989, when Prabhakaran was injured while fighting the IPKF, Seetharaman had brought the LTTE supremo to Tamil Nadu for treatment. So, while the Indian soldiers were being killed by Tamil terrorists in Jaffna, Prabhakaran was being sheltered and treated by Indians on Indian soil.

It was probably at that time that Prabhakaran saw his "Eelam" dream shattered and realised the seriousness of the situation. It was a do-or-die scenario for the LTTE . And he resolved that attack was the best defence.

This was the worst period of IPKF's presence in Jaffna. Indian troops were being butchered and in many cases, tortured to death. Perhaps this was the time when Prabhakaran had first thought of eliminating Rajiv.

Kodiakkarai serves as a highly strategic place for the LTTE. Jaffna is just about one and a half kms by speedboat from this coastal township. With the Sri Lankan government banning supply of petrol, diesel, kerosene and petroleum products in 1987 the LTTE got supply of these commodities from Kodiakkarai.

LTTE sympathisers in Tamil Nadu government have taken enough steps to help the Tigers on this count. Kodiakkarai, which has a population of just about 20,000 has more than 20 petrol pumps. Obviously, these petrol pumps are to cater to the LTTE needs. Kodiakkarai also serves as a base for arms dumping and narco-trafficking for the LTTE.

Dhanu, Sivarasan and several of the nine-member assassination squad stayed at Shanmugham's house on May 1-2, 1991. For one year between May 1990 and May 1991, Sivarasan shuttled between Jaffna and Tamil Nadu and on each occasion, he stayed with Shanmugham. Shanmugham's old wireless set was replaced with a 36-channel high-frequency wireless . This set, secretly installed at his house, had a range of 1,000 kilometres.

Barely a month after Rajiv's assassination, evidence of Shanmugham's involvement started surfacing. Known to be keeping officers of all government departments, including police, in his pocket, he had demonstrated his clout when he saved a customs officer from certain death after he was abducted by the LTTE.

When Shanmugham had disappeared without a trace, the SIT was increasingly under pressure to do something. A big catch like

Shanmugham was bound to provide a major breakthrough. SIT officers tried a psychological trick. A senior police officer of the area was told that the SIT wanted some information from Shanmugham and if the don surfaced, his arrest would be kept a secret considering his image in the area. The SIT also conveyed to Shanmugham its assurance that he would not be subjected to third degree treatment.

Besides, the officer was also politely told that it would be in his own interest if Shanmugham came overground.

The trick worked. Shanmugham surrendered before additional superintendent of police in Thanjavur east in June 1991.

Karthikeyan called Sri Kumar, a DIG from Delhi and gave him charge of Shanmugham, ignoring the officers who were instrumental in his arrest and were already investigating the case. The smuggler was brought to Madras by road and flown to Vedaranyam in a special SIT helicopter. Investigators recovered huge dumps of arms, ammunition, explosives, petrol and batteries Shanmughan had stacked away at Vedaranyam.

Though the SIT did keep its promise of not using third degree on him, it broke the other one. Shanmugham's arrest was announced in a big way .

The next morning, Shanmugham's body was found, hanging from a tree in the vicinity of tourist bungalow where he was kept. He was last seen in the company of Seetharaman, his uncle. The SIT described it as suicide. But many questions remain unanswered.

* The position of the body was rather peculiar — legs on the ground, knees bent, rope round the neck. Nobody can commit suicide in this position. Was he murdered and then "hanged" to give it a semblance of suicide?

* Where did he get the rope from at that late hour?

* Shanmugham could not have tied the knot the way it was tied.

* Why he could not be located during the six-hour search operation in which even sniffer dogs were pressed into service?

* Were the ligature marks on his body ante-mortem or post-

mortem?

* Why was the post-mortem not elaborate?

* Why was Seetharaman allowed to meet him at all and that too for over an hour and in total privacy? What did Seetharaman tell his nephew?

* Why was there no proper security arrangement for the key accused who knew too much?

* Why was Shanmugham handed over to Sri Kumar, who was not even a SIT member till then? Kumar was inducted into the SIT after this incident.

* Why was Seetharaman never interrogated by the SIT?

The Shanmugham episode was a terrible mess-up and the SIT gave all kinds of explanations. But the fact remained that all its good work came to a naught with Shanmugham's death.

Shanmugham could have led the SIT to other LTTE smugglers. Arun, Yogaratnam, Jeevratnam and Chokkan to name a few. There is enough information with the SIT of their involvement in the Rajiv case. Chokkan is said to be the most important of them all. But surprisingly, none of them finds a mention either in FIR or in the chargesheet.

The deceased could have told the investigators about LTTE's network of arms, ammunition, and infrastructural operations of the Tigers. Since his Kodiakkarai house was the hub of activities of the assassins, he could have also shed light on who were in touch with him, for what purpose. Names and identities of more conspirators could have come to light.

Most importantly, Shanmugham could have helped unravel the mystery called Seetharaman . The SIT's information was that Seetharaman had been contacted by Prabhakaran himself over wireless.

What was the latest diktat of the "Leader"? What did Seetharaman tell Shanmugham the last time they met? Inquiries into the incident showed that Shanmugham was extremely upset and tense after his uncle left him. Why he was so?

Then additional director of CBI S K Datta, who was monitoring the investigations into the Rajiv assassination and later became CBI director, flew to Madras to inquire into the incident. Datta's report indicted only junior policemen.

THE FROZEN INTELLIGENCE

How the intelligence remained frozen on such an important issue as the conspiracy to kill a former prime minister still remains a baffling question. And that too when PLO chairman Yasser Arafat had already tipped off the Indians about it beforehand?

In sharp contrast to the intelligence failure in the Rajiv Gandhi case is RAW's abilities and network. The Indian external intelligence agency gave a tip-off that a Sikh youth, clad in military uniform, was going to attack Rajiv Gandhi at Rajghat on October 2, 1986. The tip-off was given nearly a week before the incident actually took place.

Rajiv escaped getting assassinated, but the incident was not as trivial as it is made out to be. The potential assassin, Karamjit Singh was a disgruntled Sikh angry with Rajiv Gandhi over his "inaction" to stop the butchering of thousands of innocent Sikhs in the wake of Indira Gandhi's assassination.

Karamjit failed because he was an amateur and not a trained, hardcore terrorist . He wanted a telescopic rifle which guaranteed accuracy, and approached an arms smuggler at a village on the Indo-Pak border. The smuggler got caught by the security forces, and Karamjit could arrange only a countrymade pistol.

Three days before the birth anniversary of Mahatma Gandhi, Karamjit sneaked into the lush green campus of Rajghat. He hid himself atop the canopy of a cemented structure which served as a security post. The canopy was covered by a thick growth of creepers and vegetation which served as a natural smokescreen for the revenge-seeker.

Karamjit carried a toothpaste and some roasted grams, apart from his crude weapon. But he had not taken into account the mosquito menace. He came down with fever after one night with the mosquitos. The next day, he bought some tablets, a mosquito-repellant cream and a small pack of roasted cashew nuts from a nearby market. While returning to his hideout, he was stopped at the Rajghat periphery by a police constable. The *samadhi* area had been sealed after various security agencies had checked it thoroughly for possible explosives and unauthorised entrants.

Karamjit had no convincing answer to the constable's queries. He said he was an army jawan from Punjab and was going on posting to Bikaner, Rajasthan and wanted to pay his tributes to the Father of the Nation before catching his night train. But he could not produce his identity card when demanded. The suspicious constable took him to the police station. But he was let off when the police discovered he had fever.

Karamjit went back to his hide-out from the same route.

There was commotion at Rajghat when Karamjit fired his first shot at Rajiv. It sounded like a cracker burst. To some others, it appeared as if a scooter tyre had burst. Rajiv himself said that it appeared to be a gunshot. An on-the-spot alert was sounded, but none could know what had happened. The confusion prevailed for quite some time.

About 20 minutes later, Karamjit fired again and seconds later, the third shot. The quick succession in which he fired second and third shots proved to be his Waterloo. A smoke trail had been formed because of the brief time gap between the two shots . And the smoke rose from the canopy.

The game was up for Karamjit. He surrendered when security personel surrounded him.

The drama at Rajghat throws several disturbing questions. When a single-handed assassination bid is made on Rajiv Gandhi by a maniac, the plot is foiled and the conspirator caught alive. But when a foreign-based terrorist outfit is plotting Rajiv's assassination, massive arrangements are made over months, and many people are privy to the plot, intelligence is frozen.

Did this happen because of genuine operational difficulties or for political reasons? If the latter is true, it does not augur well for the democracy and unity and integrity of India. Its cause has to be examined.

But more importantly, those responsible for the frozen intelligence must be exposed and dealt with squarely. Only then can further assassinations be prevented.

12 EPILOGUE

Former cabinet secretary Zafar Saifullah was brought to Jain panel on Sept 4, 1996 by AICC counsel R N Mittal. Virtually no one got the wind of this development.

Giving a sensational twist to the probe, Saifullah told the panel he was aware of the existence of certain wireless messages of the LTTE which were intercepted by the Indian navy and IB and decoded. These messages, intercepted between 1990 and 1991 before Rajiv's assassination, had emanated from LTTE's bases in Sri Lanka and offices in western Europe and were meant for some persons in India.

These messages indicated a nexus between the LTTE, the Mossad, Chandraswami and Subramaniam Swamy, Saifullah told the Jain panel. Saifullah, who was cabinet secretary for about a year from July 1993, said this in a sworn statement on the basis of "personal knowledge".

The Central government denied there ever was any such messages and even refuted that the Navy was ever involved in wireless interception. It virtually burnt its fingers when an affidavit was filed before the commission to this effect.

Former Generals of the Indian Army and the Navy who had testified before the Jain panel on oath said the two services had been intercepting LTTE's wireless messages. Besides, from the records of the directorate general of military intelligence, which were given to the Commission for some other purpose, it was found that the navy had intercepted some important messages exchanged between the Tigers in Tamil Nadu and Jaffna during May-June, 1988.

These intercepts revealed an attempt by the LTTE to assassinate Rajiv in Madras. It was three years before they finally got him.

One message talked about planting of explosives on a bridge through which Rajiv was to pass. Another pertained to the Tigers' plan to greet Rajiv with a garland of bullets.

Why did the government lie? By this stand it effectively prevented a deeper probe into the LTTE-Mossad web which is suspected to have entangled many prominent Indians in it.

*

The Chandraswami connection is even more murky. A lot of damning reports were filed by Indian intelligence and revenue agencies regarding the activities of the self-styled godman.

According to these intelligence reports, which were put up before the Jain commission and find a mention in its final report, Chandraswami had at least seven accounts in the now collapsed BCCI*. These accounts were operated on his behalf by international arms dealer Adnan Khashoggi and Chandraswami's "disciple" R W Rowland.

The accounts were in London and tax havens like Channel Islands and Monte Carlo. Chandraswami does not have any bank account in his name.

The Jain final report which has gone into the conspiracy aspects of Rajiv's assassination, notes that both Chandraswami and Subramaniam Swamy have admitted in their depositions before the Commission that they have been regularly visiting Monte Carlo.

Inquiries by the Jain commission have shown that from Monte Carlo, massive financing was done by Khashoggi and others for gun-running from 1987 onwards.

This leads to the vital question of funding of the assassination. Former union minister Arif Mohammad Khan had in his testimony before the Jain panel implicated Chandraswami and said that the "godman" had offered huge sums of money to an Israeli for assassinating Rajiv.

---

* *For more details on BCCI read ''The BCCI Affair in chapter 'Annexures' in this book.*

It is on record that several LTTE front companies had accounts in the BCCI. During the SIT's investigations, one account of KP was found in the Bombay branch of the bank. The SIT hastily concluded that there was no link between this account and the assassination.

The Jain commission had asked for further details about this account of KP as well as Chandraswami's seven accounts. Intelligence reports confirming these were placed before the commission. The commission was suddenly growing too uncomfortable for the political system.

Which brings one to the sudden death treament meted out to the Jain commission by the Gujral government.

In the first week of February 1998, Commission secretary D R Luthra sent a letter marked "secret" to Union home secretary B P Singh. It gave a list of documents which were still not submitted by the government. These documents included Navy's intercepts from 1988 onwards, complete details of Chandraswami's BCCI accounts and all IB reports on Chandraswami from 1987 onwards. The IB and other agencies have compiled a dossier on Chandraswami's activities over the years, which contain details of his meetings with people in India and abroad.

Against this backdrop, Luthra asked for another extension for the commission, whose tenure had already been extended 12 times.

There were influential functionaries in the Gujral government who were desperate to wind up the commission. However, the authorities concerned kept telling the commission officials till the evening of February 27, 1998 that the request for extension would be granted and it was a matter of time when orders to this effect were issued.

It was the most unexpected order which lay in store for the commission. Around 11 pm on February 27, 1998, the office of Nikhil Kumar, special secretary in the ministry of home affairs, was abuzz with activity. Kumar wrote to Luthra saying the government had examined the matter and had decided not to grant any further extension to the panel. The commission was given seven days to finalise its report and was informed that during this period, the secretarial services would remain available. The letter was delivered to Justice Jain at midnight.

It was an unusual decision, more so because Gujral's was a caretaker government. It had no right to take such a major decision. The move smacked of a cover-up.

Most surprisingly, there was no official protest from the Congress party.

A campaign had already been launched to discredit the Jain commission. Statements were made to highlight the unduly long time taken by it.

Matters did not end here. A senior minister in the Gujral government asked Justice Jain over telephone to submit a "draft report" instead of a full-fledged one as the commission did not have much time left. Obviously, a draft report would have come in handy because its draft report does not have to be placed before Parliament. It also does not warrant an action taken report (ATR).

Undaunted by the stiff deadline, the Jain commission put itself into top gear and started finalising its report. Apparently, the authorities had not imagined this kind of response.

The other face of the CBI was to be seen at this time. Suddenly, a team of CBI sleuths descended on the commission secretariate and insisted on immediate questioning of the officers and staff, who were busy in finalising the report, into the "leakage" of the commission's interim report. It was only after a prolonged and fierce wordy duel that the CBI men relented and agreed to quiz commission officials after the report was submitted.

The commission's last week was the most turbulent period for the chairman and his officials. They were threatend over telephone against going ahead with the final report. Justice Jain put some of these threatening calls on record when he wrote to the home minister.

Luthra submitted 2000-page final report to B P Singh quietly on March 7, 1998. It was in stark contrast to the presentation of the interim report in August 1997 when Justice Jain himself submitted the 19-volume report to home minister Indrajit Gupta under the glare of flash bulbs and television cameras.

In a week or so after this, Justice Jain returned to his home town of Jodhpur, but not before an unexpected visit from a VVIP. Sonia Gandhi visited his residence and thanked him for his perseverance and having completed his report despite heavy odds.

Despite its unduly long tenure, the Jain commission was successful in doing what was considered unthinkable. The commission recorded the testimony of Sonia Gandhi.

It was a rare testimony. Rajiv's widow, Indira Gandhi's daughter-in-law, had never been questioned by the SIT. Nor had she ever been summoned by the trial court.

Sonia provided informtion to the commission in camera. She said Yasser Arafat had on several occasions telephoned her husband to caution him about a conspiracy by some foreign powers to kill him with the help of the LTTE or Punjab militants.

According to Sonia, Arafat said the conspirators were planning to assassinate him during election campaign and that he had got the information from two different sources — one in West Asia and another in Europe— and asked the former prime minister to get it further corroborated.

During her hour-long session, Sonia said Arafat, normally unruffled and nor given to emphasising on anything so much, seemed extremely concerned. This came at 1997-end.

The Jain panel was already aware of Arafat's warning to Rajiv and had tried hard to get a questionnaire sent to him through the ministry of external affairs. It wanted to know who Arafat's sources were? How reliable these were. And whether Arafat received any further information on the subject after Rajiv's murder. The commission could never receive a reply.

In April 1992, SIT DIG Sri Kumar went to London with sheaves of classified documents; the chargesheet in the Rajiv assassination case was about to be filed. The documents contained lists of LTTE sympathisers and other foreign-based suspects, their addresses and telephone numbers.

The DIG's briefcase was snatched in the lobby of a plush hotel. An FIR was lodged on behalf of the Indian high commission. Preliminary investigations quoted an eyewitness as describing the snatcher as having "Mediterranean looks".

The man was never caught, his identity never established. It turned out to be another case of the Indian investigators drawing a blank and the birds having flown. The SIT filed the chargesheet a month later. The briecase theft was forgotten.

Whether the Indian agencies ever suspected the LTTE's hand in the theft, and what action they took if they had, is not known. But a similar event that took place about five years later threw a new light on the theft in London. "*Time*" in its February 9, 1998 issue, reported on the LTTE's counter-intelligence.

"While finding his way through the maze of Rome's airport last March, a dapper arms manufacturer from Zimbabwe, named Tshinga Dube paused for a few seconds and put down his briefcase. It vanished. Inside were documents on the sale of 32,400 rounds of 81-mm mortars to the Sri Lankan army. With them, the Sri Lankans hoped to blast open a strategic road and break the hold of Tamil Tiger rebels in the palmyra jugles in the northern part of the island.

"At the time, Colonel Dube didn't worry much about his missing briefcase. He figured it had been grabbed by one of the airport's numerous snatch-and-run artists. Moving swiftly, Dube ordered copies of the stolen papers, and his company Zimbabwe Defence Industries, went ahead with the $ 3 million sale to Sri Lanka. On May 23, the mortars were transported to Beira, a port in Mozambique, and loaded onto a freighter bound for Colombo.

The ship docked on July 2 in Madagascar. Then, like the colonel's briefcase, it too disappeared.

"Nobody in the Sri Lankan Defence Ministry seemed too upset by the freighter's absence until July 14, when a mysterious fax arrived at the United States embassy in Colombo claiming to be from the LTTE. The message, which lacked the group's usual letterhead of a snarling tiger, seemed to be an outrageous hoax : 'We, the Tamil Tigers, inform you that on July 11, 1997 we have hijacked a vessel carrying arms , sailing under Liberian flag.' But instead of laughing at the fax, officials in the defence ministry got nervous. Checking records, they realised the shipload of mortars was nearly a month late. With growing dread, the authorities ran a check on the vessel, the *Stillus Limmasul.* Bad news : no ship by that name was registered. The mortàrs had been grabbed by the Tigers."

Is it too far-fatched to believe there were moles in the Indian security agencies who informed the Tigers about Sri Kumar's mission and the contents of his briefcase?

*

It is apparent that Rajiv's assassination is much more sinister than it is believed to be. Dhanu and Sivarasan were just the fingers, the LTTE merely the hand. The mastermind remains invisible. There are pointers they were forces beyond the Tigers.

The Rajiv assassination is yet another case in point which proves that assassinations are like Alibaba caves. Only those can enter these caves who know the magical code. To others who are outside, the caves are an impregnable mountain. And who enters these caves? Those who hide their ill-gotten treasures there. Like Alibaba, the SIT has got access to some potential magical codes. But the mysterious caves are yet to open because the codes are yet to be tried on the charmed gates.

Rajiv's assassination is just another spoke in the wheel of international conspiracy to destabilise and weaken India. The former prime minister, who gave the slogan "Mera Bharat Mahan" (My India is great), is dead. But the Indian honour is at stake.

On May 20, 1992, the SIT chargesheeted Prabhakaran as the accused number one in the Rajiv assassination case. But where is Prabhakaran? He is still at large and the warrior-king is commanding a far better organised guerilla army.

Why can't a commando operation be planned to capture Prabhakaran? When a tiny country like Israel can send its warplanes deep into Iraq which come back safely after destroying the Iraqi nuclear reactor, why can't New Delhi launch such a dare-devil operation to tame the chief of a terrorist force which may threaten the very unity and integrity of India in the not-so-distant future ?

If an American Marine is killed in West Asia or a US aircraft is shot down by Libyans or Iraqis, Washington does not hesitate to bomb the palaces of Colonel Gaddafi and Saddam Hussein. But if a former Indian prime minister is brutally killed by a foreign-based terrorist outfit on the Indian soil, softer options of seeking "extradition" of Prabhakaran and company are tried for years from a government which itself has no control over the terrorist organisation, the LTTE.

It is not impossible to launch such commando operations in this age of spy satellites.The whereabouts of Prabhakaran can be found by these spies in the skies, no matter how dense the jungles of LTTE-controlled are and how impregnable the LTTE supremo's underground concrete bunkers are.

Catching Prabhakaran alive is bound to lead to the trail of conspirators beyond him. But can we do it when we have failed to catch even an ordinary fugitive like Veerappan ?

India has competent personnel to pull off such a commando operation. All that it requires is the political will.

A more urgent imperative is to order fresh investigations into the assassination which should take into account the beyond-the-Tigers theory. Even the Jain commission has failed to totally uncover the sinister aspects of the murder, involving the high and the mighty in India and abroad. Enough evidence has already come up in this regard which has been discussed at length earlier in this book.

It is upto the political masters to take cognisance of such crucial evidences and constitute another SIT to take investigations to the logical end. I am sure that the new SIT, if given a free hand, would not require more than six months to do the job.

This will definitely peel off the mask of respectability from many influential persons. Stringent action should be taken against such persons whose otherwise clean hands are smeared with Rajiv's blood. That will send clear signals to the world that India would not leave any stone unturned to get to the root of the diabolical game of political assassinations.

It should not matter which political party Rajiv Gandhi belonged to. It is the question of salvaging the Indian honour which has been mauled by foreign forces on Indian soil.

PART V

ANNEXURES

(1) LTTE'S WIRELESS MESSAGES

Following are some of the coded wireless messages transmitted between the LTTE bases in India and abroad before and after Rajiv's assassination. These were intercepted by the Indian security agencies but decoded months after the assassination. As per the procedure after intercepting and recording code messages, transcripts are sent to the decoding section for breaking the code. After ten days of the recording of the intercepted messages, audio cassettes are used again for recording further messages.

The LTTE messages were transmitted from seven stations - Nos. 14, 31, 32, 33, 22, 91, 95 and 910. Station No. 14 was LTTE leader Prabhakaran's base, station no. 91 was Pottu Amman's base and station no. 95 and 910 were operated from Tamil Nadu. Messages transmitted from station nos. 91, 95 and 910 came to be monitored from 1991 beginning. Pottu Amman was in control of station nos. 91, 92 and 95. Station no 92 functioned from Jaffna and station no. 95 was a mobile base.

Some messages are reproduced below :

22.3.1991 (95 to 91)

-- Will come to Madras. If it is Delhi lot of time and lot of effort will be required. If Neru comes, it will be good. Set can start.

91 to 95:

If I send one of my men, can you train him to drive in a crowded town? Buy a vehicle.

25.3.1991 (91-95)

Leave on--- will reach you on (2 digits date) in the morning or evening. Better if Kodiakarai. At least 1000 litres of petrol to be sent ---- send those two people. Send medicines and other things in the boat.

6.4.1991 (91-95)—11.50 to 12.25 Hrs.

Don't use knife on Chandrahasan.* Hit with pistol. If you don't have pistol you make arrangements. I will send etc. Kittu is in touch will Ragu.

7.4.1991(91-95):7 A.M.

I cannot send you men before the date given by you. If it is beyond that, make all connections and let me know.

7.5.1991 (95-91):—9-00 to 9.15 Hrs.

She is the eldest daughter in the house of Indu Master. Moving closely. Our intention is not known to anybody except ourselves. I have told her that it is to have the support of the party who will be coming to power. Here V P Singh is coming. We are receiving. Like that we are receiving all the leaders.

I am slowly approaching. If I tell our intention there is no doubt that she will stand firmly on our side.

We are moving with her closely, have full satisfaction. Girls are telling that the intention can be revealed to her and she can be believed.

If I return I will return as your man. We are strong in powder business.

22.5.1991 (91-95):—1.00 to 1.20 Hrs..

To..**..Don't send long messages. It will create suspicion.

---

* *Chandrahasan is a Sri Lankan Tamil leader based in Madras who runs a refugee organisation called organisation for Eelam Refugee Rehabilitation (OFERR). He has been anti-LTTE.*

** *The conversation between two LTTE bases transcribed in the transcripts before and after the transmission of messages in code language is known as "Enclaire Messages" in the intelligence parlance. Most often, these enclaire messages are broken because the sender keeps changing frequencies too swiftly for the interceptor to react. That is why it is difficult quite often to make sense out of such messages.*

There is a news that there is violence in your place. What is that?

Is there any incident of attack on Sri Lankan Tamils. The vehicle will come to any place of your choice on 2nd. Start and meet me.

13.00 Hrs.

Even to our people in higher places we informed that we have no connection with this.

25. 5.1991 (91-95)—07.30 Hrs.

Is the photo of 'Anbu'* identifiable.

07.35 Hrs.

"Press cuttings" of all the newspapers are needed.

07.40 Hrs.

For Thatya+. As you told a strong foothold. I will later inform you about the task.

7.6.1991 (91-910):—8.00 to 8.25 Hrs.

To... Regarding Chandrahasan if it messes with knife finish him with pistol. If there is no facility to give pistol make arrangement and come.

9.6.1991 (910-91):—8.15 to 8.30 Hrs.

To... There is a news that one of my associates was caught at Nagapattinam and he has told all the things about me.

Tomorrow 10.6.1991 night after 7.00 P.M. we will be waiting for the vehicle. Walkie No. 5212.

At present even if there is no wireless communication vehicle can be sent.

---

* *LTTE's code name for Dhanu.*

\+ *Code name for Subha. Again, this message is apparently unintelligible. Actually, her code-name was Nitya. While decoding, 'Ni' become 'Tha'.*

10.6.1991 (91-910):—7.00 Hrs.

To... --- As directed, we have taken " Thathuvam" code sheet.

11.6.1991 (91-95) 09.00-09.17 Hrs.

Reduce the wireless communication. There will be TV disturbance during communication.

(95-91):

Persons known to us were caught. Lingam associate of Jeewaratnam was also caught. Hectic search on for Chokan.

Due to separation of Anbu, Thatya is not active. Effort by me in vain. No response unless given encouraging news.*

(91-95):

To ... Number of persons came in the vehicle --- Two were rescued. We are searching for others. I will inform after they are located.

12.6.1991 (91-910):

Nine persons including Karikalan were not rescued. Vehicle also sunk.

The code sheet name "Migaiyil" can be changed as "Thathuvam". Don't ask what for?

Thatya... Today it may not be possible to recognise our brave people and carve their victories in golden words in our group's history but their aims of goals will not change for ever. There is no need to mourn their departure, instead feel proud for their friendship. Don't get disheartened. Get ready to make a change in the pages of our history.

Without taking food, reducing the activities will create problem for you as well as for the care-takers.

---

* *This message was sent by Sivarasan to Pottu Amman when Subha gave up food for several days, mourning Dhanu's death. The message beginning with the words "Thatya...Today it may not" is Pottu Amman's reply sent next day.*

(91-910):

.....(.) Have you received three kg of gold from Shanthan. If not give the address it will be delivered there.

Is there any problem for Neelan and Indu Master?*

Can you observe the telephone communications of Neelan, Charles?

What happened to the journey of Shanthan?

Will there by any problem if Charles comes there? He wants the address.

(910-91);

.....(.) Can meet Neelan on.. come and meet at the specific data .. place...

....(.) CBI has released the photos of Thatya and officer girl.+ Hence, I am keeping Thatya with me ready with weapons without leaving her alone in any house. My LTTE name has come out.

(91-910):

.....(.) There is a radio news that nineteen year old Dhas is also involved in the assassination. Who is he? In which newspaper your LTTE name has come?

....(.) Asked to deliver five code sheets to you. Collect it if there is any contact.

(910-91):

....(.) Received gold from Shanthan.

Many were arrested in the airport. Hence, journey of Shanthan postponed. I may face problem and enquiry. Neelan is not coming out.

The name of Indu Master has come out. It is his own creation. Even if risk is taken in his problem will be difficult to meet Indu as pointed out by Ramanan.

---

* *LTTE's code name for Murugan.*

\+ *Officer girl was used as a codename for Nalini by the conspirators.*

.... losses avoided. I swear on the sweet name of my leader, no stigma will be created by me for our group or the militants who died bravely. I have not forgotten.

(910-91):

The brother of officer girl her mother were arrested.*

......(Payas) along with the family was arrested. Indiran Kutty and Gundappa were arrested.

As shown by Indiran-Kutty, Kumar has gone to the house of Chokan. No problem for Kumar.

.... (Payas) was caught. He was beaten in his house whereabout of Kanthan.

(91-910):

....(.) Many of your supporters who helped you may not have been arrested. They may mount surveillance on them. Be careful.

Be ready to go like that.

14.6.1991 (910-91):

.....(.) Starting from yesterday morning till after noon the persons arrested at Mount Road were kept for the purpose of identification.

....(.) , +For us to come many have to put in their efforts.

No news about the father of Radha who has gone to Delhi.

(91-910):

Major. David (.) Captain Karikalan.

Vehicle fitted with four engines of 150 HP sunk? The reason is bad weather.

If arrangements are made outside Madras near the shore of Pondicherry or Chidambaram, can yor go there? This is not

---

* *Yet another example of disjointed, broken wireless message.*

\+ *A full stop or a comma before an intercepted coded wireless message indicates that some words preceded which could not be decoded.*

confirmed. I am yet to take steps.

16.6.1991 (910-91):

....(.) It is true that Indu Master and officer girl were arrested. They will be produced at Chingleg at Court on 12th of 7th month.

.....(.) Came to know through newspapers regarding Kasi Anandan.

(91-910):

Whether the meeting was in Delhi or in Madras?

(910-91):

It was in Madras. The name of the CBI officer is Karthikeyan, who is next to Vijay Karan.*

(91-910)-16.08 Hrs.

......(.) We informed earlier that five boys of Ravi sent by you to me died in Ylusia. Do you remember? They were caught by Sri Lankan navy. As they have given statement saying that they are businessmen. Navy released two of them. These two at had come to India with passports.

16.08- 16.12 Hrs.

Contact them through Ravi. Be careful. Sometime surveillance on them will create problem for Ravi's men.

17.6.1991 (910-91):

To .....(.) The photos to Thatya and mine are displayed throughout Tamil Nadu.

There is a news in *Dinamani* about the confirmtion of the meeting between CBI officers and Kasi

16.02 Hrs- (910-91):

There is a Nepali friend for Roopan. Easun. Can he go with

---

* *This is factually wrong because at the relevant time, Karthikeyan was a joint director, a rank which has additional director and special director above it.*

him to Nepal, Burma border and places in Assam?

18.6.1991 (910-91)08.00 to 8.03 Hrs.

To... (.) Obtained five code sheets from Neelan.

08.05 Hrs.

There will be a problem for defending officer girl.

(91-910) 16.05 Hrs.

I am warning. It is not good to interfere in the affairs of officer girl.

19.6.1991 (91-910)-8.02 to 8.10 Hrs.

Don't interfere in the affairs of Neelan and others. They are not children. At present it will be difficult to attend to your own affairs. In the midst of this don't interfere in their affairs. Give enough money to them and ask them to look after themselves. If there is no communication for one month ask them to communicate.

(910-91) 08.11 Hrs.

To ...(.) Foreigners are suspecting. There is a news about award of 10 lakhs for information about me. Five lakhs for information about Thatya.

(91-910) 09.06 Hrs.

To.....(.) Inform whether the boys of Ravi were careful.

(91-910)09.11 Hrs.

How is the situation at Kodiakarai, Thondi and Nagapattinam.

(910-91) 09.27 Hrs.

To.... (.) Kottaipattinam was seen through Ravi. Police are alert in all the places. Anyhow, I will take the risk and come.

(91-910) 09.40 Hrs.

....(.) I will give the reply in the evening.

16.00 hrs.

.....(.) Can you not change your place in Madras through Ravi's contact?

Santhan agreed to help. If needed I will arrange for their help.

It is difficult to come in the midst of goods. For this a strong driver and cleaner are needed.

(91-910):

.....(.) Any contact with Shanthan? When and where to meet Shanthan?

16.18 Hrs ....(.) The journey of Shanthan will be on 1st July. Go via Bombay.

(910-91) 16.20 Hrs.

As instructed by Kittanna, Kasi Anandan went to CBI to help in their investigation.

16.25 Hrs.

In search of me CBI surrounded the earlier house of Jeevarathnam at Kodambakkam.

20. 6.1991 (91-910) 08.15-08.23 Hrs.

When and where to meet Shanthan at Madras? Data given to him...

07.30-08.00 Hrs.

In case of emergency my weapons will take action on the enemies. The place where Robert and others on the CBI Office is known and I have taken position. If I meet Shanthan I will hand over Nitya and follow it up. They are also co-operating in Rajiv Gandhi assassination.* Gundappa can be killed. Chandrahasan is not seen. Expecting the reply. The soul of sister "Anbu" will rest in peace. The morale of CBI will come down.

(910-91):

Yesterday I met Ravi and sent him to Pudukottai.

Decide in sending a trawler or vehicle.....

---

* *It is shocking. How could the LTTE cadres use the words ''Rajiv Gandhi assassination'' in a coded message?*

21.6.1991 (910-91) 08.00 Hrs.

.....(.)Tomorrow if I meet Shanthan I will talk to him. Further Mani is also with him.

08.30 Hrs.

More Sri Lankan Tamils are giving information. They give information when they see persons resembling both of us. Yesterday two were arrested at Dindivanam. Public attempted to kill them by beating. There is a news that both of us were arrested. The person who gave the information is Chandrasekar, Mannar district. He is now in the refugee camp at Athiyendal in Thiruvannamalai . Three children.

08.55 hrs. (91-910):

.....(.) Whether all of you have cyanide capsules? Did Indu Master have cyanide capsule? Does he know the message given by us?

16.15 Hrs.

Even if safe place is arranged after talking to Shanthan. Don't have contact with Ramanan and Neelan. If Neelan and Ramanan are not having cyanide capsules arrange through Ravi.

If vehicle is arranged only Raghuvaran, Neru and Nitya need come.

16.15 Hrs.

Contact with Shanthan need not be known to Neelan and Ravi's men.

The house of Engineer Karunakaran is a noted place. Don't use this place more than the first meeting.

(910-91):

It is understood that Ravi's men are struggling without strong base.

Expecting to meet Shanthan.

22.6.1991 (910-91) 08.00 Hrs.

.....(.) Whether our wing has done the Colombo action? Can I know?

(91-910) 08.30 hours.

......(.) This is one of the steps of Black Tigers. We will discuss it. You also come. We can do more.

32.6.1991 (910-91):

Had contact with Shanthan. Closing the wireless communication and leaving with him. He told vehicle can be arranged in a week. We will close the communication after getting your reply. Had contact with Radha. Journey on---

(91-910) 16.00 Hrs.

In Indian news it is learnt that a Special Police Force was formed to arrest both of you. Be careful about this Special Force. They are trying to capture you alive. Using tear gas, other gases they may try to thwart your attempt to consume cyanide unexpectedly.

(91-910) 16.00 Hrs.

Yesterday 60 HP engine fitted big vessel sank in the sea. Due to bad weather. No casualty. Don't expect the vehicle immediately. Inform Shanthan about this."

*

(2) IB REPORT ON THREAT FROM LANKA

DIB UO No 49/VS/87(3) dated June 5, 1987

Digest 5/87

Serious danger to VIP security also arises from the developments in our immediate neighbourhood, particularly in Sri Lanka and Pakistan. The threat potential of Sinhala elements trained and abetted by Israeli Integlligence (and other pro-western agencies) cannot be minimised. Certain elements among Sri Lanka Tamils, who feel unhappy about some aspects of Government of India's Policy, could also pose threat to the security of the Prime Minister and other VIPs.

According to an information, members of a foreign Jatha which had visited Pakistan recently were heard discussing plans to make an attempt on the life of the Prime Minister and other VIPs in the near future.

*

(3) RAW REPORT ON LTTE ACTIVITIES

CABINET SECRETARIAT UO NO. 4/1/87-VS-2306 dtd. 23.11.87 (p.8)

Sub : Threat to the security of the Prime Minister from the LTTE.

Ever since the signing of the Indo Sri Lanka Agreement on July 29, 1987, some Sri Lankan Tamil militant groups and particularly LTTE have been waging a campaign against the Agreement. While all the groups other than the LTTE seem to have reconciled themselves to the Agreement, the LTTE is continuing its campaign against it, both on the ground and in the propaganda front. The nature of this campaign against the Agreement is to some extent influenced by the increasing success of the IPKF in its operations against the LTTE in the Northern and Eastern Provinces.

Recent reports indicate that some hard core LTTE activists are keen to take revenge for the IPKF action in the Northern and Eastern provinces. There were reports that the LTTE was planning to take some dramatic action against targets in India or Indian targets abroad such as Indian missions etc. Our missions in Canberra and Singapore received threatening telephone calls, including a hoax bomb threat, relating to events in Jaffna. Some unidentified Sri Lankan Tamils in Oslo, sympathetic to LTTE, have also come to notice for trying to establish contact with Sikhs there. In a recent conversation with the Sikhs, they reportedly sought to blame our Prime Minister for the recent developments and suggested the latter should be killed.

More recently one Jayadeven, a Sri Lankan Tamil who normally resides in Hong Kong reportedly has come to notice for talking of plans to finish off the Prime Minister and a desire to make efforts to utilise the opportunity provided by the World Tamil Conference in Kuala Lumpur to canvass support for such a plan. In this connection it may be mentioned that one Jayadevan had come to notice for suspected links with drug smuggling activities of some LTTE activists. Photo copy of an article "Inside the Tamil Tigers drug racket" which appeared in the *Sunday Times* (August 30, 1987) is enclosed. On Samy working as clerk in a solicitors firm in Kuala Lumpur (Office Telephone No. 2328424 and 2320159) is known to be a contact of Jayadevan.

Enclosed is a list of the more important LTTE activists who have come to our notice in the different countries. In view of the continuing defiance and animosity displayed by LTTE, pro-LTTE men could constitute a source of threat to our Prime Minister and hence they would require to be watched closely.

Important LTTE supporters who have come to our notice:

1. Satyamurty, main organiser, LTTE, London. He had appeared on TV interview recently along with Dr Ravi Sundarasingam (EROS) in London.

2. Dr Sachidanandan, Liverpool. He is secretary, Federation of Tamil Associations in UK.

3. Ramachandran alias Ramu, accountant based in London.

4. Father Thomas, chief representative, LTTE, New York. He is Catholic and moves without cassock canvassing for LTTE.

5. Edward Bendecit, Bronx, near New York.

6. K Chelvakumar, assistant professor, Pittsburg, Pennsylvania, Recently he went on fast in USA in support of LTTE demand for cease-fire. His parents live in Madras.

7. Dr Sundarasingham, Sydney, Australia. He is secretary, Eelam Tamils Association.

8. Dr K Jagadeesan, Connecticut, tel. No. 203-7559204.

9. Sritharan, Boston, USA. He is learnt to have been a bank employee and arms dealer for LTTE.

*

(4) PRABHAKARAN'S SECRET VISIT TO SINGAPORE

DO NO. 1/17/88-VS Dt. Oct. 5, 1989.

My dear Ratan,

According to an unconfirmed report received by us, Prabhakaran, leader of the LTTE, had visited Singapore a few days ago to explore the possibility of purchasing arms and ammunition through some of his contacts there. No other details are available.

Even though this information has not yet been corroborated, it would be better to have this conveyed to the Malaysian and Singapore authorities so that they take necessary precautions in view of the forthcoming Commonwealth summit.

With regards.

Yours faithfully

Sd/

(B. Raman)

Shri Ratan Sehgal,

Joint Secretary (Pers), MEA.

*

(5) IB REPORT ON LTTE'S ACTIVITIES IN INDIA

DIB UO No. I (14) / 89 (II) 194 dated 27.12. 89

Sub : Tamil Nadu : Activities of Sri Lankan Tamil Groups.

After the Indo Sri Lanka Accord of July 1987, Sri Lankan Tamil Groups operating from Tamil Nadu had gradually withdrawn from the State to Sri Lanka, leaving only a token presence behind, mainly for purposes of liaison, propaganda and other activities. Militant groups like the EPRLF, TELO, ENDLF, PLOT EROS etc., even now function in this manner in Tamil Nadu concentrating on propaganda and related activities, including building up a lobby for their activities. The LTTE, on the other hand, while carrying on propaganda has increasingly resorted to clandestine activity like the procurement of illegal arms, ammunition and explosives and smuggling them across the Palk Straits to northern Sri Lanka.

Several LTTE cadres injured in Sri Lanka are regularly brought clandestinely for treatment in various private clinics and hospitals in Tamil Nadu.

The LTTE today maintains a small clandestine network of about 30 cadres which is active inside Tamil Nadu and Karnataka and spread over Madras city, Salem, Trichy and Madurai (in Tamil Nadu) and Bangalore city. Their activities cover a wide spectrum from kidnaping for ransom, fabrication of land mines and RP grenades, procurement and transhipment of foodstuffs, explosives and arms and ammunition to the 'struggle' area in Sri Lanka. The LTTE's underground apparatus possesses a fleet of vehicles and speed boats, and they are also able to count on the services of numerous smugglers along the Tanjore, Tirunelveli and Rameswaram coast of Tamil Nadu. The LTTE also runs a clandestine wireless station and maintains communication links with both Sri Lanka and London. Considerable dissemination of propaganda as also disinformation takes place by the Madras-based outfit of the LTTE.

Law enforcement agencies in Tamil Nadu face several difficulties in dealing with the actions of the LTTE, including its criminal activities. For one, LTTE militants are equipped with sophisticated weapons which are often superior to those possessed by the police. For another, they believe that having the latent sympathy of the population, they can flout laws with impunity. Also, that the legal loopholes give them sufficient latitude in dealing with the enforcement agencies. Third, they have little inhibition in openly confronting the authorities—the recent abduction of an Indian customs patrol on the high seas in the Palk Straits on the night intervening December 7/8, 1989, and their release off the Tanjore coast on December 24 after being in LTTE captivity for more than a fortnight well exemplifies LTTE attitudes.

The other Eelam groups such as the EPRLF, the ENDLF, both factions of the TELO, PLOT, EPDP and EROS are greatly demoralised at what they see as the dominant role accorded to the LTTE by official agencies in India, apart from the Sri Lankan government. The LTTE leadership does retain close links with the DK led by K Veeramani. Further, they appear to have overcome some of their earlier inhibitions regarding the DMK and succeeded to an extent in building a rapport with the ruling DMK in Tamil Nadu since it came to power in January 1989. Recent parleys between LTTE representatives and the Tamil Nadu chief minister have virtually marginalised the position of the other Sri Lankan Tamil groups. The latter are deeply worried about the implication for themselves, and the Tamils in north and eastern Sri Lanka, of some of the demands made by the LTTE delegation during their recent parleys viz., (i) total withdrawal of the IPKF at the earliest without insisting on the deadline of December 31; (ii) dismissal of the North-Eastern provincial government led by EPRLF and dissolution of the provincial assembly followed by fresh elections; (iii) disowning the TNA, and (iv) scrapping the Indo-Sri Lankan Accord and replacing it with a new peace treaty between the two governments for guaranteeing the safety and security of the Tamils and reasonable autonomy to the Tamil province.

The phased de-induction of the IPKF, coupled with the LTTE's 'disarming operations' against the EROS, EPRLF, ENDLF and the TELO in the North Eastern province does lead to the distinct possibility of the non-LTTE Tamil groups seeking safety and sanctuary in Tamil Nadu. This would be both for their own safety as also for subsequently re-grouping and carrying out retaliatory attacks against the LTTE. The progressive withdrawal of the IPKF from the Tamil areas is already leading to a refugee influx into Tamil Nadu through Rameswaram, Nagapattinam and Vedaranyam. During the period September-December 1989, nearly 600 Sri Lankan Tamil families comprising about 1500 persons have reached Tamil Nadu. The bulk of the arrivals (408 families and 940 persons) have been in December itself. The LTTE's quest for arms and its past record in mercilessly dealing with rival groups and opponents pursuing a moderate line thus cannot be easily overlooked.

*

(6) IB REPORT ON LTTE THREAT TO RAJIV GANDHI

Telex message sent by Madras office of IB to IB Hqrs Delhi - File No. 29/VS/89(1) Page No. 30. on the "Threat Assessment Shri Rajiv Gandhi, EX-PM" on 12.12.89.

Kindly refer to your TPM NO. 6203 Dated Dec. 8, calling for a comprehensive threat assessment concerning the former PM Rajiv Gandhi and his family members.

There could be threat to the security of the former prime minister Rajiv Gandhi and his family members mainly from Sri Lankan Tamil militants and their local supporters, Tamil chauvinist elements and the left extremists. The two political parties, viz. Dravida Kazhagam (led by K Veeramani) and Tamizar National movement (led by P Nedumaran) are also known for extending support to the Sri Lankan Tamils' causes and also for expressing anti-Rajiv Gandhi views.

Following Indo-Sri lanka Accord (July 1987) on Sri Lanka Tamil issue, the leadership of LTTE and cadres turned more violent and hostile in their attitude towards Rajiv Gandhi. The Sri Lankan Tamil militants as known for possessing sophisticated weapons, and the possibility of surprise threat to Rajiv Gandhi and his family members in the changed circumstances cannot be ruled out.

Although there has been no known camps in Tamil Nadu, the LTTE cadres continue to have clandestine place for shelter and use Vedaranyam coast for their illicit entry and exit from across Sri Lanka.

The left extremist elements and various civil liberties and human rights association spread over in several districts of Tamil Nadu have expressed time and again their resentment and opposition to Rajiv Gandhi for setting up of an atomic power station at Koodankulam (Tirunelveli district). Besides the above elements, a few Sikh service personnel have also come to notice for expressing feelings against Rajiv Gandhi after the 'Blue Star' operation in June 1984.

The spectre of threat to the person of Rajiv Gandhi and his family members from various elements listed above appears to loom large more at present than when Rajiv Gandhi was the Prime Minister of the country till recently.

A list containing various elements who may pose threat to ex-Prime Minister Rajiv Gandhi in the districts of Tamil Nadu was already sent to JD/VS vide our memo no. 1/SEC/89(1) dated August 9, 1989.

*

(7) IB NOTE ON RAJIV'S THREAT PERCEPTION

From : CREMO Bombay

To : Creminare New Delhi (JD/VS and DD/VS)

File No. Nil Dated Dec. 11, 1989.

Sub : Threat Assessment Concerning Shri Rajiv Gandhi, Ex-PM and His Family Members.

Reference IB TPM No. 6736 dated December 8, 1989.

Although there is specific information with us on the subject, as per our assessment, the threat to the lives of Rajiv Gandhi and his family members persists to the same degree as when he was PM. The Sikh extremists may feel encouraged to attack Rajiv Gandhi in the hope that the security around him would not be stringent any longer.

*

(8) IB CHIEF ON LTTE PRESENCE IN TAMIL NADU

DIB Letter No. 4/DIB/DIS/2/91-93.

Events in Tamil Nadu over the past several months have been a matter of continuing concern. More specifically, the recent turn of events and a demonstrable deterioration in the law and order situation have led to widespread apprehension as also fear in the state. The ability of the state administration to deal with the situation is being openly questioned and relative freedom with which anti-national and secessionist elements are able to function in many areas are affecting the quality of life and could disturb the democratic polity in this part of the country.

The most disturbing aspect is the widespread perception that the LTTE are operating as an independent force outside the ambit of the country's laws, and have carved out certain sanctuaries for themselves in which the state administration has no authority functioning as a kind of parallel authority in parts of Ramanathapuram, Thanjavur, Pudukottai and Tiruchirapally districts. The unwillingness of the state adminsitration to effectively deal with the menace of the LTTE has tended to give them still greater encouragement to engage in violent activities and threaten and intimidate the people in the coastal areas. This has led to several criticism of the state government and the administration.

Despite fairly extensive knowledge of clandestine boat movements along the Thanjavur, Pudukottai and Ramnathapuram coasts, no serious attempt appears to have been made by the police and the other local authorities to check such movements. There are at least 40 well-established landing points, including such well-known places as Tranquebar, point Calimere, Mallipattinam and Vedaranyam (Thanjavur district), Mimisal (Pudukottai district), Thondi, Soliakudi and Karankadu (Ramanathapuram district) and yet there have hardly been any interceptions. On the other hand, most of these areas are no longer effectively being policed nor are there any symbols of the administration's presence there. It is the writ of the LTTE which runs in these areas. The scale of operations are not small and there is nothing very clandestine about these movements, both on shore and along the coast. This perhaps suggests acquiescence in such activities. The result is that the LTTE is able to exercise unbridled influence, and fishermen and other people in the villages here have been living in great fear and dread.

Other aspects of the activities of the LTTE can have a long term fall-out. First is the presence of a fairly well-established clandestine communication network of the LTTE, using both HF and VHF facilities. Second, Tamil Nadu has become a major conduit, transit and staging point for arms, ammunition and explosives for use of LTTE militants in Sri Lanka. Some of the arms and ammunition have also found their way into underground channels within India. Encouragement by the LTTE has also led to an underground arms industry within Tamil Nadu and the 'Arul-89' and 'Pasilan-2000' (RPG shells) have today become as ubiquitous as the AK-37. Third, LTTE elements have built up an extensive network of contacts among political and economic segments of society in Tamil Nadu, using methods like bribery, corruption, influence peddling, as also coercion. The result is a thriving blackmaıket in such scarce commodities as diesel and petrol and pharmaceuticals, and smuggling of gold into the country. This has greatly vitiated the economic climate in the state and made it increasingly difficult to control blackmarket activities. Compounding this is the extensive 'hawala' transactions which have reached serious proportions of late and through which laundering of currency has become a major activity on behalf of the LTTE.

The permissive atmosphere prevailing in the state for some time is also giving encouragement to militants and secessionist forces, both within the state and elsewhere in the country. There is evidence that organisations like the Pattali Makkal Katchi (PMK), the Tamil Nationalist Movement (TNM), the Tamil Manawar Peravari (TMP), the Marxist Periyarist Communist Party and rationalist groups are now trying to create a separatist identity making common cause with the LTTE and stoking the fires of fissiparous and secessionist attitudes.

The concept of separatism being actively promoted by the above mentioned Tamil insular parties has found wide acceptability among left wing extremist groups like the People's War Group in Andhra Pradesh. Quite a few members of the TNM had reportedly participated in a PWG convention last year (1990). The growing relationship between Tamil separatist groups and left wing extremist factions like the PWG has also helped the latter to establish a beachhead with the LTTE from whom they have been able to obtain some sophisticated weapons.

Taking advantage of this situation, the United Liberation Front of Assam had established some kind of a nexus, either directly or through intermediaries in the state, with the LTTE. Very recently, some activists had used Tamil Nadu as a sanctuary and as a base for contacting the LTTE. Two prominent ULFA members were also arrested from the state. The state administration have shown a transparent lack of will to take action against elements whose professed aim has been the dismemberment of the country.

The situation in the state would not have deteriorated to this extent but for the failure on the part of the state government to provide necessary direction to its various agencies. This failure or refusal, is the result of a measure of sympathy to ethnic, linguistic and exclusivist forces. There is, hence, little possibility that such forces can indeed be contained or that the process of deterioration would be checked under the present circumstances.

A striking example of the collapse of policing in the state is the impunity with which the LTTE assailants of the EPRLF chief, Padmanabha, and 15 others were able to evade the police dragnet and escape from Tamil Nadu to Sri Lanka.

*

(9) KIRI COMMITTEE REPORT ON BCCI AFFAIR EXECUTIVE SUMMARY*

BCCI Constituted International Financial Crime on a Massive and Global Scale

BCCI's unique criminal structure—an elaborate corporate spider-webwith BCCI's founder, Agha Hasan Abedi and his assistant, Swaleh Naqvi, inthe middle—was an essential component of its spectacular growth, and a guarantee of its eventual collapse. The structure was conceived by Abedi and managed by

---

* *These are the excerpts from the Executive Summary of the Kiri report.The US select sub-committee headed by Senator John Kiri, which probed the BCCI affair, has admitted that investigations of the BCCI remain incomplete till today. BCCI activities in India and its relationship with the business empire of the Hinduja family are among the "unanswered questions" which the report talks of. Interestingly, the report is also understood to have stated that money had been transferred from the BCCI accounts of Adnan Khashoggi and Ernie Miller, a known disciple of Chandraswami, to the LTTE in 1990-91. The period mentioned is significant. Was Rajiv assassination funded through the BCCI? This is an uninvestigated area. Also mark the dubious style of functioning of the CIA as commented in the report.*

Naqvi for the specific purpose of evading regulation or control by governments. It functioned to frustrate the full understanding of BCCI's operations by anyone. Unlike any ordinary bank, BCCI was from its earliest days made up of multiplying layers of entities, related to one another through an impenetrable series of holding companies, affiliates, sudsidiaries,banks-within-banks, insider dealings and nominee relationships. By fracturing corporate structure, record keeping, regulatory review, and audits, the complex BCCI family of entitites created by Abedi was able to evade ordinary legal restrictions on the movement of capital and goods as a matter of daily practice and routine. In creating BCCI as a vehicle fundamentally free of government control, Abedi developed in BCCI an ideal mechanism for facilitating illicit activity by others, including such activity by officials of many of the governments whose laws BCCI was breaking. BCCI's criminality included fraud by BCCI and BCCI customers involving billions of dollars; money laundering in Europe, Africa, Asia, and the Americas; BCCI's bribery of officials in most of those locations; support of terrorism, arms trafficking, and the sale of nuclear technologies; management of prostitution; the commission and facilitation of income tax evasion, smuggling, and illegal immigration; illicit purchases of banks and real estate; and a panoply of financial crimes limited only by the imagination of its officers and customers. Among BCCI's principal mechanisms for committing crimes were its use of shell corporations and bank confidentiality and secrecy havens; layering of its corporate structure; its use of front-men and nominees, guarantees and buy-back arrangements; back-to-back financial documentation among BCCI controlled entities, kick-backs and bribes, the intimidation of witnesses,and the retention of well-placed insiders to discourage governmental action.

BCCI Systematically Bribed World Leaders and Political Figures Throughout the World

BCCI's systematically relied on relationships with, and as necessary, payments to, prominent political figures in most of the

73 countries in which BCCI operated. BCCI records and testimony from former BCCI officials together document BCCI's systematic securing of Central Bank deposits of Third World countries; its provision of favours to political figures; and its reliance on those figures to provide BCCI itself with favours in times of need. These relationships were systematically turned to BCCI's use to generate cash needed to prop up its books. BCCI would obtain an important figure's agreement to give BCCI deposits from a country's 'Central Bank', exclusive handling of a country's use of US commodity credits, preferential treatment on the processing of money coming in and out of the country where monetary controls were in place, the right to own a bank, secretly if necessary, in countries where foreign banks were not legal, or other questionable means of securing assets or profits. In return , BCCI would pay bribes to the figure, or otherwise give him other things he wanted in a simple quid-pro-quo. The result was that BCCI had relationships that ranged from the questionable to the improper, to the fully corrupt with officials from countries all over the world, including Argentina, Bangladesh, Botswana, Brazil, Cameroon, China, Colombia, the Congo, Ghana, Guatemala, the Ivory Coast, India, Jamaica, Kuwait, Lebanon, Mauritius, Morocco, Nigeria,Pakistan, Peru, Saudi Arabia, Senegal, Sri Lanka, Sudan, Surinam, Tunisia,the United Arab Emirates, the United States, Zambia and Zimbabwe.

The CIA developed important information on BCCI, and inadvertently failed to provide it to those who could use it.

The CIA and former CIA officials had a far wider range of contacts and links to BCCI and BCCI shareholders, officers, and customers, than has been acknowledged by the CIA.

By early 1985, the CIA knew more about BCCI's goals and intentions concerning the US banking system than anyone else in government, and provided that information to the US Treasury and the Office of the Comptroller of the Currency, neither of whom had the responsibility for regulating the First American Bank that BCCI had taken over. The CIA failed to provide the critical information it had gathered to the correct users of the information — the Federal Reserve and the Justice Department. After the CIA knew that BCCI was as an institution a fundamentally corrupt criminal enterprise, it continued to use both BCCI and FirstAmerican, BCCI's secretly held US subsidiary, for CIA operations. While the reporting concerning BCCI by the CIA was in some respects impressive— especially in its assembling of the essentials of BCCI's criminality, its secret purchase of First American by 1985, and its extensive involvement in money laundering — there were also remarkable gaps in the CIA's reported knowledge about BCCI. Former CIA officials, including former CIA director Richard Helms and the late William Casey; former and current foreign intelligence officials,including Kamal Adham and Abdul Raouf Khalil; and principal foreign agents of the US, such as Adnan Khashoggi and Manucher Ghorbanifar, float in and out of BCCI at critical times in its history, and participate simultaneously in the making of key episodes in US foreign policy, ranging from the Camp David peace talks to the arming of Iran as part of the Iran/Contra affair. Yet the CIA has continued to maintain that it has no information regarding any involvement of these people, raising questions about the quality of intelligence the CIA is receiving generally, or its candour with the Subcommittee. The CIA's professions of total ignorance about their respective roles in BCCI are out of character with the Agency's early knowledge of many critical aspects of the bank's operations, structure, personnel, and history. The errors made by the CIA in connection with its handling of BCCI were complicated by its handling of this Congressional investigation. Initial information that was provided by the CIA was untrue; later information that was provided was incomplete; and the Agency resisted providing a "full" account about its knowledge of BCCI until almost a year after the initial requests for the information. These experiences suggest caution in concluding that the information provided to date is full and complete. The relationships among former CIA personnel and BCCI front men and nominees, including Kamal Adham, Abdul Khalil, and Mohammad Irvani, requires further investigation.

BCCI actively solicited the friendships of major US political figures, and made payments to these political figures, which in some cases may have been improper.

Beginning with Bert Lance in 1977, whose debts BCCI paid off with a $3.5 million loan, BCCI, BCCI nominees, and top officials of BCCI systematically developed friendships and relationships with important US political figures. While those which are publicly known include former president Jimmy Carter, Jesse Jackson, and Andrew Young, the Subcommittee has received information suggesting that BCCI's network extended to other US political figures. The payments made by the BCCI to Andrew Young while he was a public official were at best unusual, and by all appearances, improper.

Investigations of BCCI to date remain incomplete, and many leads cannot be followed up, as the result of documents being withheld from US investigators by the British government, and documents and witnesses being withheld from US investigators by the government of Abu Dhabi.

Many of the specific criminal transactions engaged in by BCCI's customers remain hidden from investigation as the result of bank secrecy laws in many jurisdictions, British national security laws, and the holding of key witnesses and documents by the Government of Abu Dhabi. Documents pertaining to BCCI's use to finance terrorism, to assist the builders of a Pakistani nuclear bomb, to finance Iranian arms deals, and related matters have been sealed in the United Kingdom by British intelligence and remain unavailable to US investigators. Many other basic matters pertaining to BCCI's criminality, including any list that may exist of BCCI's political payoffs and bribes, remain sequestered in Abu Dhabi and unavailable to US investigators. Many investigative leads remain to be explored, but cannot be answered with devoting substantial additional sources that to date no agency of government has been in a position to provide. Unanswered questions include, but are not limited to, the relationship between BCCI and the Banco Nazionale del Lavoro; the alleged relationship between the late CIA director William Casey and BCCI; the extent of BCCI's involvement in Pakistan's nuclear program; BCCI's manipulation of commodities and securities markets in Europe and Canada; BCCI's activities in India, including its relationship with the business empire of the Hinduja family; BCCI'S relationships with convinced Iraqi arms dealer Sarkis Sarkenalian, Syrian drug trafficker, terrorist, and arms trafficker Monzer Al-Kassar, and other major armsdealers; the use of BCCI by central figures in the alleged "October Surprise", BCCI's activities with the Central Bank of Syria and with the Foreign Trade Mission of the Soviet Union in London; its involvement with foreign and foreign intelligence agencies .... the sale of BCCI Banque de Commerce et Placement in Geneva,to the Cukorova Group of Turkeym, which owned an entity involved in the BNL Iraqi arms sales, among others. The withholding of documents and witnesses from US investigators by the Government of Abu Dhabi threatens vital US foreign policy, anti-narcotics and money laundering, and law enforcement interests, and should not be tolerated.

(10) **IB NOTE ON MOSSAD AGENT IN INDIA**

TOP SECRET

Intelligence Bureau
(Ministry of Home Affairs)
Government of India
New Delhi, dt 10.6.1991

My Dear,

Kindly refer to your Top Secret note No T-233/FS/91 dated June 7, 1991.

The only concrete piece of information conveyed by the Palestinian Ambassador is regarding his knowledge of Mossad agents in India. Specifically, he had indicated that one of the employees of Pan Am was a Mossad agent. Is it possible for the Amabassador to part with this information in the utmost confidence to you or to anyone designated by you ? We would be most interested in this information.

Yours Sincerely,

(M K Narayanan)

Shri Muchkund Dubey,
Foreign Secretary,
Government of India,
New Delhi.

Copy to Shri Naresh Chandra, Cabinet Secretary.

*

(11) IB NOTE ON LTTE'S CONTACTS WITH CIA

Top Secret & Personal

N V Vathsan,
Joint Director.

No. 16-E/SZX/90-441
Intelligence Bureau; South Zone,
MHA, Government of India,
Madras

Dated the July 19, 1990

Dear Shri Saranyan,

Our fax monitoring of the Madras LTTE unit has been yielding a number of messages encripted in a complicated type of code using English alphabets and Arabic numerals for Tamil alphabets. For quite some time, we have been working on a project to break this code with the help of computer, studying the pattern of repitition. To a large extent, we have succeeded in breaking one of the many codes used by the LTTE. I use the expression "to a large extent" because we have not succeeded in making, some six/seven coded messages have yielded their secrets.

On July 12, 1990, a coded message was sent from K Padmanathan (KP) of Kualalumpur, the person in charge of raising funds abroad and also in charge of their hawala transactions, to Prabhakaran as follows :

"My friend in America who was in touch with a CIA official, contacted the latter and requested him to help us. He (CIA) expressed that he knew what was required by us (LTTE); it should be done in a way that would be helpful to both of them; and that the matter could be finalised only after meeting and discussing with KP. He (CIA), when asked, was not prepared to meet Kittu. It is possible that he (CIA) might meet me (KP) in some country other than America. Please let me know your reply. According to my friend, they (CIA) are very much interested in Trincomalee."

From the context, it would appear that the LTTE are in touch with the CIA for getting anti-aircraft guns. They are likely to exploit the American interest in Trincomalee as quid pro quo.

With regards.

Yours Sincerely,

(N V Vathsan)

Shri K Saranyan,
Additional Director (I),
IB, New Delhi.

*

(12) **IB NOTE ON LTTE'S REQUIREMENTS FOR SAMs**

Top Secret/Personal

N V Vathsan,
Joint Director

16-E/SZX/90—555
Intelligence Bureau; South Zone,
MHA, Government of India,
Madras

Dated the Sept 4, 1990

Dear Shri Saranyan,

You may recall that we succeeded in breaking a complicated code (T-1) used by the LTTE sometime ago and that we are in a position to decipher some of the important communications between the LTTE Chief Prabhakaran and K Padmanathan @ 'KP' — the underworld operative dealing in hawala transactions and weaponry. One such communication (vide my DO letter of even number dated July 19) revealed KP's inclination to seek the help of the CIA to acquire weapons to meet the onslaught of the Sri Lankan Armed Forces and, in return, cater to the American's interests in Trincomallee.

Hence we paid more attention to the communications between Prabhakaran and 'KP'. There were two more codes used in the messages exchanged between the two, namely T-2 and T-3. A sustained effort was made to break these codes and we have once again met with success. We have found the keys to the Tamil letters used in the T-3 messages which form the major part of every communication. While some of the contents of the deciphered messages are already known to us, the remaining portions offer interesting nsight into the state of affairs of the LTTE in 'land' and its requirements.

In a communication addressed to 'KP' on Sept 1, Prabhakaran has enquired from the former whether supplies as per a list (sent already) could be delivered to LTTE immediately using the one million US dollars left with 'KP'. Prabhakaran has virtually sounded the 'SOS' and has indicated that LTTE would not be in a position to sustain for long without these supplies.

Some of the messages sent by Prabhakaran to 'KP' in mid-August reveal that the LTTE was looking for 'Surface to Air Missiles' (SAM) and its accessories. Orders for purchase of 6 SAMs, a 'Candle' (?), 30 batteries used in SAMs and two pairs of spectacles worn (by soldiers) at the time of firing them have been placed with 'KP'. Interestingly, Prabhakaran had directed 'KP' to send some 'persons' who could handle the weapon system.

In a subsequent message in August '90, Prabhakaran had expressed suspicion whether it would be safe for 'KP' to send these 'persons' by himself ('KP') and had suggested that 'they' could be met by some other cadres and taken to 'land'.

With regards.

Yours Sincerely,

(N V Vathsan)

Shri K Saranyan,
Additional Director (I),
IB, New Delhi

*

(13) IB NOTE ON LTTE'S ARMS REQUIREMENTS

TOP SECRET

N V Vathsan,
Joint Director

No 16-E/SZX/90-574
Intelligence Bureau; South Zone,
MHA, Government of India,
Madras

Dated the 11th Sept, 1990

Dear Shri Saranyan,

In a coded communication dated Sept 10 to the LTTE chief Prabhakaran, K Padmanathan @ 'KP' now camping in Cyprus had indicated that the latter would be in a position to spare a sum of one million US dollars (for buying arms and ammunition), provided Prabhakaran would repay the amount within two months. 'KP' had also disclosed that his 'friend' was willing to supply the 'goods' as per the list by Prabhakaran. 'KP' had expressed hopes that he could meet the LTTE supremo soon with the 'goods'.

Another coded message originated by Prabhakaran was passed on to

'KP' the same night (Sept 10) in which emphasis had been laid on purchase of different types of optical accessories like 'Celestron' telescope, snipe sighter, parallax adjusting rifle scopes etc.

Yours sincerely,

(N V Vathsan)

Shri K Saranyan,
Additional Director (I),
IB, New Delhi

*

(14) IB REPORT ON LTTE'S FORTHCOMING ARMS SHIPMENTS

Computer/Fax Message No 40L/91 Dated 24-4-91 TTT/Crash

From : JD/SZ (N V Vathsan)
To : DIB
Info : AXI (Shri K Saranyan)
JD/V (Shri E S L Narasimhan)

PROJECT TT

According to a new contact in LTTE, Prabhakaran is planning to send an emissary to India to lobby for support among various political parties, notably the Congress-I. Kasi Anandan, who is already in Madras, is considered to be unfit to play the role in the light of his utter failure to visit Delhi and meet Prime Minister Chandra Shekhar before a crackdown was launched against the militant group in Feb '91.

(He is reported to have been given Rs 20,000 in January '91 and directed to undertake the trip to meet the PM to solicit Centre's support for LTTE. Kasi Anandan is suspected to have been prevailed upon by his DMK contacts not to make the trip.)

Ibrahim, a Lebanese Christian based in Cyprus has supplied arms and ammunition to the LTTE recently.

Another Lebanese Christian by name Charles Obed had also supplied arms and ammunition to the group and a sum of 200,000

US dollars is due to be paid to him in this connection.

Charles Obed has given his daughter in marriage to the son of a mafia 'don', Joseph of Beirut. Joseph also deals in arms and is suspected to have connections with the CIA.

K Padmanathan @ 'KP' is the LTTE representative who is in touch with these arms dealers and effects the purchases.

LTTE ship 'Yelicia' is scheduled to touch Tuticorin harbour on April 29. The other vessel, belonging to the group, 'Sunbird', is presently in a Malaysian port, Kuching.

References

1. A PTI report quoting unidentified soures in the home ministry. (*National Herald*, May 23,1991.)

2. A *PTI* report in *The Statesman*, New Delhi, dated May 28, 1991, captioned : "Police had no metal detectors".

3. A *UNI* report in *The Times of India*, dated May 28, 1991, captioned : "SP tried in vain to get venue changed".

4. *The Statesman*, New Delhi, May 28, 1991. The report by a staff reporter is captioned: "A fourth woman surfaces in Rajiv case".

5. *The Hindu*, Madras, May 28, 1991. The report by a special correspondent in New Delhi is captioned : "CBI rules out hand of Khalistanis".

6. *The Indian Express*, May 28, 1991, captioned : "Lanka student's record seized".

7. *The Indian Express*, May 29, 1991. Report datelined Madras by ENS and agencies is captioned : "Is ex-MCC girl the assassin ?"

8. *The Hindu*, Madras, May 29, 1991. A New Delhi report captioned "Probe takes new turn".

9. *The Hindu*, Madras, May 23, 1991. The report captioned : "Woman's waist had explosives."

10. *The Hindu* report by the paper's staff reporter, datelined New Delhi published on May 29 under the caption : "Rajiv's post-mortem report".

11. *The Statesman*, New Delhi, May 30, 1991. Report captioned : "Post-mortem shows vital parts missing."

12. *The Indian Express*, May 29, 1991. A Madras report of ENS and agencies captioned : "Is ex-MC girl the assassin ?"

13. A PTI report from Madras in *Patriot*, May 30, 1991, captioned : "Killer was a tough militant".

14. *The Daily*, Bombay, June 15, 1991. A PTI report captioned : "Suicide bomber could carry weights easily".

15. *The Hindu*, Madras, May 29, 1991 : "Last moments of Rajiv : photographer's claim".

16. *The Hindu*, May 30, 1991, "Leads obtained in Rajiv murder probe".

17. *The Hindu*, May 30, 1991, "Blast impact reduced because of crowd".

18. A PTI report quoted in *The Indian Express* news item "Search on for kurta-pyjama man" on May 30, 1991.

19. *The Indian Express*, May 30, 1991, "Search on for kurta-pyjama man".

20. *The Times of India*, May 29, 1991. The Dubai datelined story by a correspondent is captioned : " 'Sunday Observer' report denied".

21. *The Hindu*, May 31, 1991 : "Van driver claims having given her a lift." The news item by the newspaper's staff reporter is datelined Coimbatore.

22. *The Hindu*, May 31, 1991. Vellore datelined story by the newspaper's staff reporter is captioned : "Woman assassin visited LTTE detenue in Vellore prison ?"

23. Tharian Mathew's Vellore-datelined report in *The Indian Express* on May 31, 1991 "Did 'assassin' visit Vellore jail ?"

24. *The Indian Express*, May 31, 1991. The story of Express News Service datelined Madras captioned " 'Fourth person' may have gone to the GH, airport", suggests that the conspirators were not on the run immediately after the crime as would have been expected of them. They were instead giving a chase to the body of Rajiv Gandhi for reasons unknown. Moreover, the report suggests that there were other plotters or accomplices whose identity still remains under wraps. This report indicates that the assassins were cocksure of having committed the perfect murder. Or else, why should they

chase the body with such impunity? Or were they desperately looking for something which they believed could have spilled the beans ?

25. A Madras-datelined PTI report in *The Indian Express* dated May 31, 1991 : "No ambulance with Rajiv convoy."

26. An *Indian Express* report, datelined Madras, datelined Madras published on June 15, 1991 with the caption : "Truth is stranger than fiction"

27. *The Indian Express* report from Madras "Truth is stranger then fiction"., published on June 15, 1991. Also, the same newspaper's report from New Delhi published on June 1, 1991 with the caption : "CBI on trail of Lanka Tamil battery maker."

28. A PTI report from Madras in *The Statesman*, June 7, 1991, captioned : "Assassin's bomb made in Madras".

29. Manoj Mitta's report in *The Times Of India*, New Delhi, June 12, 1991 : "Explosive weighed less, finds SIT".

30. *The Hindu* report from Thomas Abraham from Colombo published on June 12, 1991 with the caption : "PLOT trying to identify assassin."

31. " 'Bindhi' adds to mystery", *The Hindu*, Madras, June 4, 1991.

32. "Where did the handbag come from", *The Hindu*, Madras, June 11, 1991.

33. A PTI report from New Delhi in *The Times of India*, July 7, 1991, captioned : "Sivarasan, Subha's escape plan busted".

34. An Agra-datelined report from UNI and PTI published in *The Indian Express* on June 7, 1991 with the caption : "Woman with burns being grilled in Agra."

35. *The Indian Express*, Madras, dated June 15, 1991 : "Pictures that made the probe click".

36. News item "Two injured in Sriperumbudur blast missing from hospital" in *The Hindu*, Madras, June 1, 1991.

37. A PTI news item "Car seen in video seized" in *The Indian Express*, Madras, June 1, 1991.

38. *The Hindu* Madras, June 1, 1991 : "SBI counter staff interrogated".

39. News item "Suspected assassin's accomplice 'is LTTE militant'" in *The Hindu*, Madras, June 8, 1991.

40. *The Times of India* story datelined Chengalpattu "Two held for sheltering Rajiv murder suspects", published on June 13, 1991.

41. *The Hindu*, Madras, June 12, 1991 : "SIT on lookout for man, two women".

42. "We have broken open this case—CBI chief", *The Hindu*, Madras, June 13, 1991.

43. *The Daily*, Bombay, June 15, 1991. The Madras datelined report captioned : "Suicide bomber could carry weights easily."

44. *The Hindu*, Madras, June 14, 1991 : ''Nalini had resigned her job on June 9".

45. *The Indian Express*, Madras, June 14, 1991 : ''Nalini resigned on Sunday".

46. News item "One step ahead of CBI" published in *The Indian Express* on June 13, 1991, Madras.

47. *The Hindu*, Madras, June 17, 1991 :"Nalini wanted to be rich and famous".

48. *The Hindustan Times*, New Delhi, June 20, 1997 : ''CBI arrests 2 more youths".

49. *The Statesman*, New Delhi, June 21, 1991 : "Accused got calls from 4 countries".

50. *The Indian Express*, Madras, June 27, 1991. The news item captioned "Another Lankan arrested by SIT".

51. *The Hindu*, Madras, June 27, 1991 : "Reward posters attract attention".

52. News item "Chappals of assassin identified" published in *The Hindu* on June 27, 1991.

53. *The Indian Express* , Madras, June 29, 1991 : "TADA revived".

54. A PTI news item in *The Hindu*, Madras, July 6, 1991 : "Murugan changed mind over leaving for Jaffna".

55. Jaya Menon reports from Madras in *Sunday Mail*, June 16, 1991 : "Conspirators kept a low profile".

56. Barun Mitra in *The Economic Times*, New Delhi, September 18, 1991 : "An arresting performance".

57. *The Hindu*, Madras, June 19, 1991 : "Hi-tech methods helped SIT nab suspect".

58. A PTI report from Colombo in *The Hindu*, Madras, June 25, 1991 : "SIT flooded with false leads in Colombo".

59. *The Times of India*, June 18, 1991. The Madras datelined report captioned : "Sivarasan sighted in Madras : SIT".

60. A PTI report in *The Indian Express*, Madras, June 28, 1991 : "One-eyed Jack in Porur ?"

61. A Madras-datelined UNI report in *Patriot*, July 1, 1991, titled : "One-eyed-Jack killed ?"

62. *The Indian Express*, Madras, July 4, 1991 : "Search for Sivarasan at Pulicat lake".

63. "ASI among 6 suspended in Rajiv case"— a UNI report from Raipur in *The Hindustan Times*, July 27, 1991.

64. A UNI report from Madras in *The Daily*, July 7, 1991:"Sivarasan in Bombay ?"

65. *The Times of India*, July 12, 1991. A Madras datelined report : "Another held in Rajiv case".

66. *The Hindu*, Madras, July 11, 1991 : "Search in hills on T Nadu-Kerala border".

67. A Rajkot-datelined report in *The Indian Express*, July 20, 1991, captioned : "Sivarasan 'sighted' at Jamnagar".

68. *The Indian Express*, Madras, August 11, 1991. The Rameswaram-datelined report is captioned : "Hunt for Sivarasan, Subha off Rameswaram".

69. Mysore-datelined report in *The Indian Express*, August 14, 1991 : "Sivarasan hiding in Mysore city ?".

70. "Sivarasan, Subha's escape plan busted", a PTI report from New Delhi published in *The Times of India* on July 7, 1991.

71. A PTI, UNI report from New Delhi in *The Statesman* published on July 8, 1991 with the caption : "LTTE man arrested in Nepal"

72. "Video clip on 'dry-runs'", a PTI report from New Delhi in *The Times of India* on July 18, 1991.

73. *The Hindu*, Madras, July 27, 1991 : "Entire killer squad came to V P Singh meeting".

74. A Nagapattinam-datelined report published in *The Hindu*, Madras on July 22, 1991 with the caption : "Was Rajiv case accused done to death ?"

75. Chidanand Rajghatta's report from Madras in *The Times of India* on July 22, 1991 : "Flaws, obstacles mark SIT manhunt".

76. *The Indian Express*, Madras, July 21, 1991. Thanjavur datelined report captioned " 'Harbourer' of Rajiv assassins escapes, found hanging".

77. A UNI report from Madras "LTTE had vast base in Tamil Nadu" in *the Statesman*, August 17, 1991.

78. *The Hindu*, Madras, August 5, 1991 : "LTTE squads sent with specific tasks".

79. *The Hindu*, Madras, August 19, 1991 : "The tip that paid off".

80. *The Indian Express*, August 9, 1991. A PTI story datelined Coimbatore with the caption : "Dixon's adventurous visit to theatre".

81. "Dixon's visit to Ooty being probed" in *The Hindu*, Madras, August 9, 1991.

82. Karur-datelined report in *The Hindu*, Madras, August 19, 1991 : "500 LTTE cadres came on May 10" and Tiruchi-datelined story in *The Indian Express* "LTTE sent killer squad in May" the same day.

83. *The Hindu*, Madras, August 19, 1991. Bangalore-datelined story : "5 LTTE men nabbed alive, 12 end life".

84. Mysore-datelined story "The militants were 'accountable' in *The Indian Express*, Madras, August 24, 1991.

85. A UNI report from Colombo in *The Hindu* : " 'One-eyed Jack' had escaped IPKF dragnet", published on June 17, 1991.

86. A PTI report "Sivarasan still an enigma" in *The Indian Express*, Madras on August 22, 1991.

87. A PTI report from Madras in *The Telegraph*, Calcutta on June 2, 1992 : "LTTE's aborted rescue mission".

88. PTI report from Bangalore "Message written on Sivarasan's aide's hand", published in *The Indian Express* on August 22, 1991.

89. "Did Sivarasan burn documents, records ?" a Bangalore report in *The Indian Express*, August 22, 1991.

90. The Bangalore-datelined story "'Breakfast show' for villagers" in *The Indian Express*, August 22, 1991.

91. *The Hindustan Times*, New Delhi, August 22, 1991. The Bangalore-datelined story is captioned :"An exciting Bangalore thriller".

92. *The Indian Express*, August 22, 1991, Bangalore-datelined story : "They didn't know who their neighbour was".

93. A Bangalore report in *The Times of India* on August 22, 1991 with the caption : "Murugan identifies Sivarasan, Subha".

94. *The Indian Express*, Madras, August 23, 1991.

95. *The Hindu*, Madras, February 13, 1992. The report is captioned : "Rajiv case acused moves court for Sivarasan 'diary'."

96. *The Indian Express*, February 13, 1992. The Madras report is captioned : "Sivarasan, Haribabu had links with Vazhappadi".

97. A PTI report from Bangalore in *The Indian Express*, published on August 24, 1991 with the caption "Sivarasan, Subha did not try disguise".

98. *The Hindu*, Madras, October 20 1991, report datelined Salem with the caption : "Sivarasan travelled in a tanker"; *The Indian Express*, Madras, November 10, 1991, captioned "SIT simulates

trip in water tanker".

99. *The Indian Express*, September 4, 1991 : "Sivarasan, Subha's bodies cremated."

100. "Bid to convert Sivarasan's house into Mutt foiled" : *The Indian Express*, February 2, 1992.

101. "Prabhakaran behind tip-off on Sivarasan?", a Madras datelined report in *The Indian Express*, Madras on August 23, 1991.

102. "Were they betrayed by a colleague ?", a PTI report from Bangalore in *The Indian Express*, August 22, 1991.

103. A PTI report from Madras in *The Indian Express*, captioned : "Prabhakaran sent message to Sivarasan".

104. *The Hindu*, Madras, August 30, 1991 : "Sivarasan's driver held in the nick of time".

105. *The Indian Express*, Madras, August 31, 1991 : "Sivarasan's driver is a vital catch".

106. *The Hindu*, Madras, August 30, 1991 : "Pinned down in shopping complex".

107. *The Hindu*, June 12, 1992. A PTI report from Hyderabad captioned : "21 to share reward for information about Sivarasan".

108. *Blitz* report from New Delhi : "Mossad's deadly hand in Rajiv's murder", June 23, 1991.

109. Batuk Gathani's report from London in *The Hindu*, Madras, June 3, 1991 : "Arafat tipped Rajiv about plot : PM".

110. A PTI report from Pune in *The Hindu*, Madras, June 1, 1991 : "Mossad trained LTTE and Punjab militants".

111. *Blitz* special report "Colombo connection", datelined Madras published on June 8, 1991.

112. *Blitz* report "Israel's secret troika in Lanka" published on June 22, 1991.

113. S Rajappa's Madras-datelined report : "Premadasa conspired against Rajiv" in *The Statesman*, dated September 27, 1991.

114. *The Indian Express*, Madras, September 3, 1991. A New Delhi-datelined report : "Premadasa armed LTTE, says chargesheet".

115. Coimbatore-datelined report in *The Hindu*, Madras, dated September 6, 1991 : "Colombo helped LTTE with arms, cars, funds". Also, a PTI report from the same place in *The Times of India*, published on the same day.

116. AFP report "Premadasa admits backing LTTE" in *The Hindu*, September 20, 1991.

117. "Lanka army shared arms with LTTE", a Colombo-datelined story in *The Times of India*, September 24, 1991.

118. "Payoffs to LTTE : Govt plans inquiry", an India Abroad News Service report in *The Economic Times*, November 27, 1991.

119. M K Tikku's New Delhi- datelined report "Lanka 'armed LTTE' to fight IPKF" in *The Hindustan Times*, December 17, 1991.

120. *The Indian Express*, October 1, 1991, " 'Premadasa scuttled IPKF operations' ".

121. T R Ramachandran in *The Times of India*, New Delhi, October 10, 1991 : "Premadasa explains to Rao".

122. Sanjeev Prakash's New Delhi report in *The Pioneer*, October 4, 1992, captioned "Sonia refuses audience to Premadasa".

123. "Wijeratne wanted to replace Premadasa ?" ANI report from Colombo in *The Indian Express*, June 10, 1991.

124. M D Nalapat in *The Times of India*, September 17, 1992 : "LTTE dominance due to Premadasa's partiality".

125. DPA story from Colombo in *The Hindu*, Madras, April 21, 1992, captioned "Premadasa rules out extradition of Prabhakaran".

126. "Premadasa sees threat to his life", a UNI report from Colombo in *The Times of India*, October 21, 1991.

127. "India is out to oust Premadasa : LTTE", a Colombo-datelined story in *The Indian Express*, May 25, 1992.

INDEX